The Making of a Modern Denomination

John Howard Shakespeare and the English Baptists, 1898-1924

Series Editors

Anthony R. Cross, Fellow of the Centre for Baptist History and Heritage, Regent's Park College, Oxford, UK

Curtis W. Freeman, Research Professor of Theology and Director of the Baptist House of Studies, Duke University, North Carolina, USA

Stephen R. Holmes, Lecturer in Theology, University of St Andrews, Scotland, UK

Elizabeth Newman, Professor of Theology and Ethics, Baptist Theological Seminary at Richmond, Virginia, USA

Philip E. Thompson, Assistant Professor of Systematic Theology and Christian Heritage, North American Baptist Seminary, Sioux Falls, South Dakota, USA

Series Consultant Editors

David Bebbington, Professor of History, University of Stirling, Scotland, UK

Paul S. Fiddes, Professor of Systematic Theology, University of Oxford, and Principal of Regent's Park College, Oxford, UK

Stanley J. Grenz, Pioneer McDonald Professor of Theology, Carey Theological College, Vancouver, British Columbia, Canada

Stanley E. Porter, President and Professor of New Testament, McMaster Divinity College, Hamilton, Ontario, Canada

John Howard Shakespeare, aged 34
(From the *Baptist Magazine,* September 1891)

A critical study of John Howard Shakespeare has long been overdue. He may not be to the taste of many modern Baptists, but the historically-minded will recognise in him a man of unusual stature. As a personality, as a pastor, as a denominational mover and a shaker, as a Free Church statesman, and as an ecclesiastical leader on an international stage, he commands attention and, indeed, admiration. Peter Shepherd places Shakespeare in a careful perspective. His study of the evolution of a Christian man and of a Christian denomination in a crucial period for all the Churches, is warmly to be welcomed.

Professor Clyde Binfield, University of Sheffield

A full list of titles in this series appears at the close of this book.

The Making of a Modern Denomination

John Howard Shakespeare and the English Baptists, 1898-1924

Peter Shepherd

Foreword by Roger Hayden

To Joan

Every blessing for the future ~

Peter Shepherd

July 2016

Paternoster:
thinking faith

First published 2001 by Paternoster

Paternoster is an imprint of Authentic Media
9 Holdom Avenue, Bletchley, Milton Keynes, MK1 1QR, U.K.
and
PO Box 1047, Waynesboro, GA 30830-2047, USA

03 02 01 7 6 5 4 3 2 1

British Library Cataloguing in Publication Data
A catalogue record for this book is available from the British Library

ISBN 0-84227-046-X

Typeset by the University of Derby Print Department
And printed and bound in Great Britain by
Nottingham Alpha Graphics

Series Preface

Baptists form one of the largest Christian communities in the world, and while they hold the historic faith in common with other mainstream Christian traditions, they nevertheless have important insights which they can offer to the worldwide church. *Studies in Baptist History and Thought* will be one means towards this end. It is an international series of academic studies which includes original monographs, revised dissertations, collections of essays and conference papers, and aims to cover any aspect of Baptist history and thought. While not all the authors are themselves Baptists, they nevertheless share an interest in relating Baptist history and thought to the other branches of the Christian church and to the wider life of the world.

The series includes studies in various aspects of Baptist history from the seventeenth century down to the present day, including biographical works, and Baptist thought is understood as covering the subject-matter of theology (including interdisciplinary studies embracing biblical studies, philosophy, sociology, practical theology, liturgy and women's studies). The diverse streams of Baptist life throughout the world are all within the scope of these volumes.

The series editors and consultants believe that the academic disciplines of history and theology are of vital importance to the spiritual vitality of the churches of the Baptist faith and order. The series sets out to discuss, examine and explore the many dimensions of their tradition and so to contribute to their on-going intellectual vigour.

A brief word of explanation is due for the series identifier on the front cover. The fountains, taken from heraldry, represent the Baptist distinctive of believer's baptism and, at the same time, the source of the water of life. There are three of them because they symbolize the Trinitarian basis of Baptist life and faith. Those who are redeemed by the Lamb, the book of Revelation reminds us, will be led to 'fountains of living waters' (Rev. 7.17).

This book is dedicated to the members of
Middlesbrough Baptist Church

Contents

Foreword   ix
Acknowledgements   xi
Introduction   xii

Chapter 1
Background   1
1.1   The Baptists   1
1.1.1   *Origins*   1
1.1.2   *The Evangelical Awakening*   4
1.1.3   *The Baptist Union*   7
1.1.4   *Nonconformity in Late Victorian England*   10
1.2   John Howard Shakespeare   13
1.2.1   *Childhood and Preparation for Ministry*   13
1.2.2   *St Mary's Baptist Church, Norwich*   15

Chapter 2
The Strengthening of the Union   25
2.1   The Twentieth Century Fund   25
2.2   Denominational Development   29
2.2.1   *Baptist Church House*   29
2.2.2   *New Departments and Societies*   31
2.2.3   *A New Constitution*   35
2.2.4   *The Baptist World Alliance*   38
2.3   Shakespeare as Denominational Leader   41
2.4   Congregationalism and Unity   47

Chapter 3
The Sustenance of the Ministry   53
3.1   Union Recognition   53
3.2   The Ministerial Settlement and Sustentation Scheme   61
3.2.1   *Putting the Scheme Together*   61
3.2.2   *Gaining Support from the Churches*   71
3.2.3   *Implementing the Scheme*   75
3.3   The Union Supreme   84

Chapter Four
The Search for Unity   93
4.1   The National Council of the Evangelical Free Churches   93
4.2   The Impact of the War   96
4.2.1   *The United Chaplaincy Board*   96
4.2.2   *The Federal Council of the Evangelical Free Churches*   103

4.2.3   *Conversations with the Church of England*   110
4.3   The Lambeth Appeal   114
4.4   Shakespeare and Reunion   129

Chapter Five
Final Years at the Baptist Union   139
5.1   The Ministry   139
5.1.1   *The Ministry of Women*   139
5.1.2   *Ministerial Support*   144
5.1.3   *Lay Ministry*   145
5.1.4   *Accreditation*   147
5.1.5   *Evangelism*   151
5.2   Resignation   153

Chapter Six
Shakespeare's Legacy   169
6.1   Shakespeare and the 'Dissolution of Dissent'   169
6.2   Changes in Baptist Church Polity   175
6.2.1   *Denominational Leadership*   175
6.2.2   *The Union*   177
6.2.3   *Baptist Ministry*   179
6.2.4   *Superintendency*   180
6.2.5   *Baptists and Ecumenism*   182
6.3   Conclusion   185

Bibliography   191
1   Primary Sources   191
1.1   *Archival Sources*   191
1.2   *Newspapers*   192
1.3   *Books, Articles etc. published before 1930*   192
2   Secondary Sources   197

Appendices   213
1   John Howard Shakespeare: some key dates   213
2   Baptist Union Presidents 1898-1924   214

Abbreviations   215

Index   216

FOREWORD

John Howard Shakespeare's overall passion for the effective mission of the church in Britain brought him to a growing and deepening conviction that this could only be accomplished by church reunion. As General Secretary of the Baptist Union for the first quarter of the twentieth century, he consciously set about making the national Baptist organisation one that could play its rightful part in a future united English Free Church. His own position was clear: 'No one could ever call me an indifferent Baptist. I plan and toil for the Church of my own faith, that when the grand festival of union comes she may be led to the altar in radiant beauty...yet the days of denominationalism are numbered. There is nothing more pathetic or useless in this world, than clinging to dead issues, worn-out methods and antiquated programmes.'

However, the trauma of the First World War marked Shakespeare so deeply that he realised even Free Church union was just not radical enough. His book The Churches at the Cross-Roads (1918), is still a vibrant forward looking book eighty years on. It spelled out his profound conviction that denominationalism was dead because its members no longer believed in it! It had to be decently buried if mission to post-war England was to be successfully accomplished. 'The plain fact is that the vast tree of sectarian divisions is rapidly becoming hollow: it is propped up by iron bands of trust deeds and funds...One day, in a general storm, the hollow tree will come down with a crash...' p.79. He was personally prepared for reunion with the Church of England. 'It is no use concealing my conviction that reunion will never come to pass except on the basis of episcopacy. I did not think so once, but that was simply because I did not understand it' p.178. That was a step too far for English Baptists then, and probably still is. But is there now any more relevant alternative than total church reunion if the missionary challenge facing the church is to be met?

Peter Shepherd's book presents the continuing challenge of the mysterious, enigmatic, now little-known J. H. Shakespeare for to-day's English churches, including Baptists, as they search for a meaningful Christian identity. Part of this ignorance arises from his request that no biography be written. The varied source material brought together here provides us with an intriguing, properly critical, wide-ranging portrait of Shakespeare, who with consummate skill and imagination created a new interpretation of Baptist life and thought which shaped the denomination he loved to be ready for reunion when it came. It reveals the challenge

Shakespeare faced and the essentially non-Baptist answer he provided when confronted with the disparate Arminian and Calvinistic Baptist family that had finally come together in 1891.

For Baptist Christians who have spent the last decade looking towards 2000, conducting an in-depth review of their life and mission, in an agonising search for a new Baptist identity, Peter Shepherd's well-researched and penetrating study of Shakespeare is essential reading. It also has relevance at the end of a decade of evangelisation that according to Peter Brierley's recent series of church censuses, shows the English church is still bleeding to death. Certainly, if Baptists are reluctant to concede Shakespeare's ecumenical challenge faced with the death throes of denominationalism, or fail to understand his original and as yet largely unacknowledged re-interpretation of their identity, or are unable to discover a vital mission strategy for the present day, it will make present Baptist discussions of a denominational future about as effective as moving deck chairs on the Titanic.

ROGER HAYDEN, President, Baptist Historical Society.

AKNOWLEDGEMENTS

During the researching and writing of this book I have been helped financially by the Dr. Williams's Trust, the Baptist Union of Great Britain Scholarship Fund, the Whitley Lectureship Trustees and the Particular Baptist Fund. I have also received practical assistance in the form of accommodation from Regent's Park College, Oxford, and several friends and relations, including Priscilla, Myrtle, Reg and Brenda. I have been indebted to the generous co-operation and assistance of several libraries, including the Dr. Williams's Library, the House of Lord's Record Office, the City of Norwich Archives, the Lambeth Palace Library, the British Library newspaper collection and the libraries of Spurgeon's College, St. John's College, Cambridge, and St. John's College, Durham. Susan Mills, librarian and archivist at Regent's Park College has enabled me to make the most of the very limited time available to me on my trips to Oxford. A number of other individuals have given their time to help me, including the late Sir William and Lady Shakespeare, Mr. Ken Hipper, archivist at St. Mary's Baptist Church, Norwich, and my PhD supervisor at Durham University, Dr. Sheridan Gilley. I am grateful to all of these.

The preparation for this book has been done on a part-time basis, mostly while I was minister of Middlesbrough Baptist Church. The church was generous and supportive, allowing me time to study and write, and their part in the project deserves acknowledgment. Any fruit that may come from the outcome is in large part due to them. I have also, during the past six years, been a husband, and father to five growing children. I am afraid I have been a bore at times. My family's tolerance and interest have been wonderful. They have generously backed me from start to finish. The project has been demanding of money, energy and time, and I am conscious that they have given at least as much as I have. Without the love of Rita and the children I could not possibly have seen it through to a conclusion.

PETER SHEPHERD

Introduction

The main purpose of this book is to evaluate the work of John Howard Shakespeare, the leading figure in English Baptist church life during the first quarter of the twentieth century, and to explore his place in the history of the Baptists. He made a vitally important contribution to the development of his own denomination, and also played a significant role as a leader of Nonconformity as a whole, particularly with regard to its relations with the Church of England. His importance to Baptists is the primary concern of what follows, but I have also given attention to his wider significance in English church life.

Shakespeare was appointed Secretary of the Baptist Union of Great Britain and Ireland in 1898, and remained in that position until poor health enforced his retirement in 1924. His personality was a dominant feature of Baptist life from the beginning of the century. In the immediate post-war years he was also, as architect and first Moderator of the Federal Council of the Evangelical Free Churches, a leading figure within English Nonconformity. His influence continues to be felt to this day through the institutions with which he is associated, especially the Baptist Union and the Federal Council. He was described by a contemporary as 'the maker of the Baptist denomination',[1] and by another commentator as 'the architect of the Baptist Union as we know it'.[2]

No other individual has played as major a part as Shakespeare has in the shaping of the overall pattern of Baptist denominational life in England throughout the twentieth century. Features of that pattern that he set in place include: the leadership of the General Secretary of the Baptist Union in denominational life; the accreditation of ministers by the Union; the centralised system of grant-aiding ministers; the work of senior regional ministers employed by the Union (Area Superintendents) to co-ordinate questions of ministerial settlement and provide leadership in other areas of church life. These features of Baptist life are now frequently taken for granted as part of the Baptist way of doing things. In fact they were all twentieth-century innovations.

As far as Nonconformity as a whole is concerned, Shakespeare's importance as the creator of the Federal Council of the Evangelical Free Churches in 1919 is indisputable. It was his vision and leadership that, for the first time, brought all the main denominations of Nonconformity together into a single body. His long-term influence within Nonconformity has been less marked than that within his own denomination, and he was unable to achieve his ambition of developing the Federal Council into a United Free Church of England. The impetus he gave to co-operation among the denominations of Nonconformity is nonetheless important. It is still felt today through the work of the present Free Church Council.

His leadership and vision were important contributory factors in the improvement of relations between the Nonconformists and the Church of England. He was involved in the early Faith and Order movement following the 1910 Edinburgh Missionary Conference, and was at the heart of the Free Church response to the 1920 Lambeth Appeal.

It is an injustice to Shakespeare that his contribution to English church life has not been more generally recognised. Anthony Cross has written recently that his importance ecumenically 'has seldom adequately been acknowledged'.[3] Adrian Hastings has been one of the few to give him credit for the part he played in the early ecumenical movement, describing Shakespeare's *The Churches at the Cross Roads* as 'in principle one of the most important books of English Christianity because it sets out so clearly the logic of the forthcoming ecumenical movement'. Hastings paid tribute to Shakespeare's courage in standing virtually alone as he attempted to overcome the divide between the two largest sections of the English Church.[4]

Baptists themselves have sometimes been slow to recognise the importance of his part in their own recent history. This is partly because Shakespeare himself asked that no biography of him be published.[5] His wish has so far been granted, and this has no doubt had its part in limiting recognition of his work. His personal papers have disappeared, and seem to have been destroyed after his retirement or death, possibly at his own request. He rarely spoke about personal or family matters. There are occasional glimpses of Shakespeare's personality in his published writing, in the official record of the events he was involved in, and in correspondence that has survived in the collections of other people, but overall, information about his personal life is very hard to come by. He told his friend J. C. Carlile that he 'wanted his life's story to remain his own as a sacred thing which belonged to his family and himself',[6] and, by and large, this is what has occurred. The most obvious memorial to his work was, until the Union moved its offices out of London in 1989, Baptist Church House on Southampton Row. Now that that particular building, with its close associations with Shakespeare, is no longer in Baptist hands, and the portrait of him by John Collier is no longer on public display in the new office building in Didcot, it seems especially appropriate to acknowledge how much the denomination owes to him.

Most of Shakespeare's own published work can be found in the pages of the *Baptist Times*, of which he was the editor from 1901, and most of this is related directly to the immediate needs and opportunities facing the denomination at the time. He was more a man of action than thought, an organiser rather than a theologian, and rapidly grew impatient with those who did not see the urgency of getting things done as he did. Apart from several articles, sermons and contributions to larger volumes, he only produced two substantial publications. These were _Baptist and Congregational Pioneers_ (1906) - an historical work covering the late sixteenth and early seventeenth centuries - and _The Churches at the Cross Roads_ (1918) - a forceful plea for church unity. There is a short autobiographical chapter in the latter, as there is in his son Geoffrey's own autobiography _Let Candles Be Brought In_ (1949). These are seriously inadequate, however, for gaining any real insight into Shakespeare on a personal level. C. M. Townsend's unpublished and undated biography, currently in the possession of the Shakespeare family,[7] and the various newspaper obituaries of 1928, are also of limited value. Any biographical work must come to terms with the fact that there are few means of making contact with him as a private rather than as a public figure.

The steady twentieth-century decline in the social and political importance of Nonconformity has also affected the subsequent assessment of Shakespeare's significance. As well as its numerical decline, Nonconformity lost its coherence as a political force following the Great War, largely as a consequence of the fragmentation of Liberalism under Lloyd George. In late Victorian and Edwardian England, the Free Churches had been a major component of the strength of the Liberal Party, and exerted a powerful influence in the nation, but by the time of Shakespeare's retirement, their influence was negligible, and has since remained so. Shakespeare himself was always consistently loyal to Lloyd George, but of the other Nonconformists who remained politically minded, some supported the non-coalition Liberals under Asquith, and still more, like the veteran Baptist campaigner John Clifford, drifted towards Labour. Shakespeare's career, in fact, coincided with the watershed in Nonconformist political fortunes, encompassing their brief flowering during the Liberal Governments between 1905 and 1916 and their sudden demise afterwards.

The war was undoubtedly the dominant event for this whole period, and as well as helping shape Shakespeare's life and work at the time, has had an impact on his reputation since. Some of his most important achievements, both within the Baptist denomination and more widely, occurred during the war years. He was accused at the end of the war by at least one critic of pushing through denominational and ecumenical reforms while the attention of those who might have resisted them was diverted elsewhere.[8] It is certainly true that he found himself freer to implement his plans during those years than he had before, or did afterwards. He was not able to build on these achievements after the war as he wanted, and although many of them proved of lasting importance, doubts and suspicions grew about the direction he was taking.

He associated himself very forcibly with the war effort, and, together with William Robertson Nicoll, the editor of the *British Weekly*, used his position among the Free Churches to promote the struggle against Germany as a battle for Christian civilisation.[9] The war, however, cast a dark shadow over many who lived in the years immediately before and after it, and tainted the reputation of many of those who were associated with it. In general, the churches emerged from the war deeply scarred, and Shakespeare probably suffered more than most in this regard.

In the analysis that follows, one of the primary objectives will be to assess how far Shakespeare's reforms were consistent, or in conflict, with the Baptist ecclesiological tradition he inherited. It will therefore be necessary to give a brief sketch of this tradition. Shakespeare was motivated more by pragmatic concerns than theological ones, but the changes in church polity he brought about have important implications for the Baptist view of the church. Changes in church polity are sometimes helpful in revealing underlying and unarticulated changes in thinking. Disagreements over organisation can also be symptomatic of hidden theological tensions.[10] Baptist ecclesiology is inevitably an imprecise subject. Not only was the Baptist denomination in the latter stages of the nineteenth century an amalgam of several theological and ecclesiological traditions, but it was also by its very nature diffuse and lacking in any centralised control. These characteristics are actually in themselves an important part of Baptist tradition. Shakespeare's attempt to harmonise these disparate elements into a single national system was an important, and rather unBaptist, aspect of his work.

Particular ecclesiological issues raised by the reforms in church polity under Shakespeare included one that was familiar to all congregationally organised church bodies, the tension between the autonomy of the local church and denominational unity. This tension was brought sharply into focus during this period. Other important issues were the Baptist ministry, especially the nature of the distinction between ordained and lay ministry and the recognition and support of ministers. Shakespeare's work also highlights the difficulties posed for denominations holding different ecclesiologies, and committed to different forms of polity, pursuing a greater degree of organisational unity. These became increasingly obvious, both within the Free Church movement, and in Baptist and Nonconformist relations with the Church of England. In more general terms, it is also important to consider Shakespeare's part in the churches' attempt to meet the challenge of the new century. As that century has now drawn to a close, an evaluation of his approach to this task is possible.

In the chapters that follow, the first is concerned with the historical and personal background to Shakespeare's period of office. A brief outline of English Baptist history, especially as it relates to patterns of church polity, is given, in order to provide the necessary context for Shakespeare's reforms. This is followed by a description of the challenges and opportunities facing Nonconformity at the turn of the century. The first chapter ends with a survey of Shakespeare's personal background, leading up to his appointment as Secretary of the Baptist Union. The second chapter describes the development of the Baptist Union and the creation of the Baptist World Alliance, and considers Shakespeare's style of leadership. It covers the years from 1898 until about 1907. The third chapter explores the changes that took place in the Baptist ministry under his leadership, including ministerial training, accreditation, support and settlement, up to the end of the First World War. The most important aspect of this was the adoption of the Ministerial Settlement and Sustentation Scheme in 1916, which gave the Union a dominant and unchallenged place in denominational life. In the fourth chapter, the centre of interest is Shakespeare's involvement in the pursuit of church unity during and after the war. This includes the creation of the United Army and Navy Chaplaincy Board, the formation of the Free Church Federal Council and the response of the Free Churches to the Lambeth Appeal. The fifth chapter deals with post-war developments within the denomination, especially in regard to the ministry, and the circumstances surrounding Shakespeare's resignation in 1924. The sixth and final chapter attempts an evaluation of Shakespeare's contribution to Nonconformity and to his own denomination.

Some word of explanation may be in order concerning the restriction of this study to England, in view of the fact that Shakespeare was secretary of the Baptist Union of Great Britain and Ireland. In the early years of the Union, there were no equivalent organisations in the other three countries of the British Isles, but in the second half of the nineteenth century, independent Unions were formed in all of them (in Wales in 1866, in Scotland in 1869 and in Ireland in 1895). Although there were a few churches in all four nations in membership with the Baptist Union of Great Britain and Ireland, the existence and growing strength of the other national Unions meant that it became fundamentally an English institution. The character and history of Baptists and their institutions in the four nations differed significantly. The Welsh revival in 1905, for example, which deeply affected the Baptists of Wales, had virtually no impact in England. The raising of the Sustentation Fund between 1912 and 1914 and the organisation of the 1916 Ministerial Settlement and Sustentation Scheme were, as far as the Union was concerned, limited to England, although the other Unions undertook parallel initiatives at the same time. To attempt to include Ireland, Scotland and Wales in the pages that follow would be to add a degree of complexity that would be unhelpful.

Where quotations from some early documents include archaic spelling, these have been modernised.

1. *BT*, 15 March 1928.

2. F. Townley Lord, *Baptist World Fellowship: A Short History of the Baptist World Alliance* (The Carey Kingsgate Press Ltd.: London, 1955), p. 53.

3. Anthony Cross, 'Revd. Dr. Hugh Martin: Ecumenist', *BQ* vol. 37 (April 1997) p. 71. Two recent publications from Baptist authors have helped meet the need for a more fitting acknowledgement of Shakespeare's importance in the history of the denomination. These appeared while the thesis on which this book is based was being prepared for publication. They are W.M.S. West's *Baptists Together* (Baptist Historical Society: Didcot, 2000), which inludes a chapter on Shakespeare, mainly describing his involvement with the three denominational Funds he helped raise, and Anthony Cross's *Baptism and the Baptists: Theology and Practice in Twentieth Century Britain* (Paternoster Press: Carlisle, 2000). Cross deals at some length with the implications of Baptist baptismal practice for Shakespeare's attempts to achieve church unity (see especially pp. 42-59).

4. Adrian Hastings, *A History of English Christianity 1920-1985* (Collins: London, 1986), pp. 98-9.

5. J. C. Carlile, *My Life's Little Day* (Blackie and Son Ltd.: London, 1935), p. 169.

6. *Ibid.*.

7. C. M. Townsend, *The Life and Work of J. H. Shakespeare*. It was probably written in about 1971, or soon after.

8. By Robertson Nicoll in *BW*, 5 December 1918.

9. *BT* 25 September 1914.

10. See Paul M. Harrison, *Authority and Power in the Free Church Tradition: A Social Case Study of the American Baptist Convention* (Princeton University Press, Princeton: 1959), pp. 5-6, whose analysis is very helpful in this regard.

CHAPTER 1

Background

1.1 The Baptists

1.1.1 Origins

For the first English Baptists, ecclesiology lay at the heart of discontent with the national church.[1] This was largely true of the radical reformation in general, but was especially important for those who, like the Baptists, embraced Separatism. There was considerable diversity and fluidity in ecclesiology within the various radical congregations and groups in the early seventeenth century, but once believers' baptism had been adopted, the result was inevitably a separatist ecclesiology. It emphatically undermined the whole concept of a united national church.

Two main Baptists groups developed independently of each other in the early seventeenth century. They were theologically different, in spite of their common Separatist inheritance. The General Baptists emerged from the exiled Separatist congregations in the Netherlands. The congregation led by John Smyth developed close links with the Anabaptist Mennonites, from whom it learned believers' baptism. When Thomas Helwys returned to London in 1612, having broken with Smyth, leading a small group of English Baptists, it became the first such church on English soil. Tolmie describes them as the 'only significant survivors in England of the early separatist tradition'.[2] This may be something of an overstatement, but it is true that their first leader, John Smyth (who, like Robert Browne, was prepared for the Church of England priesthood at Cambridge University), was a direct product of Elizabethan Separatism. While in the Netherlands, the Smyth/Helwys congregation not only became Baptist, but also abandoned Puritan Calvinism and embraced Arminianism. It was the start of the General Baptist movement.

The Particular Baptists, on the other hand, remained true to their Calvinistic inheritance, emerging gradually, over the course of several years, from the Separatist church founded by Henry Jacob in 1616. They first appear as a distinct and recognised group, committed to the practice of believers' baptism, with the publication of the London Confession of Faith in 1644. Seven London churches co-operated in the production of this document. Their primary aim in doing so seems to have been to assert their fundamental orthodoxy among the independent reformed churches.

It is possible to identify some common and important themes in early Baptist ecclesiology, many of which they shared with the non-Baptist Independent congregations. One central principle was the competence of each individual congregation to seek the will of Christ and acknowledge Him as its Lord. The 1644 London Confession described each particular congregation as 'a compact and knit city in itself',[3] following Henry Jacob's view that a true church consists of believers voluntarily coming together, these believers 'having the power to exercise ecclesiastical government and all God's other spiritual ordinances'.[4] Barrie White, writing of the signatories of this Confession, says, 'their primary conviction was that the Church on earth was manifested in individual congregations of believing men and women each of which had authority committed to it for the ordering of its life immediately from the Ascended Lord'.[5] Thomas Helwys was no less committed to this principle than the Particular Baptists. Every congregation, he believed, 'though they be but two or three, have Christ given them, with all the means of their salvation'.[6] The members of each individual congregation were bound together by their faith in Christ and their commitment to each other, and were collectively responsible for their life together, under the Lordship of Christ.

This congregational ecclesiology was shown in various ways, such as in the refusal to allow any outside body jurisdiction over the local church, and the limitation of the authority of church officers to the particular congregation that had called them. The Particular Baptists were in general more eager to protect the autonomy of each local church than the General Baptists, and the latter tended to give relatively more authority to the associations of churches as the seventeenth century progressed. However, this was more a matter of differences in emphasis than a significant divergence of principle.[7]

A related Baptist distinctive practice was the participation of the laity in all forms of ministry. In this respect Baptists differed from most of the Independents, who were more inclined to limit certain functions to the ordained clergy. This blurring of the distinction between lay and ordained leaders among Baptists is seen in the 1644 Confession. One of the ways in which it differed from the 1596 Separatist Confession was its weakening of ministerial authority.[8] Practice varied, but the view of the Midland Baptist Association in 1655 may be taken as fairly typical. Non-ordained members who were already preaching could be called by the church to baptise and administer the Lord's Supper, as long as this did not lead to the church's neglect of the search for an 'official minister'.[9]

This acceptance of the autonomy of the local church, and its ability to function fully even without an ordained minister, enabled small and sometimes isolated and persecuted congregations to survive. It also reflected their total rejection of a separated priesthood, and a desire to avoid any form of ecclesiastical hierarchy, which were two elements of the established church they most despised as unscriptural. One of the consequences of this was uncertainty about the precise status of the ordained ministry. Baptists were committed to its importance, as the Particular London Confessions of 1677 and 1688 clearly indicate:

A particular church gathered, and completely organised, according to the mind of Christ, consists of officers and members; and the officers appointed by Christ to be chosen and set apart by the church . . . are bishops or elders and deacons . . .. The way appointed by Christ for the calling of any person . . . is that he be chosen thereunto by the common suffrage of the Church itself, and solemnly set apart by fasting and prayer, with imposition of hands of the eldership of the church, if there be any constituted therein.[10]

The church representatives of the Abingdon Association, at a meeting in 1654, had in like manner concluded that the offices of elders and deacons were 'ordained of the Lord for the good of his church' and that it was 'the duty of every church very diligently to endeavour, and very earnestly to seek unto the Lord, that they may enjoy the benefit of these his gracious appointments'.[11]

Ordination was understood as a function of the local church, but there was considerable variation in the way it was practised. The exercise of a ministry beyond the bounds of a single congregation was generally rejected. Baptists insisted on seeing the minister's own local congregation as the context for his ministry. However, a degree of flexibility was sometimes required. Churches would sometimes seek the help of a neighbouring minister, and this was encouraged in early association life.[12] They also ordained and commissioned ministers for the work of forming new churches in new areas, who would exercise responsibility for them until their own ministers were ordained.[13] Among General Baptists, this practice developed, towards the end of the seventeenth century, into the acceptance of itinerant ministers, known as Messengers, alongside the pastors and deacons of the local churches.

Baptist collective identity and fellowship was predominantly expressed by means of associations of churches, which can be seen as a partial modification of strict congregational independence. Much of the surviving Baptist material from the seventeenth century is in the form of association records, and it is difficult to know just how many Baptist churches existed apart from the associations. They were, without doubt, one of the characteristic features of the early Baptist movement. The 1644 Confession is itself an example of co-operation, and affirms the importance of its member churches walking 'by one and the same rule', and having 'the counsel and help one of another in all needful affairs of the church, as members of one body in the common faith under Christ their only head'.[14] The records of the first Particular Baptist associations show the high value placed on mutual support and help by their member churches.[15] The Abingdon Association began its meetings in 1652 with representatives of just three churches, with the objective of enabling churches to care for each other as fellow members of the same body of Christ.[16] The Midland Association, formed in 1655, consisted initially of 17 churches. They agreed to help each other by giving advice, financial and other practical assistance and 'watching over each other'.[17] The associations were, however, careful to disown any jurisdiction over the churches, and their deliberations and decisions were subject to confirmation by the churches.[18] Henry Ainsworth's *The Communion of Saints*, first published in 1641, and widely read by Baptists and other Independents, expressed the relationship between like minded churches in the following way:

> . . . the particular churches are sisters each to other . . . Churches owe help, comfort, and refreshing one to another, as they have need and ability . . . although we may advise, exhort, warn, reprove, etc., so far as Christian love and power extends: yet find we no authority committed to one congregation over another . . .[19]

Over time, the General Baptists increasingly diverged from the Particular Baptist pattern, so that by the early part of the eighteenth century they had developed a more connexional ecclesiology. Church representatives met at a national Assembly as well as on a regional basis. The Assembly was given authority to hear appeals from individuals and churches, and to resolve differences. The originally evangelistic Messengers gradually assumed a supervisory function among the churches. The Particular Baptists developed no national body until the nineteenth century. It was they, however, who provided the main stream of denominational development, and it is from among them that the two most important Baptist institutions of the nineteenth and twentieth century (the Missionary Society and the Union) emerged. These institutions were both products of the Evangelical Awakening.

1.1.2 The Evangelical Awakening

Initially, the Methodist revival had little effect on the churches of Old Dissent. This was partly because it began as an essentially Anglican movement. John Wesley, himself a priest in the Church of England, was hostile towards Dissenters in general, and Baptists in particular. The Arminian theology, which underlay his evangelistic activity, alienated him from the bulk of Nonconformists. Even George Whitfield, with his more congenial Calvinism, was closely linked to the Establishment and regarded with suspicion. The organisation of Methodism, with its national Conference and circuit system, was entirely alien to congregational polity. Indeed, the whole spirit of Methodism, with its emotional fervour and emphasis on personal experience, was one that even the most open and evangelistic of the dissenters of the eighteenth century (men such as Philip Doddridge for example) found disturbing.

The General Baptists, whose background had more in common with

Methodism (especially their more connexional organisation and Arminian theology), were in no position to take advantage of the new movement. Numerically weak, and divided by doctrinal controversy, many of their churches were, by the middle of the eighteenth century, moving away from orthodoxy to embrace Unitarianism. However, the General Baptists did have close ties with a new group of Baptist churches that was to play a crucial role in the subsequent history of the denomination, the so-called New Connexion of General Baptists.

The New Connexion was a child of the Methodist Revival, and had its origins among Methodist converts who became convinced of the invalidity of paedobaptism in the 1750's. Two groups of churches that were comprised of such believers, one in Yorkshire and the other in the Midlands, were drawn into the orbit of the Lincolnshire Association of General Baptists. Their leader was Dan Taylor, and he was ordained as a General Baptist minister in 1763. Increasingly dissatisfied with a general lack of enthusiasm for evangelism and doctrinal unorthodoxy within his denomination, Taylor formed the New Connexion of General Baptists in 1770. Relationships with the old General Baptists remained cordial until a complete break was made in 1803. Taylor's dynamic leadership continued well into the nineteenth century, and while the original General Baptists continued to decline until they became an insignificant force, the New Connexion grew rapidly, establishing its own academy for ministerial training and overseas missionary society, as well as many new churches.

The New Connexion introduced a Methodist element into Baptist denominational life, particularly with respect to church polity. This became increasingly important as it grew closer to the Particular Baptists during the course of the nineteenth century. The principle of congregational autonomy was officially adopted by the Connexion, but there was also, along with this, a clear commitment to the importance of unity and co-operation among its churches. Unlike the Particular Baptists, whose organisations and activities lacked any effective central direction, it had a coherent corporate identity, and acted as such. This was largely due to the personal unifying influence over many years of Dan Taylor himself. The college, home and foreign missionary societies and magazine operated under the sanction of the Connexion as a whole, acting through their annual meeting (known as the 'Association'). There were also local district conferences that exercised a degree of authority over the local churches. The New Connexion did not, however, adopt the General Baptist practice of appointing Messengers. The ordained ministry was understood in congregational terms, as was the case with the Particular Baptists.[20]

Among the Particular Baptists, two centres in particular caught the revivalist spirit during the last quarter of the eighteenth century, and from these it spread to influence the whole denomination. The first was the Baptist college in Bristol, the only Baptist institution for training ministers until the General Baptists' 'Society for the Education of Young Men for the Ministry' started its work in 1792 and the New Connexion's academy opened in 1798. Its tutor, Caleb Evans, founded the Bristol Education Society in 1770 in order to widen support for the work of the college. This was the first example among Baptists of a single purpose voluntary society, and acted as a stimulus for later co-operative activity, especially in training and mission. John Rippon and William Steadman were two of the ministers trained at Bristol at this time who went on to play leading roles in the revitalisation of the denomination. Rippon created the *Baptist Annual Register* in 1790 and continued to edit it until 1802, an important step in giving Baptists a sense of denominational identity. Steadman became the first President of a new Baptist Academy in Bradford in 1804.

The second main centre of revivalist activity among Baptists was the Northamptonshire Association. In about 1780, Andrew Fuller, minister of the Kettering Baptist Church, came under the influence of the writings of the American Congregationalist preacher, Jonathan Edwards. Edwards was a leading figure in the New England revival of the 1730's, and theologically a Calvinist. Fuller became convinced that Calvinistic doctrine could be reconciled with issuing appeals to the unconverted to accept Christ. His *The Gospel Worthy of All Acceptation*, which became a foundational book for nineteenth-century evangelical Calvinism, set out this view. William Carey was a fellow minister in the Northamptonshire Association. His *An Enquiry into the Obligations of Christians to use Means for the Conversion of the Heathen* (1792) led directly to the formation of the Baptist Missionary Society. Fuller became its secretary and chief advocate. The founding of the missionary society hastened the transformation of the Baptists' approach to the evangelistic task of the churches, both at home and abroad.

An explosion of co-operative activity, especially in evangelism, occurred in the closing years of the eighteenth century. It involved the formation of many new societies, as well as new associations. This constituted an important new development in Baptist church polity. The concept of ministry was broadened, with the appointment of missionaries for mission work overseas and itinerant preachers for mission work at home. They were chosen and supported variously by churches, associations, societies and colleges. This response to the opportunities Baptists saw around them was not systematic, but spontaneous and haphazard. It met with remarkable success. The years between 1780 and 1830 saw unprecedented numerical growth among Baptists, with a mushrooming of churches, church members and attendance.

The excitement and change of those years had a profound effect on the Baptists' approach to church life. There was little desire among most of them to think through the ecclesiological implications of what was happening. It is not necessary to go all the way with Sellers, in his assessment that 'theological system was brushed aside, cast into the shade by the irrefutable witness of a multitude gathered in by rhetoric alone'.[21] It seems indisputable, however, that Briggs is right in writing that 'the theological under-pinning of church activity became less well focused, less clearly identi-fied'.[22] This, together with the emergence of new societies, tended to weaken commitment to the traditional Baptist model of the self-governing gathered church. Those who wanted to hold on to the denomination's eccle-siological roots were challenged by the success of those who were pioneer-ing new methods, and the flood of new converts unfamiliar with the denom-ination's history.

1.1.3 The Baptist Union

The haphazard spontaneity of the early years of the nineteenth century grad-ually gave way to a more centralised and institutionally elaborate denomi-nation as time went by. The most important sign of this was the develop-ment of the Baptist Union. It was formed as a 'society of ministers and churches' in 1813 when 45 Particular Baptist ministers in London signed the agreed constitution as inaugural members. Its primary aim was the support of Baptist missions, particularly the Baptist Missionary Society.[23]

The way the missionary society itself was supported and managed also changed, as it moved away from its Northamptonshire roots to a more gen-uinely national, London based organisation. Andrew Fuller always resisted this development, and it was not until after his death in 1815 that the move to London took place. Soon afterwards the society's first salaried secretary was appointed. A similar development took place in the field of home mis-sion. The Baptist Society in London for the Encouragement and Support of Itinerant Preaching was formed in 1797, and was one of a number of such societies in different parts of the country, mainly enabling local ministers to engage in preaching tours. By 1820, it had become a national body, employ-ing its own full-time staff and supported by auxiliaries throughout the coun-try. In 1822 it was renamed the Baptist Home Missionary Society, in recog-nition of its developing status and role. These developments reflect the fact that evangelism was increasingly becoming regarded as a 'denominational rather than a local responsibility'.[24]

The Baptist Union made no significant contribution to denominational life until its reconstitution in 1832, and even then its impact on most churches was small. The new 1832 constitution abandoned the original Calvinistic statement of faith. This enabled churches and ministers of the New Connexion to become members. The theological diversity of Baptists made genuine unity difficult to achieve. There were divisions between inde-pendently minded Calvinists and connexionally minded Arminians, as well as differences over conditions of church membership and admission to the Lord's Supper. The imprecise 1832 doctrinal basis of the Union was an attempt to embrace everyone who went under the name Baptist, but it did not constitute a very adequate foundation for meaningful denominational unity. As long as 30 years later, with the Union established as an important feature of denominational life, its secretary was forced to admit that:

> Denominational union among Baptists has been slow in manifestation, and difficult of cultivation. We have long been a divided body, and we are so still; and if any progress at all has been made, it is unquestionable both that much remains to be done, and that the most recent efforts have met with little success . . . The Baptist denomination, while, in name *one*, is in *fact* many. If it were an evil spirit it might say, 'My name is Legion'.[25]

Insofar as the denomination had any organisational coherence, it was made up, in effect, of a number of overlapping circles of co-operative effort and allegiance. The New Connexion (which soon came to be usually known as the General Baptist Association), with its associated organisations, was an important such circle, as were the Particular Baptist colleges, the associations and the Baptist Missionary Society. Each of these drew support from particular groups of churches within the denomination. Many churches, however, were fiercely independent, maintaining only superficial wider ties. Practice and principles varied considerably, and insofar as the Union brought unity to Baptists, it did so without attempting to harmonise these differences. When a new constitution was agreed in 1873 it specified only two principles upon which the Union was based: that 'every separate church has liberty to interpret and administer the laws of Christ, and that immersion of believers is the only Christian baptism'.[26] Many churches were prepared to associate themselves with the Union, and their members to attend its annual meetings, but its ecclesiastical significance and authority, like its financial resources, were minimal.

From the 1860's onwards, however, there were increasing signs that Baptists valued the Union and the contribution it made to denominational life. The number of churches joining it increased, autumn Assemblies outside of London were instituted, in addition to the spring London meetings, and its secretary began to be seen as a significant figure in national Baptist life. A number of developments took place in the 1870's and 80's that strengthened the Union's position. The 1873 constitution made it possible for the first time for colleges and associations, as well as churches, to become members. The bringing of these important institutions under the umbrella of the Union helped instil a new sense of denominational unity. In 1875, in a move the importance of which Sparkes says, 'can hardly be exaggerated',[27] a Union Annuity Fund for ministers was established. In 1877 the Union appointed its first full-time secretary, Samuel Harris Booth. In 1882 the Home Missionary Society was incorporated into the Union, making the latter for the first time an evangelistic agency in its own right. This period was an important formative period for John Howard Shakespeare. Between 1875 and 1883 he was a young man in London, preparing for the Baptist ministry. The Principal of Regent's Park College, where he received his theological training, Joseph Angus, was an active participant in Union life.

Shakespeare's call to his first pastorate at St. Mary's Baptist Church in Norwich came in 1883. In the decade following this, two other highly significant events took place that were to be crucial in shaping the Union's future development. The first was the departure from the Union of Charles Haddon Spurgeon following the Downgrade controversy of 1887-8. Spurgeon's typically vigorous attack on what he considered to be liberal tendencies within the Union led to a vote of censure by the Union Council, and, in spite of efforts by Booth and others, no reconciliation could be brought about. It is surprising that this event did not split the Union. In spite of Spurgeon's immense popularity, only a handful of churches followed him out of the Union. Payne regards this as a sign of the importance of the Union to Baptists.[28] The effect of the withdrawal was to deprive the Union of the most powerful Baptist figure in the country, and to make it easier for those who disliked his flamboyant and unsophisticated Calvinism to determine its future. In particular, it enabled the General Baptist Association (i.e. the New Connexion), and especially its most influential minister, John Clifford, of whose theology Spurgeon was openly critical, to assume a prominence that would otherwise have been much less likely.

One of the people Spurgeon almost certainly had in mind in his accusations of Baptists' departure from Scriptural truth (he refused to name the culprits himself) was the Rev. James Thew of Leicester. Thew did not hide his aversion for Spurgeon's theology. Writing at the time of the Downgrade controversy, he declared that 'the God of Mr. Spurgeon is not my God . . . Mr. Spurgeon's doctrines concerning Jesus, alas! came nigh to robbing me of Him altogether'.[29] Thew was a leading liberal in the denomination, and, as minister of the church attended by Shakespeare as a boy, was a prime influence on him.[30]

The second significant event that took place during Shakespeare's first decade in the pastorate at St. Mary's was the absorption of the New Connexion by the Baptist Union in 1891. The Union had welcomed New Connexion Baptists into its life at every level for many years, their theological differences having ceased to matter for most people on both sides. The main difficulty in achieving unity was organisational, as the two bodies were constitutionally quite different. The formation of the Baptist Union Corporation Ltd. in 1890 was one of the steps taken by the Union to enable it to absorb the Association. This event also had wider significance for future denominational development in facilitating the Union's adoption of greater financial and legal powers.

Rinaldi says that the influence of the General Baptists in the denomination was 'simply overwhelmed in the merger' with the Union.[31] It is true that as an institution they disappeared in 1891, but Rinaldi's view does not do justice to their impact on the Union and their influence over its future development. The Union was still, in 1891, as much a collection of different Baptist groups as it was a coherent ecclesiastical body. Among these groups, the General Baptist Association was one of the strongest. The formal amalgamation brought into the Union the novel experience of a Model Trust Deed for local churches, a Board of Reference to help place ministers in churches and a centrally administered Sustentation Fund. These were not immediately adopted by the Union, but in time, they all found their way into national Baptist life. The Association's 'well-developed sense of denominational cohesion and the development of appropriate instruments to secure it'[32] were to be highly significant for the future. Both the 1891 amalgamation and the Downgrade Controversy had a great effect on the denomination, preparing the way for many of the subsequent events for which Shakespeare was responsible.

1.1.4 Nonconformity in Late Victorian England

Four denominations dominated English Nonconformity at the end of the nineteenth century: the Wesleyan Methodists, the Primitive Methodists, the Congregationalists and the Baptists. There were also important smaller groups, including several other branches of Methodism (three of which united in 1907 to form the United Methodist Church), the Presbyterian Church and the recently formed Salvation Army. The nineteenth century had seen substantial numerical growth for most of them and an increase in status as disadvantageous legislation was steadily removed. In spite of the entrenched privileges of the Church of England in many areas, they had gained a secure and influential place in national life. Middle class suburbia had proved fertile ground for their evangelistic activity, and they were comfortable with the liberal, entrepreneurial values that lay at the heart of Victorian society. Numerically, attendance at Nonconformist places of worship matched that of the Established Church, the four major denominations claiming about one and a half million communicants among them. Their political hero was Gladstone, of whom the *Freeman* wrote, at his death in May 1898, 'no public man since Oliver Cromwell has been more loyal to his conscience, the Bible and the Saviour'.[33]

The rise of the Free Church movement in the 1890's gave enormous confidence to Nonconformists and a boost to their sense of unity. The National Council of Evangelical Free Churches was formed, and held its first Congress in Manchester in 1892. Local Councils multiplied rapidly throughout the country, united missions were held, a catechism published and several full-time staff appointed. At the 1900 National Congress, the incoming President addressed the gathered delegates as representatives of 'the great Free Church of Great Britain'.[34] In 1905, describing what he saw as revival within Nonconformity, the author and journalist W. T. Stead wrote that 'the birth in our time of a new National Church, not established by the

State, but created and sustained by the people, is one of the most unexpected and reassuring events of the last decade'.[35] In similar vein, the leading Congregationalist minister, Silvester Horne, in his *A Popular History of the Free Churches*, published in 1903, concluded with the following assertion:

> This massing of the Free Church forces for the defence of the interests of religious liberty and Christian truth is the most influential factor in the present ecclesiastical situation in England. . . .The Free Churches, which have been so largely instrumental in establishing the principle that the final authority in the State is the people, are now concerned to establish the principle that the final authority in the Christian Church is the Christian people. They have triumphed in the former issue; they will triumph in the latter.[36]

As Kent points out, it is difficult, from the perspective of a hundred years later, and looking back over two World Wars and almost constant religious decline, to appreciate the sense of hope and excitement with which the Free Churches embarked on the twentieth century.[37] Men like Shakespeare believed they were living in times of unprecedented opportunity.

There was an ambiguity about the Nonconformists' position, however, even then. The stigma of dissent was still felt, and evidence of social exclusion not difficult to find. The fact that only 10 tickets were offered to Free Church leaders for the coronation of Edward VII was one example.[38] Intellectual challenges to the Scriptural basis of their faith also troubled some. The greatest sense of threat, however, came from the increasing evidence that their attempts at mission to the urban working classes and the poor were failing dismally. The publication of *The Bitter Cry of Outcast London* in 1883, General Booth's *In Darkest England and the Way Out* in 1890, and the evidence published by Charles Booth in his exhaustive survey of *Life and Labour of the People of London* (finally published in full in 1902) together with numerous other local surveys, were deeply disturbing. English society in the twentieth century seemed destined to be increasingly urban in character, and if Nonconformity could not 'square chapel going with urban life',[39] the outlook could only be a bleak one.

Several of the key figures in Baptist life (including F. B. Meyer and John Clifford in London, and, indeed, Shakespeare himself, in the centre of Norwich) were engaged in trying to meet this challenge. Throughout Nonconformity, a wide range of activities grew up around many of the larger urban churches, inspired in many cases by the example of the Wesleyan, Hugh Price Hughes. Central Halls and Missions were established, often at great expense and with enormous effort. Institutional churches, embracing a wide and complex array of social and educational activities, grew increasingly elaborate. Charles Booth's view was that the Baptists were the most successful of the Nonconformist denominations in many parts of London, especially in the

South where the influence of Spurgeon was still felt. 'Whatever this master workman put his hand to seems to have been well and solidly accomplished', he wrote, 'and to have been endowed with lasting life'.[40] The mass of the urban poor and the working classes, however, still remained untouched.

As well as attempting to meet the challenge of the urban poor and working classes, Nonconformity was also eager to rise above its reputation of being uncultured and poorly educated. Great efforts were made in the erection of elaborate Gothic buildings, the pursuit of the best ministerial education and the improvement of worship. Nonconformity's apparent readiness to abandon its intellectual and cultural heritage in the pursuit of social acceptance has often been commented on.[41] Jeffrey Cox describes late nineteenth-century Nonconformity's frequent condescension towards its own intellectual heritage as one of its least attractive aspects.[42] Baptists, whose predominantly lower middle and upper working class congregations put them towards the lower end of the social spectrum within the major Nonconformist denominations, were sometimes especially prone to this tendency. Ironically, If Booth was right, and probably unfairly, Spurgeon was one of the chief victims of this disparaging of the more 'vulgar' elements of their past.

Calculating the numerical strength of Baptists in England in the nineteenth century is a notoriously difficult task.[43] The figures for churches in England were not usually separated from those of Wales in official publications. The majority of churches belonged to their local association, but a substantial minority did not, and the associations differed in their constitutions and the care taken in collecting and publicising membership statistics. There were several national denominational bodies and publications, and many independent churches were unaffiliated to any wider organisation. Even those that were affiliated did not always submit reliable statistical returns. A further complication is over defining the term 'Baptist'. Some churches owed allegiance to more than one denomination; some moved in and out of the Baptist 'fold'; others (particularly among the older General Baptists) drifted towards Unitarianism.

The 1851 census of religious worship identified four major groups of Baptists in England and Wales: General Baptists (of whom total attendance on Census Sunday was 22,000), Particular Baptists (741,000), New Connexion Baptists (64,000) and undefined Baptists (101,000). Deducing the total number of attenders from attendance figures is not straightforward, as many people attended twice or even three times. On census day, however, there were probably about 600,000 attenders in total, of whom about one third attended churches in Wales. Membership returns from associations to the *Baptist Manual* suggest that this was five or six times church membership, but these returns were almost certainly a substantial underestimate of the real figure. Briggs suggests that membership (for England and Wales) was actually about 150,000, a quarter of the number of attenders.

Figures for England given in the *Baptist Handbook*, and followed by Currie, indicate that total Baptist membership in 1875 was about 171,000, rising to 239,000 in 1900.

The changing ratio of members to attenders or adherents is difficult to ascertain with any degree of certainty. This is unfortunate, as it is an important (and sometimes neglected) factor if the significance of official membership figures is to be properly assessed. As we have seen, it probably stood at about 1:4 in 1850, and if Alan Gilbert's suggestion that by the early twentieth century membership actually exceeded attendance is correct, this is as dramatic an indication of Baptist (and Nonconformist) decline during that period as any.[44]

An accurate evaluation of changing Baptist strength in the country must also take account of the rise in the general population.[45] The number of church members, as a proportion of the population aged over 15, was at its highest between about 1850 and 1890, at about 1.3%.[46] The percentage for Nonconformity as a whole started to fall from about 1880.[47]

1.2 John Howard Shakespeare

1.2.1 Childhood and Preparation for Ministry

Shakespeare was born on 16 April 1857 in Malton in the East Riding of Yorkshire, the second of three children. His father, the Rev. Benjamin Shakespeare, had become the minister of Malton Baptist Church earlier in the same year.[48] Both his father and his mother were the children of Baptist ministers. The whole family was thus steeped in the Baptist faith, and Shakespeare's early upbringing was shaped by the restricted and narrow outlook of rural Nonconformity in the North of England. He was no doubt all too familiar with both the idealism and the struggles of the manse.

Surviving references by Shakespeare to his family background are extremely rare, and such details as are available very sketchy. In 1918 he described it in the following terms:

Religiously, I was born in an austere land, and I travelled in boyhood through a narrow and rugged defile. If St. Paul was a Pharisee of the Pharisees, I was reared as a Baptist of the Baptists, a dissenter of the dissenters. In my childish ignorance, it was a matter of continual surprise to me that any good or intelligent person could be anything but a Baptist. Of course, there were degrees of remoteness from the true faith, but I do not remember any kind of fellowship outside the pale of the denomination. As for attending a service in another chapel, such an idea never entered the mind.[49]

Shakespeare's son Geoffrey, in his autobiography *Let Candles Be Brought In* (written over twenty years after Shakespeare's death) admits to ignorance about his father's early life. He imagines an education in small private schools.[50] In the autobiographical chapter in his *The Churches at the Cross Roads*, Shakespeare himself passes over this period in his life with only the scantiest of information. Some helpful background is provided by J. F. Makepeace, whose autobiography *All I Could Never Be*, published in 1924, describes an upbringing that must have been very similar to Shakespeare's. Makepeace was the son of a Baptist minister with pastorates in Luton and Bradford when he was a child. Speaking of his childhood in the 1860's, he describes it as a happy time, in spite of its restrictions and poverty. 'We had no social life except for an occasional tea-meeting or 'entertainment' at the chapel, or a formal invitation to the houses of the most prosperous members', he writes. Makepeace's elementary education, undertaken before the 1870 Education Act, was 'meagre . . . inefficient . . . uninspiring'.[51]

Shakespeare's later passion for improving the lot of the ordinary Baptist minister, particularly in the rural churches, must have sprung at least in part from his own family background. One of the few occasions when he spoke publicly about it was at the Baptist Assembly in the spring of 1904, when, in an appeal for more effective support for village pastors, he described in emotional terms how he had once read the Gospel of John at the bedside of his dying grandfather.[52]

In 1863 the family moved to Derby, and soon afterwards to Leicester. Shakespeare attended Wyggeston's Hospital School in the city, and worshipped at the Baptist church on Belvoir Street. The minister at Belvoir Street was James P. Mursell, one of the most prominent Baptist leaders of his day and a keen advocate of the amalgamation of the Baptist Union with the New Connexion.[53] Shakespeare was also greatly influenced by Mursell's young assistant, who later succeeded him as minister, James Thew. The impact of a large and progressive city church, led by two gifted preachers, made a lasting impression on him, and he remained an admirer of Thew's liberal and cultured ministry throughout his life.[54] The *Baptist Magazine*, in a biographical article on Shakespeare in 1891, stated that Shakespeare experienced his call to the Christian ministry under the influence of the preaching of the Belvoir Street ministers, referring to the 'enkindling fire of Mr. Thew's ministry'.[55]

At the age of 18, Shakespeare moved to London, his father, having left the ministry, being in business there.[56] He was baptised and joined the Regent's Park Church. He was engaged in clerical work for a short time. In 1878 he failed the Civil Service examination, his hand apparently shaking so violently that he was unable to write.[57] According to Geoffrey, he saw this as God's guidance away from a secular career, and later in the same year he entered Regent's Park College to train for the Baptist ministry. At that time the College was housed in 'a private mansion . . . of stately Georgian proportions', and was presided over by its 'courteous, scholarly, saintly' Principal, Rev. Joseph Angus.[58]

Shakespeare received a rigorous academic training over the course of the next five years, of which he was later critical as being too academic and insufficiently concerned with developing the skills needed in the pastorate, preaching in particular. This included instruction in Hebrew, Latin and Greek. According to the *Baptist Magazine*, he gave a 'speech of remarkable brilliancy' advocating the merits of Tennyson during a debate in his first year as a student, and became secretary of the college debating society.[59] It was possibly during his time at Regent's Park that he developed his love of the poet Browning.[60]

Regent's Park College was affiliated to University College, part of London University, and his training included the acquisition of an MA degree in philosophy from the University. Shortly before his training was due to be completed, he accepted a call to the pastorate of one of the leading Baptist churches in the country, St. Mary's Baptist Church, Norwich, having conducted several services there as a visiting student. He commenced his ministry at St. Mary's in March 1883, shortly before his 26th birthday.

1.2.2 St Mary's Baptist Church, Norwich

Shakespeare's fifteen years of ministry in Norwich gave him the opportunity to exercise to the full his preaching and organising gifts, and introduced him to a wider sphere of church life than he had experienced before. The first really significant event, however, was a personal one. In September 1883 he married Amy Gertrude Goodman, the daughter of a Kent Baptist minister. Shakespeare and his wife threw themselves energetically into the task of leading a large and busy church. Membership grew steadily, more than doubling in size to about 500 by the time they left Norwich in 1898.

One of Shakespeare's first major initiatives was a joint evangelistic venture with the other Nonconformist churches of the city. In December 1883 he told the deacons that he hoped to form a union of churches for evangelistic work,[61] and in the following year a united mission in the city was undertaken, led by the prominent young Wesleyan minister, Hugh Price Hughes. At about this time Hughes was embarking on his leadership of the Methodist 'Forward Movement', with its promotion of strategic mission initiatives in large cities by means of Central Halls, and was in 1895 to create the *Methodist Times*. Ten years older than Shakespeare, he provided a pattern of denominational leadership that influenced Shakespeare considerably in the years to come.

There were a number of other united Nonconformist events in subsequent years, including the visit of the American evangelist D. L. Moody in 1892, and Shakespeare consistently sought to nurture close relationships with other churches in the city. This interest in ecumenism was boosted by his involvement in Sir Henry Lunn's seminal conferences in Grindelwald, Switzerland, during the late 1880's. These led, largely under Hugh Price Hugh's leadership, to the formation of the National Free Church Council in the following decade.

Shakespeare had a reputation for preaching that was 'eloquent, dramatic, intensely evangelical and marked with great power'.[62] 'To accept Christ as Saviour is . . . the only necessity', he told his congregation at the end of 1884, 'before which education, position, wealth, everything, fades away'.[63] A Logic Class, Bible Class and a 'First Day School' for working men were among the activities he established at St. Mary's. In 1885 an ambitious programme of building renovation was undertaken, involving, among other things, the construction of a 'first rate organ' and the installing of choir seats and a pulpit platform. Extracts from the booklet published by the church when the premises were re-opened in 1886 gave an impression of the ambitions and ideals that lay behind the work that had been done.

> First, an enlargement of the building by the construction of an apse at the south end for an organ-loft and choir-gallery . . . a handsome pulpit of tre-foil form in the Italian style . . . some amount of decorative art . . . exquisite carvings in Spanish mahogany. . . . New cast-iron fluted columns with coloured and gilded Corinthian capitals . . .The seats, . . . covered with crimson Axminster Wilton seating, are most comfortable. . . . A beautiful stained-glass window, chaste in design and colouring, has been inserted at the north end.[64]

Shakespeare was eager not to be left behind in the cultural advance that was taking place in many leading Nonconformist places of worship.[65] A fine organ, ranking 'third in importance to all the public organs in Norfolk' replaced the old harmonium.[66] Further substantial building improvements were done in 1896, including the introduction of electric light. He was also keen to reform the administrative procedures of the church. In 1891 he formed a 'Church Council' to streamline decision-making in the church and handle controversial issues.

As the minister of the leading Baptist church in the county, Shakespeare soon got involved in the life of the Norfolk Baptist Association. At the annual meetings in 1887, in a move typical of his desire for administrative efficiency, he proposed 'that any church which receives a grant from this Association shall pledge itself to obtain the concurrence of the committee before appointing a minister'.[67] This provoked considerable opposition, on the grounds that it took away 'the rights and privileges of our poorer brethren', and it was not put to a vote. A watered down version, strongly urging upon churches 'the desirability of conferring with the committee before finally deciding upon the choice of a pastor' was eventually agreed at the following year's meetings.[68]

Shakespeare's abilities and achievements soon brought him to the attention of the denomination nationally. He was elected to the Union Council in 1885. This was the year before the storm surrounding the Downgrade Controversy broke over the Union. An indication of Shakespeare's view of this can be seen in the resolution passed by the deacons of St. Mary's in Norwich in 1888. Showing little sympathy with Spurgeon, it expressed the view that the matter had been 'wisely dealt with' by the Council.[69] Shakespeare had spoken at Assembly meetings before 1889, but his sermon at the autumn Assembly of that year on 'The Issues of Agnosticism and Faith' brought his preaching ability to the attention of the denomination as a whole, and showed his willingness to tackle the difficult issues facing the churches in their mission to contemporary society. Speaking of the necessity of supernatural revelation, he said, 'do not mock the drunkard and the harlot with the Christ of Strauss'.[70]

In 1891 Shakespeare provoked controversy by questioning the adequacy of the ministerial training provided by Baptist colleges in two articles in the *Baptist Magazine*. In these he expressed his view that preaching was the primary task of the ministry, and criticised the colleges for their failure to produce good preachers. Often, he wrote, they did the reverse, so that, after a college course, 'the burning evangelist has shrivelled into the maker of elegant sermons, pretty sentences, and dull platitudes'.[71] He characteristically outlined a detailed seven-point programme for improving college training, in which the emphasis would be on preaching. He also spoke of his dream for a Baptist college at either Oxford or Cambridge University, which alone, he believed, could provide the right theological atmosphere for the highest standard of training.[72]

Two other events during these years contributed significantly to Shakespeare's future career. One was the invitation to present a paper at the 1892 national spring Baptist Assembly on 'Baptist Church Extension in Large Towns'. His address made a great impression, and brought him forcibly to the fore in denominational life. It was delivered with passion, and included specific practical proposals for advance. The ability to combine vision with an awareness of what was needed to see it realised was one of Shakespeare's greatest gifts. When published, his address included several pages of statistics reinforcing his argument. His aim was to urge Baptists, alongside the other main Nonconformist denominations, to tackle the challenge of mission more effectively, especially in the growing cities. This would, he believed, require united effort and organisation. It was 'the organised churches which have a hierarchy or a central authority' that were best able to meet the challenges of the day. In ways that would find an echo in many later pronouncements, Shakespeare pleaded for radical changes to Baptist church polity, including the development of a 'One Town, One

Church' approach to church life in larger towns and cities. He believed that
without such a strategy, whereby several congregations could be regarded as
constituting a single church, the promotion by older town centre churches of
new causes in the suburbs, drawing away some of their best supporters, was
unrealistic.[73] He asked for the establishment of a Baptist Union Church
Extension Society for the whole country, with 'an imposing central fund'.
'We must be interested in the towns . . . we must feel at home with the stir
and rush of civic life, and welcome the bracing air of cities', he told his audience. His appeal concluded with this stirring challenge to his fellow
Baptists:

> Multitudes have died in spiritual darkness almost as deep as that of India,
> to whom by the exercise of a little thought and energy we might have car-
> ried the message of the grace of God, but now it is too late . . . God for-
> give us that we have been in the midst of a perishing multitude, not like
> the compassionate Master, but enjoying our religious privileges, rapt in
> glorious memories and clutching at a dead idol, the brazen and deceptive
> serpent of an extreme and selfish independency[74]

The denomination did not at that stage take up the challenge as
Shakespeare would have wished, but a Church Extension Fund was set up,
and Shakespeare's continued promotion of Church Extension prepared the
way for his later reforms.

The second influential event also involved an address by Shakespeare to
an ecclesiastical gathering. The occasion, however, was of a very different
nature. In 1895 the Anglican Church Congress met in Norwich, and
Shakespeare was invited to give an address of welcome to the gathered
clergy of the Church of England, on behalf of the city's Nonconformist
churches. In it, he spoke warmly and generously of the feelings of
Nonconformists about 'the greatness, the influence and the achievements of
the English Church'.

> We recall with gratitude our debt to you, for the thoughts of your great
> preachers and teachers have entered like iron into our blood, and have
> coloured and inspired our whole ministry. It is your inalienable glory that
> generation after generation you have maintained the unfailing use of com-
> mon prayer and the regular reading of the Word of God.[75]

He was not prepared to admit that the differences between
Nonconformity and the Anglican Church were 'final and hopeless', and
asserted that, whatever the outcome of any discussions about possible
reunion at the Congress might be, 'the realities which unite us infinitely
transcend our differences'.[76] Such an ecumenical spirit is remarkable, especially given Shakespeare's background.

The experience of addressing the Congress had a considerable impact on him. One thing in particular that stood out in his memory of the event was the coldness of the reception he received. 'Never shall I forget the appalling sense of dismay which came over me when I rose to speak at the call of the bishop,' he later wrote of the experience, describing the sense of 'intense disapproval' and 'deep gloom' he felt from his audience.[77] This saddened him, for he had a deep longing, expressed three years later on his departure from St. Mary's, to, whenever possible, 'stand side by side with all the other followers of Christ in winning the world to God'.[78]

In February 1898, Samuel Harris Booth informed the Council of the Baptist Union that he was resigning as Secretary, having served with distinction for over twenty years.[79] Three weeks later Shakespeare told his deacons at St. Mary's that he had been unanimously invited by the Council to take up the position.[80] The deacons were distressed at the possibility of his leaving, but in April received a letter from their pastor indicating his intention to accept the invitation.[81] There followed a confusing sequence of events, related in the deacons' Minute Book of the St. Mary's Church. Ten days after Shakespeare wrote the letter to the deacons, they received another from his doctors saying that he was seriously ill, and that his fragile state of health ruled out his taking up the position of Secretary of the Baptist Union. With proper precautions and rest, the letter continued, he should be able to resume his duties as pastor of St. Mary's.[82]

As Shakespeare's health improved, the expectation was that he would return to the church in September, and the 25th was set for the date when he would once again occupy the pulpit. On the 16th of that month, however, the deacons received a further letter from Shakespeare announcing that he was leaving the church after all, having decided to accept the renewed invitation from the Union Council 'on medical grounds'![83] The medical opinion had now been reversed, having come to the conclusion that it would be ill-advised for Shakespeare to continue in Norwich. Shakespeare told the church at his farewell services a few weeks later that God had led him 'without my intention, to a kind of entanglement in denominational movements. But beyond all that, He has sent sickness, which is now driving me out'.[84] This was the second time that he sensed the direct hand of God in his life leading him to make a major and unexpected change in direction (the first was his inability to complete the Civil Service examination in 1879, which led him into the ministry). His son Geoffrey saw this as evidence of 'a strong mystical strain in his character'.[85]

In its report of his appointment as Union Secretary at the autumn Assembly of 1898, the *Freeman* quoted Shakespeare as saying that his doctors had not at first understood the nature of his sudden illness, the onset of which had occurred on the very day he had first received the invitation from the Union in March. Changed medical opinion, and the unexpected renewal of the offer from the Council, had led him to accept. He said, 'I wish it to be clearly understood that I leave on medical grounds alone'.[86]

It was not the first time that he had suffered an extended period of ill health, nor was it the last. For several months in 1888 and 1889 he had been almost unable to sleep, eat or study, and had suffered from constant headache. His physician described his condition as involving 'no active disease, only a delicacy of organisation'.[87] From time to time throughout his 26 years as Union Secretary he had to stop work for lengthy periods, suffering from what was sometimes described as 'nervous exhaustion'. The precise nature of Shakespeare's recurring health problems is one of the central mysteries of his career. When he was well, however, he worked with formidable energy, as the denomination was soon to discover.

It was agreed to entrust to Shakespeare 'the entire direction and control of the staff of the Union'.[88] Baptists were quickly made aware that the man they had invited to lead them had dramatic and far-reaching ambitions for the Union. There were hints of this in his acceptance speech at the 1898 autumn Assembly. The *Freeman* reported him as saying that:

> If in any way he could promote the extension of their churches in the town, and if he could quicken the denominational conscience to play its proper part in the national life . . . and if he could retain the great, or lessen the burden of the humblest village minister, he would have his reward. He knew . . . he was a man of too strong opinions to make a good secretary, but a man is not wanted simply to register the decisions of other people. He had had a great deal of his own way during the last fifteen years, and he hoped to have some of it still.[89]

His occupancy of the office of Union Secretary would show that, significant though they were, the changes that had taken place in the last quarter of the nineteenth century were minor compared with those that occurred in the first quarter of the twentieth.

1. See Stephen Brachlow, *The Communion of Saints: Radical Puritanism and Separatist Ecclesiology 1570-1625* (Oxford University Press: New York, 1988), pp. 3-4.

2. Murray Tolmie, *The Triumph of the Saints: The Separate Churches of London 1616-1649* (Cambridge University Press: Cambridge, 1977) p. 69.

3. The Particular Baptist London Confession, 1644, section 47 (in William L. Lumpkin, *Baptist Confessions of Faith* (The Judson Press: Philadelphia, 1959) p. 168.

4. Brachlow, pp. 136-7.

5. B. R. White, 'The Doctrine of the Church in the Particular Baptist Confession of 1644' *Journal of Theological Studies* vol. 19 (1968) p. 590.

6. 'A Declaration of Faith of English People remaining in Amsterdam' (1611) section 11 (in Lumpkin, p. 120).

7. Lumpkin describes the General Baptist's *Orthodox Creed* of 1678 as exceptional in

being the only confession of the century to 'elevate the association above local churches'. (Lumpkin, p. 296).

8. White, *Doctrine* p. 590.
9. B. R. White (ed.), *Association Records of the Particular Baptists of England, Wales and Ireland to 1660* (BHS: London, 1971) pp. 23-4.
10. 'Second London Confession ' (1677 and 1688) chapter 26 (in Lumpkin, p. 287).
11. White, *Association Records*, p. 134.
12. Within the Midland Association, for example (see White, *Association Records*, pp. 24-5).
13. Within the Western Association, for example (see White, *Association Records*, pp. 56 and 103-4). Thomas Collyer was one of the best known Particular Baptists to exercise this kind of ministry.
14. Lumpkin, p. 169.
15. White, *Association Records*, pp. 20-1.
16. *Ibid.*, p. 26.
17. *Ibid.*, p. 21.
18. The procedures for association debates among the Particular Baptists carefully preserved the precedence of the churches, with resolutions being subject to confirmation by the churches. See, for example, White, *Association Records*, pp. 129-30.
19. Henry Ainsworth, *The Communion of Saints* (1641) p. 384.
20. The history of the New Connexion is given by Frank W. Rinaldi in his *PhD* thesis *The Tribe of Dan* (Glasgow University: 1996). Its emergence in the eighteenth century is also described in Raymond Brown, *The English Baptists of the Eighteenth Century* (BHS: London, 1986).
21. Ian Sellers, *Nineteenth Century Nonconformity* (Edward Arnold: London, 1977), p. 3.
22. J. H. Y. Briggs, *The English Baptists of the Nineteenth Century* (BHS: Didcot, 1994), p. 14.
23. The Union's first constitution is given in Ernest Payne, *The Baptist Union: A Short History* (Carey Kingsgate Press: London, 1959) pp. 24-5. It is interesting, in the light of subsequent developments, that it specifically disclaimed 'all manner of superiority and superintendence over the churches'.
24. Deryck W. Lovegrove, *Established Church, Sectarian people: Itinerancy and the Transformation of English Dissent, 1780-1830* (Cambridge University Press: Cambridge, 1988) p. 142.
25. John Hinton, speaking in 1863 (cited in Payne, *Baptist Union* p. 85).
26. Payne, *Baptist Union* p. 109.
27. Douglas C. Sparkes, *The Constitutions of the Baptist Union of Great Britain* (BHS: Didcot, 1996) p. 17.
28. Payne, *Baptist Union*, p. 127.
29. Cited in M. R. Watts, 'John Clifford and Radical Nonconformity 1836-1923' (*DPhil* thesis: Oxford University, 1967) p. 139.
30. See p. 14.
31. Rinaldi, p. 268.
32. Briggs, *English Baptists*, p. 144.
33. *BT* 27 May 1898.
34. *Free Church Yearbook* (1900) pp. 19-20.
35. W. T. Stead's pamphlet 'The Story of Gipsy Smith and the Missions of the National Free Church of England' in his *The Revival of 1905* (NCEFC: London, 1905) p. 115.

36. Silvester Horne, *A Popular History of the Free Churches* (James Clarke and Co.: London, 1903) p. 426.
37. John Kent, 'A Late Nineteenth Century Nonconformist Renaissance', in Derek Baker (ed.), *Renaissance and Renewal in Christian History* (*Studies in Church History* vol. 13) (Basil Blackwell: Oxford, 1977) pp. 352-3.
38. *Free Church Yearbook* (1903) pp. 262-3.
39. James Munson, *The Nonconformists: In search of a lost culture* (SPCK: London, 1991) p. 303. Munson's view is that the Nonconformists' failure to rise to the urban challenge has been a key reason for their twentieth century decline.
40. Charles Booth, *Life and Labour of the People of London (Third Series: Religious Influences)* (MacMillan and Co.: London, 1902). Part 4: Inner South London, p. 74.
41. For example, by Clyde Binfield in 'Hebrews Hellenised? Evangelical Nonconformity and Culture, 1840-1940' in Sheridan Gilley and W. J. Sheils (eds.), *A History of Religion in Britain: Practice and Belief from Pre-Roman Times to the Present* (Blackwell: Oxford, 1994) pp. 322-45, and Mark Johnson, *The Dissolution of Dissent 1850-1918* (Garland Publishing: New York, 1987).
42. Jeffrey Cox, *The English Churches in a Secular Society. Lambeth 1870-1930* (Oxford University Press: London, 1982) p. 147.
43. Payne says it is 'impossible' (*Baptist Union*, p. 267).
44. See Robert Currie, Alan Gilbert and Lee Horsley, *Churches and Churchgoers: Patterns of Church Growth in the British Isles since 1700* (Clarendon Press, Oxford: 1977) pp. 147-52 and 216-7; Briggs, *English Baptists* pp. 248-268; Alan David Gilbert, 'The Growth and Decline of Nonconformity in England and Wales, with Special Reference to the Period Before 1850: An Historical Interpretation of Statistics of Religious practice' (Oxford University *DPhil* thesis, 1973) p. 448).
45. The population of England and Wales rose from about 9 million in 1801 to 18 million in 1851, and to 32.5 million in 1901.
46. A. Gilbert, 'Growth and Decline' p. 41. Gilbert's figures indicate that, at their highest point, 1.5% of the population over fifteen years of age were members of Congregational churches (between about 1850 and 1870), and 1.3% members of Baptist churches (between 1850 and 1890).
47. *Ibid.*, pp. 93-4.
48. Benjamin Shakespeare's six year ministry at Malton began after a period of considerable growth in the church after what J. Brown Morgan called 'a remarkable revival' in the town as a result of a mission conducted by the itinerant Baptist evangelist Thomas Pulsford. Charles Spurgeon preached at the church in 1860 (J. Brown Morgan, 'The present Baptist Churches of Yorkshire' in *Baptists in Yorkshire, Lancashire, Cheshire and Cumberland (augmented edition)* (Baptist Historical Society: 1913) p. 208.
49. John Howard Shakespeare, *The Churches at the Cross Roads: A Study in Church Unity* (Williams and Norgate: London, 1918) p. 201.
50. Geoffrey Shakespeare, *Let Candles Be Brought In* (MacDonald: London, 1949) p. 336.
51. J. F. Makepeace, *All I Could Never Be* (Basil Blackwell: Oxford, 1924) pp. 1-7.
52. *BT* 6 May 1904.
53. See A. C. Underwood, *A History of the English Baptists* (Carey Kingsgate Press: London, 1947) p. 214. Mursell was President of the Union in 1864.
54. In one of Shakespeare's last public engagements, he spoke at a memorial service for

Thew, at which he said, 'I have heard many preachers but none who ever moved me as he did' (*BT* 21 September 1923). The Thew started his ministry as assistant to Mursell in the Belvoir Street Church at the beginning of 1872, a few years before Shakespeare moved to London (Sheila Mitchell, *'Not Disobedient . . .': A history of United Baptist Church, Leicester* (United Baptist Church: Leicester, 1984) p. 73).

55. *Baptist Magazine* (September 1891) p. 387. Arthur Porritt (editor of the *Christian World*) also speaks of Thew's example as leading to Shakespeare's desire to be a preacher (*CW*, 15 March 1928).
56. *Baptist Magazine* (September 1891) p. 386.
57. *Daily Sketch*, 13 March 1928.
58. Makepeace, pp. 12-13.
59. *Baptist Magazine* (September 1891) p. 388.
60. Referred to by his son Geoffrey (in *Let Candles*, p. 345).
61. St. Mary's Deacons, 7 December 1883.
62. According to M. E. Aubrey, writing in the *Baptist Quarterly* vol. 17 (July 1957) p. 100.
63. Sermon preached by Shakespeare at St. Mary's on 28 December 1884 (Angus Library, Regent's Park College, Oxford).
64. 'Re-Opening Services: Renovated St. Mary's' (St. Mary's Baptist Church, Norwich: 1886) pp. 3-4.
65. See the writing of Clyde Binfield, especially 'Hebrews Hellenized?'.
66. 'Re-Opening Services: Renovated St. Mary's', p. 5.
67. C. B. Jewson, *The Baptists in Norfolk* (Carey Kingsgate Press: London, 1957) p. 96.
68. *Ibid.*.
69. St. Mary's Baptist Church Norwich, *Deacons' Minute Book*, 16 March 1888.
70. John Howard Shakespeare, *The Issues of Agnosticism and Faith* (Norfolk News Company: Norwich, 1889).
71. John Howard Shakespeare, 'The Colleges and the Ministry' *Baptist Magazine* vol. 83 (February 1891) p. 73.
72. John Howard Shakespeare, 'The Colleges and the Ministry' *Baptist Magazine* vol. 83 (June 1891) pp. 261-9.
73. John Howard Shakespeare, 'Baptist Church Extension in Large Towns' in *Baptist Magazine* vol. 84 (February 1892) p. 81
74. *Ibid.*, p. 83.
75. C. Dunkley (ed.) *The Official Report of the Church Congress held at Norwich* (Bemrose and Sons: London, 1895) p. 26.
76. *Ibid.*, p. 27. The Lambeth Quadrilateral had been published seven years earlier.
77. Shakespeare, *Churches* p. 204.
78. Cited in C. M. Townsend, *The Life and Work of J. H. Shakespeare* (unpublished manuscript in possession of the Shakespeare family: no date) p. 6.
79. BU Minute Book, 28 February 1898.
80. St. Mary's Deacons, 18 March 1898.
81. St. Mary's Deacons, 5 April 1898.
82. St. Mary's Deacons, 14 April 1898.
83. St. Mary's Deacons, 16 September 1898.
84. *St. Mary's Magazine* vol. 3 (November 1898) p. 86.
85. Geoffrey Shakespeare, *Let Candles*, p. 337.
86. *BT* 7 October 1898.

87. St. Mary's Deacons, 8 February 1889.
88. BU Minute Book, 27 September 1898.
89. *BT* 7 October 1898.

CHAPTER 2

The Strengthening of the Union

Shakespeare's appointment as secretary brought a man of vision, energy and superb organisational skills to a Union full of ambition for the new century. The Free Church movement had given Nonconformity as a whole new confidence about its future prospects. The previous 10-20 years had seen the Union develop into a body that had the potential for embracing the denomination as a whole, and as the main vehicle for future Baptist growth. Hopes were high for several proposed initiatives, including the creation of a proper denominational headquarters, the establishment or purchase of a denominational newspaper, and the raising of major central funds for Baptist expansion. Shakespeare was a man who could turn these dreams into reality.

2.1 The Twentieth Century Fund

It is difficult to exaggerate the importance of the Twentieth Century Fund for the subsequent pattern of Baptist denominational life. The principle sources of information about it are the two denominational newspapers of the time - the *Freeman* (after 1899 the *Baptist Times and Freeman*) and the *Baptist*. Shakespeare's personal account of its history was published by the Baptist Union in 1904.[1] The Fund was formally proposed by the Rev. Samuel Vincent, President of the Union, at the 1898 autumn Assembly (the same Assembly at which Shakespeare became Union Secretary). The Wesleyans and the Congregationalists had also set up funds to mark the beginning of the new century. As often seemed to happen during this period, the main Nonconformist denominations kept in step with each other.

The financial target for the Baptists' fund (£250,000), and the purposes for which it was to be used, were agreed by the Council during the course of the months following the Assembly, and it was officially launched in the spring of 1899. The setting up of the Twentieth Century Fund thus coincided with Shakespeare's first months in office, and although responsibility for its conception lay elsewhere, its design and implementation were predominantly his doing. The *Freeman* described Shakespeare's achievement in getting unanimous Council support for the committee's plans for the Fund as 'well-nigh phenomenal', in view of not a little controversy about it in the denomination.[2]

Several features of the Fund were notable. A very important one was that it was to be administered centrally by the Union. The Congregationalists had decided that responsibility for the use of money raised in connection with their equivalent fund would largely rest with local associations and churches. In practice this meant that a significant proportion of it was used to pay off existing debts. The Congregationalists' fund also contained a significant element designated for foreign missions. Decisions about the allocation of the Baptist Fund, on the other hand, were entirely at the discretion of the Council of the Union. Neither local churches and associations, nor committees administering existing denominational funds (such as the Annuity Fund, Church Extension Fund and Home Mission Fund), nor the missionary society were directly involved in deciding how the money would be used. There was, it appears from the minute book, no controversy about this at the Union Council and committee meetings, and no suggestion of a joint appeal with the missionary society.[3] This is a remarkable indication of the desire, at least in official circles, for a greater degree of denominational consciousness and unity under the aegis of the Union. Another significant feature of the fund was its size. Although smaller than the Congregational and the Wesleyan funds, it was, nonetheless, a huge sum for a fragmented and generally less affluent denomination. It far surpassed any previous appeal by the Union.

The objects of the Fund reflected some of Shakespeare's personal interests. By far the largest proportion, half the total, was designated for 'evangelisation and church extension'. £34,000 was allocated to pay for the erection of a denominational headquarters. A further £30,000 was designated for assisting poorer churches in maintaining their pastors and the same amount for the Union's Annuity Fund. The remainder (£31,000) was to be used mainly for the support of ministerial training and education.

Shakespeare's ability as an organiser lay behind the systematic approach that was taken to the task of raising the money. As well as a strong national committee, every association and church was encouraged to appoint officers with responsibility for promoting the Fund. Ministers were urged to include appeals for gifts and pledges in their preaching. Shakespeare won the enthusiastic support of the three Union Presidents who served during the years the Fund was being raised, and he constantly travelled the country with them appealing for support.

Early in 1899, Shakespeare grasped an opportunity for promoting the Fund, and his other ambitions for the Union, as a result of the financial difficulties being encountered by one of the two denominational newspapers. In February it was announced by the *Freeman* that it was changing its name to the *Baptist Times and Freeman*, and in July that it had been acquired by the Baptist Union, and would henceforth be 'the organ and channel of information and progress' for the denomination.[4] From then on it became Shakespeare's primary means of promoting the Fund.[5]

It was soon clear that the money was not coming in as quickly as was necessary to meet the target. Most churches did not contribute anything at all in 1899. Critical voices were occasionally raised, especially in the *Baptist*, the other Baptist weekly newspaper. The *Baptist* represented the more conservative wing of the denomination, and was unhappy about the decision to appoint John Clifford Union President in 1899, a decision hurriedly made following the sudden death of the President-elect, James Spurgeon, and often about the Union's leadership in general. Its lack of enthusiasm about the Twentieth Century Fund came to a head after the 1900 spring Assembly, at which the needs of the Fund were vigorously urged upon the delegates, when a leading article asked, 'may it not possibly be said just now that one's soul may be saved and one's life sanctified even though we contribute not to the deservedly popular Twentieth Century Fund?'[6]

Raising the Fund dominated Shakespeare's mind more and more. Early in 1901 he took two months holiday, admitting 'he was getting very tired, for the one idea of the Century Fund had been like a mania with him for the past year'.[7] It had originally been planned to close the appeal at the spring Assembly in 1901, but the decision was made to extend it until 1902 in order to achieve the target. *The Baptist Times and Freeman*, in its account of the 1901 Assembly, reported that

> The Secretary asked, solemnly and seriously, desiring to place the matter upon their hearts and consciences - that from 1st October next, to 31st of the following December, the churches should, apart from immediate and pressing local claims only, clear all else out of the way, and work entirely for the Baptist Twentieth Century Fund.[8]

Shakespeare was very keen to recruit the women in the denomination to help with fund raising, and a Baptist Women's Century Fund League was formed. The progress of its Million Shilling Scheme was regularly reported.

In the summer of 1901 Shakespeare was forced to cancel all his engagements because of illness, brought on through 'the strain of the past few months', according to the *Baptist Times and Freeman*.[9] He was out of action for several months. This seemed to stimulate a last great effort on the part of his supporters to get the remaining money in. At the autumn Assembly that year, a friend reported that when Shakespeare weighed himself on a public weighing machine 'he hardly weighed anything. I was dreadfully afraid he was going to heaven'. 'The more you give to the Century Fund, the longer you will keep Mr. Shakespeare down here below', he pleaded.[10] The Fund increasingly took on an importance greater than simply a money raising exercise for good Baptist causes. It 'may be said to have caused the Denomination to embody itself', a *Baptist Times* leading article asserted.[11]

The last few weeks of the appeal, leading up to the 1902 spring Assembly, make dramatic reading in the pages of the *Baptist Times*. 'The effort to raise the last £70,000 was very strenuous and severe', admitted Shakespeare in his own account.[12] A simultaneous collection was arranged for 23 March 1902. In a leading article on 18 April, just a fortnight before the closing date at the end of the Assembly, Shakespeare was 'at his wit's end' to know how to raise the last few thousand pounds.[13] On the first day of the Assembly, he reported that £235,000 had been promised or given, and a further £6,000 promised on condition that the target was reached. Appealing for the £9,000 still required, he urged the delegates to be generous. 'Is it not worth while, brethren? When we have got so near, and after all we have done?'[14]

On the final morning of the Assembly, the delegates watched the pale figure of Shakespeare mount the rostrum with bated breath, and heard him announce that the target had been successfully reached. They rose spontaneously to sing the doxology. For Shakespeare, it was 'undoubtedly the most wonderful meeting at which I have ever been present'.[15] £5,000 had been offered on the previous day by the family of William Chivers (a leading Baptist laymen who had recently died) in his memory. This left just £326 to be found for the target to be reached, and two laymen agreed to provide this late in the evening.

Generous tributes were made to Shakespeare. Samuel Vincent reminded delegates of Shakespeare's 1892 appeal for a fund to aid church extension, a wish now amply fulfilled. John Clifford attributed the successful outcome 'to the much faith, to the fine tact, to the unsleeping devotion, to the rich courage of our dear friend'. 'We give thanks to God for this great and precious gift to us as a Baptist Union of our beloved secretary',[16] he said. Even the *Baptist* was quite effusive, sincerely congratulating Shakespeare for 'a marvellous achievement'. The task of raising such a sum was for 'financially feeble' Baptists 'a quite Herculean enterprise'. It made the occasion 'a historic, and probably epoch making, assembly, since nothing succeeds like success, and the Baptist Church now feels it has the strength of a young giant'.[17] Shakespeare himself said that the financial benefits were not the most important. The Fund was intended to 'promote Baptist unity, intensify Baptist sentiment and enthusiasm, bring our leading laymen into closer touch with the Union, and better equip the Baptist Denomination to take its part in the work of God in the twentieth century',[18] and this, he believed, it had done. Even more significantly, it had dramatically increased the financial resources and therefore the power of the Union.

Nothing would ever be the same for Shakespeare and the Union after the success of the Twentieth Century Fund. It did indeed play an important part in changing the whole concept of the term denomination for Baptists. Their sense of corporate unity, which had been developing gradually under the banner of the Union for several decades, had now become a practical reality. Crucial as the Twentieth Century Fund was, however, it was not by any means the only factor responsible for this change of perception. A breathtaking array of other changes was taking place under Shakespeare's leadership that reinforced this movement towards a strong, centralised denominational organisation.

2.2 Denominational Development

2.2.1 Baptist Church House

Between 1877 and 1903 the Baptist Union was housed in rooms rented from the Baptist Missionary Society at its headquarters on Furnival Street. Before 1877 it had no full time secretary, and no office accommodation at all, its affairs being conducted from the secretary's home or vestry. The growing financial and publishing responsibilities of the Union and its developing importance within the denomination from the mid-1870's onwards mean that a settled London base became essential. By 1890, a need was felt for more adequate accommodation than the missionary society could provide, especially for the sale of Union publications. An abortive attempt to purchase premises adjoining the missionary society's offices was made in the early 1890's, and as the decade wore on, the urgency of the situation became more and more apparent. Further discussions took place in the summer of 1898 between the Union and the society about a possible new joint headquarters, either in Furnival Street, or in Kingsgate Street, where proposed major re-developments by the London County Council, involving the Baptist chapel there, opened up the possibility of a suitable site. The two organisations failed, however, to agree on a joint project.[19]

It is clear that the impetus for a worthy denominational headquarters in London, something the Congregationalists had possessed in Memorial Hall for many years, as with the Twentieth Century Fund, was something Shakespeare inherited rather than originated. He soon brought his organising genius to bear on the problem. At the Union Council meeting in January 1899 it was agreed to designate part of the proceeds of the Twentieth Century Fund for a London 'Baptist Church House'. The decision was also made to go ahead with a major new development at Kingsgate Street without the missionary society.[20] The process of getting plans drawn up began in March, and soon an agreement was signed between the Kingsgate Street church and the Union for a large new building, with a frontage on Southampton Row, adequate for both.[21]

During the 1901 spring Assembly, the incoming President, Alexander MacLaren, performed a stone laying ceremony for the new Baptist Church House. In the speech he made on that occasion, Shakespeare said that the Union's position in Furnival Street had become intolerable.[22] Steadily, over the course of the next two years, the true significance of the new building began to be felt in the denomination. Its size and style was out of all proportion to what had gone before. A leading article in the *Baptist Times* said it would be 'the hub of our ecclesiastical universe', to 'express and foster Denominational unity'.[23] It was officially opened on 28 April 1903, and from then on 'Baptist Church House, 4, Southampton Row' became the address of the Union and its departments. Its Council Chamber was first used by the Council for its meeting in July of that year.

In its first issue of 1904 the *Baptist Times* treated its readers to a series of photographs and descriptions of their new headquarters, in which could be found the new Council Chamber, 'richly panelled in oak and elaborately decorated' and the library with its 'very elaborate ceiling'. There were also a visitors' room, chapel and book saloon, linked by the 'vaulted ceilings and marble floors' of its corridors.[24] Although the building, like its name, represented a striking departure from the spirit of traditional Nonconformity, attention was given to a celebration of dissenting and Baptist history, with statues of Bunyan and Spurgeon commissioned and erected. The building had four floors, and had cost £50,000, considerably more than the £34,000 allowed for it in the Twentieth Century Fund. This was a far cry indeed from a few offices rented on an upper floor from the Baptist Missionary Society. Initially, most of the office space was let to tenants.

The erection of Baptist Church House was not without its critics, but following hard on the heels of the success of the Twentieth Century Fund (which made it possible), it seems to have been met with general approval by the denomination. It had many practical benefits, and also met another need - for a worthy and public statement of the status Baptists felt they had achieved as a prominent section of national religious life. It thus helped fulfil one of Shakespeare's personal ambitions for his denomination. In Clyde Binfield's words, 'Baptists were now woven into the fabric of the world's greatest capital city. They were a national force in an international setting'.[25] The symbolism of 4 Southampton Row was not altogether straightforward, however, as Binfield goes on to point out:

> A defiantly congregational denomination which refused to see itself as a church had built a Church House, facing Kingsway; . . . Such tribute to Caesar was ambiguous, for which king did baptists serve?[26]

As Sellers more pointedly remarks, the very name Baptist Church House 'would have been incomprehensible to Baptists of a former age'.[27]

The combination of ambition and ambiguity inherent in the new denominational headquarters was typical of many of Shakespeare's achievements. It remained a monument to his drive, energy and vision, in both the breadth of their scope and the uncertainty of their direction, for the 86 years that it remained the possession of the Union. Its design and construction was largely his responsibility, and it was to become the nerve-centre for all his future endeavours and creations. These included the multiplying new Union departments, the Baptist World Alliance, the United Army and Navy Board for Free Church chaplains, Area Superintendents and the Federal Council of the Evangelical Free Churches. It was, over the next twenty years, a familiar centre of ecclesiastical activity in London and throughout the country, not simply for Baptists, but for the leading figures of the other Nonconformist denominations, and indeed, for the bishops and archbishops of the Church of England. J. C. Carlile was right, perhaps, in expressing his regret at Shakespeare's request for no biography to be written, to describe it as his true memorial.[28]

2.2.2 New Departments and Societies

A comparison between the departmental structure of the Union, together with its associated societies, in 1898, with that in 1908, shows the scale of the changes during Shakespeare's first ten years in office. The Union became a much more elaborate and complex institution. There were several completely new departments, including one for administering a ministers' home of rest in Brighton, given to the Union in memory of J. A. Spurgeon; one for the promotion of theological scholarship; one for local preachers; one for young people's work and one for advising churches about chapel property. New Baptist societies listed in the 1909 *Baptist Handbook* included the Historical Society and the Fire Insurance Company. Most of the departments in existence in 1898 had also changed in important ways. The Literature Fund had been transformed into a large Publication Department; the originally separate Home Mission, Church Extension and Augmentation Funds had been reorganised and amalgamated as the Home Work Fund; and the Board of Introduction and Consultation had evolved into the Advisory Committee for Ministerial Removals.

When the Publications Department was formed in 1902, one of its main responsibilities was the publication of the weekly *Baptist Times and Freeman*. Mention has already been made of the Union's acquisition of the *Freeman*, and the importance of this for the promotion of the Twentieth Century Fund.[29] It is clear from discussions at the Union in 1899 that the publication's financial difficulties were in danger of resulting in its disappearance, and in July the Council agreed that £500 be borrowed from the Twentieth Century Fund to purchase and develop it as an official Union newspaper.[30] For several years feeling had grown within the Union that the two independent Baptist newspapers, the *Freeman* and the *Baptist*, no longer met the needs of the denomination, and that the Union required a publication of its own to reflect its growing importance. The new title of the newspaper, the *Baptist Times and Freeman*, implied that the change involved not merely a transfer of control to the Union, but the formation of a new publication altogether. It seems likely that the creation of the *Methodist Times* in 1885 by Hugh Price Hughes was one of the factors lying behind the choice of title.

Initially, the editor of the *Freeman*, A. H. Stockwell, continued to edit the *Baptist Times and Freeman*. Dissatisfaction with his performance was very quickly evident, and in October 1899 the Union's Literature Committee wrote to him with instructions to take more care and time in his editorial duties.[31] It cannot have been a surprise when, little over a year later, he announced his intention of resigning.[32] In January 1901 the Council supported a recommendation from the Literature Committee that Shakespeare himself be entrusted with the editorship. In line with instructions to 'make the best arrangements for the devolution of all clerical work in connection with the position',[33] he arranged for his brother Alfred to act as sub-editor.[34] From the beginning of 1902 the newspaper boldly claimed itself to be 'The Official Organ of the Baptist Denomination' on the front page of each issue. It was actually the official organ of the Union, rather than the denomination, and this very public identification of the two was more an expression of Shakespeare's ambition than a statement of fact. Many Baptists, and many Baptist churches, did not regard their commitment to the Union and their denominational identity as one and the same thing, and a substantial minority (those belonging to the more strictly Calvinistic wing in particular) would have found such a suggestion positively offensive.

Shakespeare saw control of the denominational press as vital in the promotion of his plans for the Union, and when the opportunity came, he eagerly grasped it. It is impossible, then, to regard the *Baptist Times* as providing an independent voice as far as his reforms are concerned from 1901 onwards. This makes the role of its rival, the *Baptist*, especially important in helping provide a more complete picture of denominational opinion. The *Baptist* claimed to offer its readers columns that were 'free, independent and unofficial'.[35] The *Baptist Magazine* was another source of information and comment on Baptist affairs, but it ceased publication at the end of 1904, citing the increase in the number of religious periodicals of a general nature, the establishment of 'weekly denominational organs' (the creation of both the *Baptist* and the *Freeman* post-dated that of the *Baptist Magazine*) and increased numbers of localised magazines as reasons for the decline in its readership.[36]

In 1905 the *Baptist* embarked on a direct assault on the editorial policy and management of the *Baptist Times*. A correspondent alleged that Union funds intended for other purposes were being used to subsidise the *Baptist Times* unfairly, in particular profits from the sale of the *Baptist Church Hymnal*, some of which were handed over to the Baptist Union by its publishers, the Psalms and Hymns Trust, under an agreement made between the two bodies. The 'exclusiveness and monopolising tendency' of the *Baptist Times* in promoting only official Union publications was severely criticised, as was its claim to be the 'official' organ of the denomination. Contradicting Shakespeare, the *Baptist* expressed the view that the Union should not to be identified thus with the denomination. The *Baptist Times* was accused by the same correspondent of existing

> for the purpose, among other things, of advocating methods of narrow and
> centralised denominational government, 'preference' plans for officially

controlling our pulpits and pastorates, and other systems of class favour and privilege utterly foreign to the entire conception of that free and open administration which is traditionally Baptist, as it is distinctly Scriptural.[37]

In an editorial message to pastors and church secretaries later in the year, John Clifford's support for the *Baptist*'s place in denominational life and its campaign for survival was claimed (a somewhat surprising claim in the view of their divergent theological positions).[38]

The *Baptist* faced an increasingly difficult struggle to exist in the face of competition from the *Baptist Times*, and ultimately this was to no avail. It did not prove possible for a denominational newspaper to survive outside the official structures of the denomination. It continued to provide an important alternative commentary on denominational affairs for another five years, but on 29 September 1910, 40 years after it had first appeared, it published its final issue and announced its 'self extinction'. Describing itself as 'the pioneer penny journal in our denomination', and still proud of its 'absolutely independent and unofficial' reputation, it disappeared from Baptist life.[39] Valedictory tributes to, and reminiscences of, the newspaper were printed in the *Baptist*'s final issue. Shakespeare was not among the contributors.

The copyright of the *Baptist* was sold to the *Baptist Times*, which described its demise as the result of a friendly agreement to amalgamate the two newspapers. This left the official newspaper, in its own words, as 'the only, as well as the official, weekly organ of the Denomination and the Union'.[40] It reassured its readers that its pages were available for the publication of views other than officially sanctioned ones. The move from three national publications independent of the Union (the *Baptist Magazine*, the *Baptist* and the *Freeman*) to one firmly under its control, in little more than ten years, represented a significant transformation of denominational life. The *Baptist* had constituted an alternative viewpoint, tending to report more on non-Union aspects of Baptist life, such as those aspects reflecting the tradition of Spurgeon and the work of the missionary society, and was an independent channel for discontent over official Union policy. After 1910, Baptists who were not happy about the direction being taken by the Union were even more isolated from the mainstream of denominational life than before.

Apart from its responsibility for the *Baptist Times*, the Union (either through its Literature Committee, or the Publications Department, as it became) was involved in other significant publication projects. In conjunction with the Psalms and Hymns Trust, the *Baptist Church Hymnal* appeared in 1900. The Baptist Tract and Book Society, founded in 1841, was taken over by the Union in 1902, and a bookshop opened in Baptist Church House the following year. A growing stream of printed material issued from the Union, reflecting its growing strength and confidence under Shakespeare's leadership.

The reorganisation of the Union's three funds for home mission in 1904, and the resulting creation of the Home Work Fund, was another important development in Shakespeare's early years in office. At first, the Council had serious doubts about his proposals for the reorganising of denominational finances, not regarding them as 'either final or fully satisfactory'.[41] Shakespeare nonetheless persuaded it to support his presentation of them at the 1904 spring Assembly, where the scheme won unanimous backing. It was in part simply a rationalisation of Union accounts, involving the amalgamation of three separate funds (those concerned with Home Mission, Augmentation and Church Extension), but it also involved more significant changes in the use of the Union's financial resources. The new scheme gave Shakespeare the opportunity to reaffirm and redefine the Union's right to control the funds at its disposal. Most of the remaining Twentieth Century Fund money, some of which was still arriving at Baptist Church House in the fulfilment of promises, became subject to the new rules.

The new Home Work Fund had three sections, roughly corresponding to the funds it replaced, for the purposes of Church Aid, Church Extension and Evangelisation. To qualify for help under the Church Aid or Church Extension sections, a church had to be in membership of the Union, and its pastor 'must have satisfied the Council as to his ministerial efficiency'. According to the new rules, the appointment of such pastors 'shall be made jointly by the Baptist Union, the Association and the aided Church - the Baptist Union and the Association having power to terminate the engagement whenever they may decide to do so'.[42] It is not clear to what extent these rules were enforced, and the number of churches affected must have been limited, but complaints received by the editor of the *Baptist* indicate that the Union's powers were used in some cases at least. D. Ff. Dafis accused the Union of breaking faith with the weaker churches by insisting the minister of any aided church should be properly trained, and that the church should be paying at least £80 a year towards his stipend.[43] The Evangelisation section gave the Union the power to appoint evangelists and colporteurs - either on its own or in conjunction with the associations.

The effect of the growth and elaboration of the Union's departmental structure was twofold. First, it widened the scope of the Union's involvement in the affairs of local Baptist churches. Churches had not, before 1900, considered the Union as relevant in matters such as church property, young people's work, hymn books or local preachers. Nor had the Union had much control over the denominational material Baptists might choose to read, other than the annual *Handbook*. Within a few years of Shakespeare's appointment, however, it had a stake in all these areas. Its influence was being felt in many unfamiliar areas. Its institutional structure was rapidly becoming more comprehensive of denominational life and concerns.

Not only was the scope of the Union's involvement broadened, but its authority and power were strengthened as well. This was partly a question of the increased financial resources it gained as a result of the Twentieth Century Fund. It was also, however, the result of its greatly expanded role as a publisher, and its growing status as a significant ecclesiastical body in the country. Since its formation it had been unique in being both national in scope and general in its interests, unlike the other major Baptist institutions such as the missionary society and the colleges, which had specific and limited aims, and the geographically defined associations, but it was only in the first ten years of Shakespeare's period in office that its potential for denominational dominance became evident. Increasing numbers of churches and ministers found themselves drawn into the orbit of the Union as never before. It had no power to coerce, and churches could in theory ignore its programmes and policies, but in practice it was becoming increasingly difficult for them to do so.

2.2.3 A New Constitution

In order to cope with its expanding role, the need was felt early in the new century for a more adequate and up-to-date constitution and set of bye-laws for the Union. The Council agreed to the formation of a Constitution Committee in 1901, and this body first met in February 1902 to discuss possible changes. It assembled several times during the course of 1902, and at its meetings Shakespeare brought forward some radical ideas. These included a reduction in the number of national Assemblies from two to one each year (to be held in the autumn) and a complete overhaul of the Council, including a reduction in its size, changes in the way it was elected to make it more democratic and an increase in its powers.[44]

There are parallels between Shakespeare's proposals for the Union, and the ones that he had brought forward at St. Mary's when a Church Council was put in place.[45] At St. Mary's, the aim was to avoid the arguments and delays that sometimes occurred at the large and unwieldy church meetings. In the same way, he wanted to streamline the decision-making processes within the Union, and make the Council less dependent on the unpredictable, and in some ways unaccountable, proceedings of the Assembly. Shakespeare set out the principles that lay behind the proposals in a leading article in an April 1902 issue of the *Baptist Times* entitled 'Centralisation and Democracy'. 'Democracy and centralisation are complementary', he wrote, pleading for Baptist institutions to be co-ordinated and directed centrally, and for more power to be vested in the central executive. Without efficient organisation, democracy, wearying of discussion and despairing when deliberation is demanded, 'yields to the masterful mind of the clear sighted individual', and runs the risk of tyranny, he believed. He outlined an organisational structure for the denomination involving associational districts ('the unit of our organisation'), associations, provincial committees and the Council of the Union.[46]

The two annual Assemblies were the main events in Baptist national life, originally occurring once a year. The Assembly had begun as the Union's annual meeting, and was constitutionally its governing body. In 1864, because of its growing popularity, and the desire not to have every meeting in London, a second annual Assembly was inaugurated, to be held outside the capital. They developed into gatherings spread over several days, involving far more than matters directly related to the Union. They were arranged jointly with the missionary society, and had a range of functions within denominational life, with different sessions designated for different purposes. Leading Baptist figures, and sometimes those of other Nonconformist denominations, were given a national platform from which to speak, and resolutions on matters of public concern were brought forward for debate. Some of the meetings were open to the public. They were, above all, the occasions when the diffuse Baptist denomination embodied itself, and at which most of its various factions came together to express a sense of a common identity.

Prior to 1903, membership of the Assembly was decided in a variety of ways, the bulk being appointed by member churches in proportion to their size. The seriousness with which this responsibility was taken varied, depending on churches' interest in Union affairs, the venue of the Assembly and the attractiveness of the Assembly programme. The majority of the Union's Council was elected by ballot at the spring Assembly. The Union President, who served for one year, was elected in the same way. When controversial issues were being discussed, or passions raised by the eloquence of a popular speaker, sessions could become very lively and noisy occasions.

Shakespeare was an eloquent and persuasive public speaker, and was capable of using the Assembly to his own advantage, as his address on church extension in 1892 had demonstrated. He was also a capable enough organiser to use his position as Union secretary to avoid many of the inherent dangers of the Assembly system. However, eager as he was to transform the Union into an effective ecclesiastical body, he found the situation very unsatisfactory. Informed and reasoned debate over complex ecclesiastical, moral or doctrinal issues was difficult, if not impossible, to achieve. The audience was swayed more often by passion than by rational argument. The Council was responsible for the routine oversight of the rapidly expanding affairs of the Union, but because of the way it was elected, it did not reliably represent the churches. Its authority and freedom of action was also limited because of its dependence on support from the six-monthly Assemblies.

The Constitution Committee supported Shakespeare's suggested solutions to these problems, which were incorporated into a new draft constitution he presented to it. As well as the elimination of the spring Assembly, Shakespeare wanted the Council to be elected by the churches, on the basis of geographical regions, and to be given the constitutional power to determine what resolutions could be debated at the Assembly meetings. The effect of these proposals was to make the Council more independent of the Assembly, and to transfer power over Union life from it to the Council. The Council itself demanded some minor modifications to the proposed changes, then allowed them to be presented to the 1903 spring Assembly.[47] The intention was for the autumn Assembly to vote on the new constitution.

The Council was still uncertain about the proposed changes, and Shakespeare was asked to prepare a statement for the 1903 July meeting explaining why they were necessary.[48] A letter along similar lines was sent to all the churches during the summer of 1903. The reduction in the number of annual Assemblies from two to one was justified by Shakespeare by 'the enormous multiplication of Conferences, Assemblies and Committees', the growth of the work of the associations, and the fact that the other Nonconformist denominations had only one such national meeting. The proposed direct election of the Council by the churches, on a regional basis, would be a sounder method than the 'varied and somewhat chaotic' existing arrangements, and give the Council the increased authority and freedom of action it needed.[49]

Reaction to the proposed changes was mixed. In the *Baptist*, Richard Glover, one of the most respected figures in the denomination, expressed his concern that the proposal to abandon the spring Assembly had not been given enough time for proper consideration. Glover was closely associated with the Baptist Missionary Society, and he believed the consequence of having only one assembly would be to make it a predominantly Union affair. This would have the effect of distancing the Union from the missionary society.[50] Although the *Baptist* itself, in a leading article, expressed general support for the changes, many letters in its pages showed a distrust of Shakespeare's motives and uneasiness about the speed with which they were being pushed through.[51]

When the time came for Shakespeare to introduce the proposals to the 1903 autumn assembly, he received a critical reception, and they were referred back to the Council without being put to a vote. According to the *Baptist*, the main objection was that the concentration of power in the hands of the Council was considered to be undemocratic, and therefore 'more fitted for a Presbyterian synod' than a Baptist assembly.[52]

The failure to secure agreement for the proposed new constitution in the autumn of 1903 was Shakespeare's first major setback in his programme of reforms for the Union. While the denomination was given time to reflect further on a modified set of proposals, the *Baptist Times* ran a series of articles in November and December in favour of radical denominational change.[53] In the end, however, most of Shakespeare's most innovative ideas were dropped, and, after the new constitution was adopted at the 1904 autumn assembly, the workings of the Council and the Assembly continued broadly as they had before. Apart from an expanded, and much improved,

Declaration of Principle (not much commented on at the time), the main step forward, as far as Shakespeare was concerned, was that the Council was made more genuinely representative. The idea of churches being involved directly in its election on a regional basis was dropped. Instead the associations were given the right to elect Council representatives, on the basis of one for every 50 churches in their membership.[54]

Although the 1904 constitution has been revised on a number of occasions since, it remains the basis of that which governs the affairs of the Union today. This is a tribute to the skill of Shakespeare, who, in spite of his disappointment over the rejection of several of his earlier suggestions, was able to put together a document that served the needs of the denomination well. It shows an aspect of his character that was to become evident in the years ahead - a willingness to compromise for the sake of making progress. A notable feature of his leadership of the Union was his ambitious and expansive vision for its future, but this was tempered by a pragmatism that enabled him to accept and put in place less than he wanted when his ambitions proved unrealisable. A report in the *British Weekly* some years later summed up this feature in his character by describing him as 'that most interesting and successful of combinations, a practical mystic'.[55]

2.2.4 The Baptist World Alliance

The General Baptist leader Thomas Grantham first suggested the idea of a global fellowship of Baptists as early as the seventeenth century. This was also part of John Rippon's expansive vision of Baptist life at the end of the eighteenth century.[56] In more recent times, the Congregationalists had convened a world conference in 1891, at which the International Congregational Council was formed, as the Methodists had a decade before. In 1901 the Baptist Assembly had included for the first time an 'ecumenical session', at which representatives of ten overseas Baptist Unions were present. The ability to travel and communicate internationally was improving rapidly, and it was natural for Baptists to wish to express their world-wide identity. When a definite proposal was made for a global gathering of Baptists in 1904, Shakespeare threw all his considerable organising skill into making it a reality. The London Congress of 1905, and the Alliance to which it gave birth, are among his greatest achievements. For the first time, he moved beyond the circle of the Union into a broader sphere of work. He was to remain closely associated with the Alliance and involved in all its major events for as long as he remained in office.

The suggestion for a world Baptist Congress first came from an editorial written by A. T. Robertson in the *Baptist Argus*, an American journal, in 1903. In January of the following year, the *Argus*'s editor, J. N. Prestridge, sent copies of the article to Baptist leaders around the world. Shakespeare took the idea to the Union's General Purposes Committee in June, and it was resolved to have a 'Pan-Baptist Conference in London' in the summer of 1905.[57] With support from the Union Council and the missionary society, Shakespeare embarked upon the huge amount of work required to prepare invitations and make the necessary arrangements. It was decided to dispense with the 1905 spring assembly, and to allow some time during the conference to conduct necessary domestic business. The 1904 autumn assembly was unanimous in ratifying these decisions and formally issued an invitation to Baptist Unions and Missions throughout the world to London.

During the first half of 1905, the Baptist press was full of exhilarating reports of the Welsh revival, the increasingly intensive Free Church campaign against the 1902 Education Act, and the huge London mission led by the American evangelists Torrey and Alexander. In July, however, these events were eclipsed in the *Baptist Times* by news of the World Congress. It opened on 11 July in Exeter Hall in London. Shakespeare, as the Congress secretary, welcomed the delegates with the ambitious, if not arrogant, claim that 'we are probably . . . the greatest Protestant evangelical community on earth'.[58] According to his introduction to the *Authorised Record of Proceedings*, the tone of the Congress was 'distinctly evangelical' and 'optimistic'.[59] The Congress President was Alexander MacLaren of Manchester, and notable Baptists delivered addresses and sermons from both sides of the Atlantic. E. Y. Mullins, President of the Southern Baptist Convention, spoke of the 'six religious axioms' that distinguished Baptists from other Christians. David Lloyd George and John Clifford, recently sentenced to a prison term for refusing to pay rates in connection with the campaign of Passive Resistance, delivered stirring speeches on the British education controversy. Richard Glover gave an address on 'The Inadequacy of Non-Christian Religions to meet the needs of the World'. The gathering closed at the end of a week of meetings with a 'demonstration' in the Albert Hall, and excursions to Baptist heritage sites in Bedford and Cambridge.

All in all, it was an occasion for Baptists to congratulate themselves on their global strength and to make their presence felt. As Shakespeare wrote:

> We have travelled far when it has become possible to federate the great Baptist community for common purposes, and as a demonstration of the fact that there is now in existence, and to be reckoned with, a Baptist world consciousness.[60]

Before the Congress closed, it was resolved to appoint Prestridge and Shakespeare as convenors of a committee to arrange future Congresses, and to form a Baptist World Alliance. The same two men were also appointed joint secretaries of the Alliance, and John Clifford the President.

The co-ordination of continuing activities was inevitably problematic in a global organisation like the Alliance. One of the most significant benefits was the development of a greater sense of unity among European Baptists,

and Shakespeare naturally assumed responsibility for that. At the next
Congress, in 1911, this was explicitly acknowledged when he was given the
title of European Secretary. He was involved in two important European
events during the three years following the 1905 Congress. The first was a
visit to Hungary, with John Clifford and Newton H. Marshall, in 1907. The
objective was to help Hungarian Baptists resolve their differences over
whether or not to seek official State recognition - a potentially sensitive
issue because of the traditionally strong Baptist commitment to the separation of Church and State.

The outcome of this visit was important for Shakespeare partly because
it provided a model for the centralised national organisation of Baptists. The
three-man delegation helped the Hungarian Baptists to draw up a constitution for a Union in which the country was divided into 'convenient geographical areas'. Baptists in each area formed a single church, 'though these
may be attached to different local meetings or preaching stations'. The payment of all ministerial stipends would be the responsibility of these areas,
rather than the individual local churches.[61] Shakespeare's comments in the
Baptist Times on his return are revealing. He hoped the new constitution
would enable the Baptists of Hungary to:

> avoid the faults and the weaknesses which Independency exhibits among
> ourselves. We trust that the work of the Commission may . . . serve as an
> object lesson to ourselves. Independency here would be all the stronger
> and far more beautiful, if it were tempered with that 'dash of
> Presbyterianism' which has been infused into the constitution of the new
> United Hungarian Church.[62]

The second important event arising out of the formation of the Alliance
that occupied much of Shakespeare's time was the Congress of European
Baptists in Berlin in the summer of 1908. He described it as 'one of the
three great Baptist events since the twentieth century began',[63] and saw it as
the beginning of a new era for European Baptists. Shakespeare was supported in his growing international responsibilities by Marshall, and by
another young minister who was destined to play a leading role among
world Baptists in the future, J. H. Rushbrooke. Rushbrooke was, at that
time, the minister of the Archway Road Baptist Church in Highgate where
Shakespeare and his family themselves were members.[64]

Through Shakespeare, English Baptists were thus drawn into an awareness of the global and the European dimension of Baptist life. They were
regularly kept informed of developments on the continent in the pages of the
Baptist Times, frequently through the writing of Rushbrooke. Shakespeare's
reputation among English Baptists received a boost because of his official
position within the Alliance. Even when they felt uneasy about the direction in which he was leading them at home, their sense of pride in his

achievements was enormous.

There was one aspect of the Alliance that was not obvious in 1905, but would pose problems for Shakespeare in later years. This was the different doctrinal emphasis of most American Baptists compared to their English counterparts, particularly concerning relationships with other denominations. The fiercely non-ecumenical stance of many American Baptists was in harmony with the anti-Church of England feeling in England in 1905, brought about by the controversy over education. Attacks on 'priestism' and 'sacerdotalism' were frequently heard, and the possibility of finding any common ground with the Established Church seemed remote indeed. On the other hand, however, Shakespeare was in sympathy with closer relationships with the other churches, in line with his generally more liberal outlook. The link between England and America, which was fundamental to the Alliance, was one which would, in time, create tensions that ultimately posed a significant threat to Shakespeare, and contribute to the undermining of his vision for the English Baptists.

2.3 Shakespeare as Denominational Leader

Because of the unstructured nature of the denomination, personal qualities had always been important for Baptist leaders. This was so within individual congregations because of the lack of any recognised external source of human authority. The office of pastor, however, generally carried with it a dignity and standing quite apart from the individual holding it. Leadership qualities were even more important in the denomination as a whole. Baptists have often gathered around particular individuals, either regionally or nationally, who have demonstrated the strength of personality capable of commanding allegiance, Spurgeon being one of the most obvious examples. There have been few, if any, official positions possessing a recognised authority by virtue of their own inherent ecclesiastical importance. Shakespeare's predecessor as secretary of the Union, Samuel Harris Booth, had attracted considerable respect, largely because of his ability and personality. Under his leadership, as the Union became a more influential body, the office of Union secretary inevitably attracted increased status. It was still true, however, that Shakespeare's qualities as a leader were far more important than any supposed dignity in the office in enabling him to achieve what he did. The *Times* called him 'one of the ablest and boldest of leaders'.[65]

Shakespeare did not possess the personal charisma of Spurgeon, or even of MacLaren, Clifford or Meyer. What he lacked in this area, however, he made up for in other ways. Those who worked with him during his first years in the Baptist Union were amazed at his drive and energy. His personal secretary, W. H. Ball, looking back over 25 years of working together, described their labours at Baptist Church House as often lasting for fifteen hours a day.

As I look back . . . I am almost appalled by the stupendous tasks which were not only undertaken but achieved . . . To be in his room was to be in a whirl . . . He was never really at rest either asleep or awake but was ever striving after what seemed the impossible to many people but not to him. His body was frail but he had a wonderful and tenacious will.[66]

M. E. Aubrey, who eventually took over the secretariat after Shakespeare's resignation in 1924, acknowledged that his predecessor had been intense and autocratic,[67] and J. C. Carlile, who was as familiar with his personal style as anyone, described his strength and single-minded leadership in the same way:

It was amazing to see that even in those early days Shakespeare took the reigns and drove the team. I was among those who were sometimes doubtful of the way the driver was taking, and seriously objected to the crack of the whip . . . (he was) an autocrat to his finger-tips.[68]

On his appointment in 1898, Shakespeare hoped to direct the affairs of the Union in as forceful a way as he had grown used to in his St. Mary's pastorate.[69] He greatly admired the leadership qualities of Hugh Price Hughes, the dynamic Wesleyan minister who was, at the time, President of the Wesleyan Methodist Conference. After Hughes's death in 1902, Shakespeare wrote a tribute to him in the *Baptist Times*. His manner of leadership within his own church was 'conservative, aristocratic and episcopal', and at times audacious, according to Shakespeare. 'Such men are God's greatest gifts and they must be taken as they are', he said. Hughes shook Wesleyanism out of 'the deadly routine into which it was in danger of settling'.[70] Shakespeare showed by his actions from the start that he believed many in his own denomination needed shaking out of their deadly routines as well. He wanted to get things done, and with as little delay as possible. As time went on, he increasingly felt that

there is not the slightest danger that anything great and good will advance too quickly. Sometimes I feel like a passenger in a crowded thoroughfare, who has urgent business and who cannot get along, hindered by those who saunter with a leisurely step and casual air as if time were of no account.[71]

This sense of urgency and pressure for change attracted resentment, and even fear, at times. Those who were uneasy about the direction in which he was leading Baptists accused him of abusing his position and of officialism. On more than one occasion he was dubbed the Baptist Pope,[72] which was about as insulting a charge as Baptists could make.

For the most part, however, Baptists were proud of their Secretary, and more than prepared to follow his lead. The success of the Twentieth Century

Fund, the opening of Baptist Church House and the creation of the World Alliance were all remarkable achievements. They were not only hugely impressive from an organisational standpoint, but also gave Baptists a more secure sense of their denominational identity and significance. No one could doubt Shakespeare's sincerity, nor his total commitment to the Baptist cause, and these qualities, when coupled with his administrative abilities, were enough to silence most critical voices and calm most anxious minds. An illustration of the high regard in which Shakespeare was held can be seen in an event that took place in November 1905. A dinner was given in honour of Shakespeare and his wife by a number of leading figures in the denomination, at the Holborn Restaurant in London. John Clifford proposed Shakespeare's health, describing him as 'God's gift to the denomination'. An appreciative address was read by the Union treasurer, Herbert Marnham, who also handed over a cheque for £500 as a gift from Shakespeare's admirers. Alexander MacLaren, chairing the proceedings, said that Shakespeare had 'in extraordinary degree evoked and regulated our sense of unity'. He gave Mrs. Shakespeare a gift of £50 'to be spent in utter selfishness'.[73]

Shakespeare's acquisition and use of the *Freeman* also strengthened his personal position significantly. He understood the power of the popular press, which for Baptists meant particularly their weekly denominational newspapers (although he occasionally made use of other publications to good effect as well). Throughout his career he exercised personal control over the *Baptist Times*. He was thus able to orchestrate to a large degree how denominational debates were conducted. In society as a whole, the importance of the press in influencing popular opinion, and its resulting political power, was increasing dramatically in the late Victorian and Edwardian period. Baptists had always prided themselves on their democratic methods of denominational government, expressed primarily through the six-monthly Assemblies. The importance of being able to influence opinion through the press was therefore considerable. In time, and especially after the war, the partiality of the *Baptist Times*, both on denominational and other social and political questions, became more evident, and Shakespeare's critics made increasing use of other newspapers, such as the *British Weekly*, to express their views.

Not only did Shakespeare have the *Baptist Times* at his disposal as a means of communication; he also possessed considerable skills as a preacher and public speaker. According to Arthur Porritt, editor of the *Christian World*, he did not preach often following his appointment in 1898, and his appearances on public platforms were infrequent.[74] The response to his addresses from the Assembly platform, and elsewhere, however, was generally enthusiastic, and sometimes he generated considerable excitement. He was a 'powerful and persuasive advocate'.[75] The ability to inspire and persuade from the pulpit or platform was, of course, vitally important in a denomination for whom preaching lay at the very centre of church life. A sense of humour does not easily fit with Shakespeare's intense personality, but there are occasional signs of it in both his speaking and writing. During the delivery of a report at an Assembly, for example, he said, with subtle irony, 'I always do what I am told by good Baptists, in the hope that they will always be equally compliant with my wishes'.[76] Shakespeare's description of the Union President's golfing ability, as displayed on the links of Cornwall in the summer of 1908 shows a lighter side of his character. 'The President bore himself with serenity in nearly all the bunkers on the course, and presented a most admirable picture of a good man bearing up cheerfully under adversity', he wrote.[77] The Baptists, like the Liberal Party with which most of them identified politically, were a coalition of different groups, and holding them together was a challenge for any leader. The power to use language, whether spoken or written, was one of the indispensable tools for this task.

Apart from his contributions to the *Baptist Times*, Shakespeare did not write a great deal for publication, and evidence of the development of his theological ideas is sparse. What he did write, however, shows him to be evangelical and scholarly. A series of articles that appeared in the *Baptist Magazine* in 1899 on 'Sin', 'Grace', 'The Incarnation' and 'The Meaning of the Cross' demonstrate this. On the Incarnation, he wrote:

> From the scientific and materialistic point of view, the Copernican system has thrust human life into insignificance and littleness. But the Incarnation still makes it possible for us to believe in the value and greatness of human life.[78]

Those who worked with him often acknowledged another side to Shakespeare's personality. This was the ability to gain not only the respect but also the affection and loyalty of those he worked with. The co-operation he received from all three Union Presidents during the Twentieth Century Fund appeal, and the generous personal tributes when it succeeded, are evidence of that. A contemporary described him as 'genial, approachable and sympathetic',[79] and M. E. Aubrey, a prominent younger minister destined to become Secretary of the Union after Shakespeare's resignation, described his friendship as 'a privilege and delight'. 'We can recall his gaiety', said Aubrey at Shakespeare's memorial service in 1928, 'the affectionate grip or tap on the arm, that frank word of love'.[80]

Shakespeare played a 'fine game of golf ', and was a keen participant in the regular matches between Free Church ministers and journalists before and after the war.[81] He had great ambitions for his denomination, but little personal ambition. He was determined and persistent, but not stubborn and inflexible. More than once, he was able to win over opponents by personal kindness and courtesy. One of the most striking examples of this was the change of heart of J. Moffat Logan during the debates on the Ministerial

Settlement and Sustentation Scheme in 1909 and 1910. Logan was at first one of Shakespeare's most vociferous antagonists, and his speech explaining how Shakespeare's courtesy and patience had helped lead him to change his mind made a considerable contribution to the outcome of the debate.[82] Shakespeare's friend and colleague in the ministry, J. C. Carlile, described him as 'a curious combination' of dictator and clinging man, 'depending so much upon the sympathy and affection of those about him'.[83]

Shakespeare's eagerness to avoid confrontation and controversy was reflected in his attitudes to those outside his own denomination. When he addressed the congregation of St. Mary's at his farewell services in October 1898, he acknowledged that he had, when he was younger, attached too much importance to the questions that divided Christians from each other. This was a consequence of the 'very strict school of ecclesiastical thought' in which he was raised. 'I trust that I respect the sincere convictions of other Christians more than I did', he said.[84] The ecumenical spirit that he later became famous for was based on a profound personal dislike of conflict and division.

In 1906 the National Council of Free Churches published Shakespeare's first major book, *Baptist and Congregational Pioneers*. It described the contribution of nine late sixteenth/early seventeenth-century dissenters to the early history of Nonconformity. It provided more evidence for his essentially eirenic spirit. The period covered by the book was characterised by the principled and obstinate dissent from the established church by a small number of clerics and their congregations, and their experience of cruel persecution. When the book was being written, and at the time of its publication, feelings of hostility between Nonconformity and the Church of England were running high. Shakespeare commended the lasting value of the stand of the dissenting pioneers, but there is no suggestion in the book that the historic conflict bore any relation to the contemporary one. In fact he was at pains to distance contemporary Nonconformity from the more extreme elements of its past.

Ian Sellers has pointed out that Shakespeare's book was written at a time when interest in the Anabaptists had just been awakened.[85] A number of publications had appeared in the 1890's, and an earlier volume in the same series as Shakespeare's book on the Anabaptists had appeared in 1904 (the series was published by the Free Church Council under the title 'Eras of Nonconformity'). These portrayed the Anabaptists in a positive light, demonstrating a pride in the radical roots of contemporary Nonconformity. Sellers sees the conflict with the Church of England, especially over education following the 1902 Education Act, as an important part of the historical context for this. The Free Churches were keen to demonstrate confidence in their historical roots.[86]

Shakespeare's book showed a reversal of this trend. It deals with the Anabaptists only in passing, but such references as there are leave no doubt as to the author's view of the matter. 'It is entirely unhistorical and mis-leading to confuse the English Baptists with the Anabaptists', he writes, for example.[87] In Shakespeare's view, the connection was negligible, and the rise of the Baptist churches in the early seventeenth century was 'wholly independent' of continental Anabaptism.[88] A similar view was put forward in subsequent years by other Baptist writers, such as Henry Clark in 1911 and Champlin Burrage in 1912. Sellers is of the opinion that this change of heart took place because of the discrediting of the Anabaptists' record by historians at about this time, together with Baptists' 'search for academic and social respectability, not least in respect of origins and history', under Shakespeare.[89] It also reflects Shakespeare's desire to distance Edwardian Baptists, and the Free Churches generally, from the more radical and abra-sive elements of their past, and thereby to soften any sense of inherent con-tradiction between Nonconformity and the Established Church.

This wish to affirm Nonconformity's essential respectability is also seen in other sections of Shakespeare's book. In the chapter on Robert Browne, he asserts that when Congregationalism parts from 'love and kindness', as happened in the later stages of his leadership of the exiled separatist con-gregation in Middleberg, it is 'only fit to be cast out and trodden under foot of man'.[90] Francis Johnson's experiences showed that 'Congregationalism had a weary path to tread before it discovered the bond of Church life, which consists not in knowledge, but in love'.[91] The most relevant chapter in the book for Baptists is the one dealing with John Smyth, who, according to Shakespeare, was 'the founder of the modern Baptist churches'.[92] Shakespeare finished it by quoting Smyth as he 'drew very near to the gates of death', by which time Smyth was no longer pastor of the English Baptist congregation, which under Thomas Helwys had returned from exile to face persecution in London. Smyth wrote:

> All penitent and faithful Christians are brethren in the communion of the outward Church, by what name soever they are known; and we salute them all with a holy kiss, being heartily grieved that we should be rent into so many sorts and schisms; and that only for matters of no moment . . . From this day forward do I put an end to all controversy and question about the outward Church and ceremonies with all men, and resolve to spend my time in the main matters wherein consisteth salvation.[93]

In these words, wrote Shakespeare, the 'sweetness and beauty' of Smyth's character could be seen. Doubtless he would have liked the same qualities to be evident in his own life. The fact is, of course, that Smyth would never have become pastor of the Separatist congregation in Gainsborough, nor led it to exile in the Netherlands, nor embraced believers' baptism, if this spirit had been the directing force in his life and ministry from the start. Shakespeare's remarkable commitment to the search for compromise and the avoidance of conflict is one of the most characteristic features of his ministry.

Another aspect of Shakespeare's leadership during his early years in office is worth noting, especially in view of his later involvement in the search for church unity. Apart from his writing of *Baptist and Congregational Pioneers*, his work was almost exclusively limited to his own denomination, and he had little to do with the Free Church movement. This is surprising, in view of his obvious interest in, and knowledge of, the other Nonconformist denominations. He frequently cited them (particularly the Wesleyans) as showing the way forward for Baptists, and was an admirer, not only of Hugh Price Hughes, but also of Joseph Parker, the leading Congregationalist minister. Both Parker and Hughes were prominent in leading the Free Church movement around the turn of the century. It is striking how limited Shakespeare's own personal involvement was. He played very little, if any part in the great Simultaneous Mission of 1901, being on vacation in the South of France for the two main months of the campaign,[94] and seems to have contributed nothing of any significance to the campaign against the 1902 Education Act. Perhaps if the leadership of Parker and Hughes had continued for a few years longer (they both died in 1902) he would have been drawn more actively into the wider Free Church scene. Perhaps, on the other hand, it was simply a matter of already having enough to do at Baptist Church House. Shakespeare's standing as a Free Church leader inevitably grew as the years went by, but it was not really until 1910 that he began to play an active part in the affairs of the National Council and the Free Churches in general.

2.4 Congregationalism and Unity

Ecclesiology lay behind most of the debates and developments in the Baptist Union during the early years of Shakespeare's time in office. The fundamental issue was the place and role of the Union itself. How could the concept of a strong Union be reconciled with the historical Baptist concept of the church? This question was becoming increasingly relevant during the final decades of the nineteenth century, but it was the forceful leadership of Shakespeare that gave it greater urgency. His reforms implied a shift in perspective, lessening the traditional emphasis on the local congregation and increasing the emphasis on the national dimension of the church. Baptists had generally expressed their sense of belonging to the wider church in relatively informal ways, or through societies with specific objectives. Under Shakespeare, the Union took on a more systematic and powerful institutional form and authority. Its increasing status within the denomination changed the way Baptists thought about themselves. The denomination began to be spoken of as an ecclesiastical body, and there began to be a growing number of calls to adopt the term 'Baptist Church' to describe it.[95]

For Shakespeare, this development had more to do with pragmatism than with any question of principle. If Baptists were going to use their ministerial and financial resources efficiently to meet the challenge of twentieth-century urban society, they needed to organise themselves effectively. He strongly believed that a localised, fragmented denomination was wasteful and could never make a real impact, as his address to the Union in 1892 made clear, as did many subsequent addresses and articles. He had little sympathy with those who argued for the retention of local church autonomy, believing that they were timid, or motivated by self-interest. Many Baptists, particularly those who wrote to the *Baptist*, felt the ecclesiological ground shifting beneath their feet, and sensed that the denomination was being transformed into an unfamiliar body. Some had the uneasy feeling that efficiency did not lie at the root of the new century's challenge, and that the changes that were occurring involved more than simply the effective marshalling of Baptist resources.[96]

The two autumn Assemblies in 1905 and 1906 illustrate the denominational tension well, and provide a useful introduction to the main topic for the next chapter, the Baptist ministry. The 1905 spring Assembly was cancelled because of the World Congress, so the Union President for that year, Judge William Willis, had only one opportunity to give a presidential address, in the autumn. Willis had a reputation for eccentricity, as well as embodying the unusual combination of being both a King's Counsel and a Baptist. Underwood, rather disparagingly, described him as 'a simple-hearted Christian of the Puritan type'.[97]

Willis took as a theme for his address 'The Christian Pastor and his Claims', and it amounted to a vigorous and eloquent plea for the autonomy of the local church, especially in regard to its choice of minister, and for the essentially congregational nature of the Baptist ministry. It contained echoes of Baptist statements of the seventeenth century. The honour and dignity of the pastor, according to Willis, arose from the fact that he was 'the pastor of an assembly of converted men'. His authority, according to Willis, was based solely on his election by the members of such a congregation, and no other ordination or sanction was required. Training was valuable, but could never be insisted upon as a condition for being appointed pastor. If a church needed financial help to support its pastor, application for such help to neighbouring churches or associations could be made. Such gifts, however, should 'never justify any interference in the affairs of the church; still less, in the appointment, or removal, of the pastor'.[98] There is little doubt that Willis intended this as criticism of Shakespeare's ambitions for the denomination and the ministry.

The *Baptist Times* expressed its disapproval, the most forthright criticism of Willis being made in a leading article in December 1905, written by Walter Wynn. Wynn described the kind of congregational autonomy which the judge advocated as 'wicked', and in practice as a form of 'inverted popery' more contemptible, in some churches, 'than any Rome could produce'.[99]

The year following Willis's address, at the 1906 autumn Assembly, the Council presented, for discussion, suggestions for a centrally regulated roll of Baptist ministers as a 'guide' to the churches as to 'who were thoroughly fit for the pastorate'.[100] This was part of the preparation for the adoption of a system of ministerial accreditation by the Union the following year. In a later session at the same Assembly, the Principals of two Baptist theological colleges, William Henderson and Henry Wheeler Robinson, delivered papers on 'The Interpretation of Congregationalism'. They argued that ample justification could be found for the modification of congregational independence in both Scripture and the practice of the Early Church. Henderson spoke of the New Testament pattern of a single church in one town incorporating several congregations, in which material resources and leadership were shared. Wheeler Robinson urged that 'we should encourage the new convert to believe that he is joining the whole Baptist Church', and that there was a need to recognise a minister as God's gift to the whole Church, not just the local congregation.[101]

Shakespeare, responding to the two Baptist scholars, expressed agreement with their views, confessing that he had 'lost faith in the current interpretation of Congregationalism'. He had come to the conviction that 'Independency' was unequal to the tasks facing the denomination.[102] The papers were published as a pamphlet by the Union's Publications Department, with an introduction by Shakespeare. Describing them in his introduction as 'sensational', he advocated an ecclesiastical arrangement whereby churches in particular towns and districts should unite in 'a common church', with one eldership and shared ministers.[103] The *Baptist*, responding to the whole tone of the 1906 autumn assembly, but in particular to the proposals for a Union roll of accredited ministers, commented, 'they might well, for their pedagoguishness and the Synodical prerogative they assume, be sufficient to cause some of our good old Baptist forefathers to turn in their graves'.[104] It was clear by then that the main battleground over which the campaign for a change in Baptist polity was being fought was the ministry.

1. John Howard Shakespeare, *The Story of the Baptist Union Twentieth Century Fund with the Financial Report* (BUGBI: London, 1904).
2. *BT* 27 January 1899.
3. BU Minute Book, 15 November 1898 - 17 January 1899.
4. *BT* 10 February and 7 July 1899.
5. See pp. 31-2 for further information about the Union's acquisition of the Freeman.
6. *B* 4 May 1900.
7. *BT* 4 January 1900.
8. *BT* 26 April 1901.
9. *BT* 2 August 1901.
10. *BT* 18 October 1901.
11. *BT* 23 August 1901. It will be convenient to use the abbreviated title *Baptist Times*

from now on, although the official name of the newspaper continued to be the *Baptist Times and Freeman*.

12. Shakespeare, *Story* p. 50.
13. *BT* 18 April 1902.
14. *BT* 2 May 1902.
15. Shakespeare, *Story* p. 54.
16. *Ibid.*, pp. 59-60.
17. B 9 May 1902.
18. Shakespeare, *Story* p. 54.
19. BU Minute Book, 16 January 1899.
20. *Ibid.*, 17 January 1899.
21. See Douglas C. Sparkes, *The Offices of the Baptist Union of Great Britain* (Baptist Historical Society, Didcot: 1996) pp. 4-11 for a more detailed account of these events.
22. *BT* 3 May 1901.
23. *BT* 11 April 1902.
24. *BT* 1 January 1904.
25. Clyde Binfield, 'English free churchmen and a national style', in Stuart Mews (ed.), *Religion and National Identity (Studies In Church History* vol. 18) (Basil Blackwell, Oxford: 1982) p. 532.
26. *Ibid.*.
27. Sellers, *Nineteenth Century Nonconformity* p. 12.
28. Carlile, *My Life* p. 169.
29. See p. 26.
30. BU Minute Book, 17 July 1899.
31. BU Minute Book, 16 October 1899.
32. BU Minute Book, 17 December 1900.
33. BU Minute Book, 15 January 1901.
34. Payne, *Baptist Union* p. 160. It is noticeable how few references there are in the Union's records to Alfred's role, or indeed to any other members of the Union's staff (such as Shakespeare's personal secretary, W. H. Ball), during Shakespeare's time in office.
35. *B* 29 December 1904.
36. *Baptist Magazine* vol. 96 (December 1904) p. 471.
37. *B* 3 August 1905.
38. *B* 21 December 1905.
39. *B* 29 September 1910.
40. *BT* 30 September 1910.
41. BU Minute Book, 21 April 1904.
42. *HB* (1905), p. 229.
43. *B* 11 August 1904.
44. BU Minute Book, 26 May 1902 and 8 December 1902.
45. See p. 16.
46. *BT* 11 April 1902. It is noteworthy that even at this early stage Shakespeare had in mind the division of the country into Provinces. Eventually, these were to become a reality with the creation of Areas under the 1916 Ministerial Settlement and Sustentation Scheme.
47. BU Minute Book, 17 March 1903 and 23 April 1903.

48. BU Minute Book, 16 June 1903.
49. BU Minute Book, 20 July 1903.
50. *B* 17 July 1903.
51. See, for example, *B* 24 July 1903, in which a letter from 'Anti-Oligarchy' criticised the lack of consultation over the proposed abandoning of the spring Assembly.
52. *B* 16 October 1903.
53. *BT* 6 November, 13 November, 20 November and 18 December 1903. A key issue was expressed by W. E. Blomfield, Principal of Rawdon College, in the last of these, when he wrote, 'nothing will be done until the Assembly is prepared to give its Council some executive power'. The critical question, however, was whether the Council would have belonged to the Assembly at all in any meaningful way, if Shakespeare had got his way.
54. The 1904 Constitution, together with a description of the events that led up to its acceptance, is given in Sparkes, *Constitutions*, pp. 19-27.
55. George Eayrs in *BW* 9 March 1916.
56. Both men are quoted in H. Leon McBeth, *The Baptist Heritage: Four Centuries of Baptist Witness* (Broadman Press: Nashville, 1987) pp. 522-3. See also Lord, *World Fellowship*, p. 2.
57. BU Minute Book, 21 June 1904.
58. *Authorised Record of Proceedings, First Baptist World Congress, July 11-19, 1905* (Baptist Union: London, 1905) p. 1.
59. *Ibid.*, p. vi.
60. *Ibid.*, p. ix.
61. *BT* 27 December 1907.
62. *Ibid.*.
63. *BT* 18 September 1908.
64. Bernard Green, *Tomorrow's Man: A Biography of James Henry Rushbrooke* (Baptist Historical Society: Didcot, 1997) p. 41.
65. *Times* 13 March 1928.
66. An unpublished appreciation of 'Dr. Shakespeare' by W. H. Ball, in the E. A. Payne collection, Angus Library, Regent's Park College, Oxford. No date.
67. M. E. Aubrey, 'John Howard Shakespeare, 1857-1928' in *BQ* vol.17 (July 1957) p. 107.
68. Carlile, *My Life* p. 152.
69. *BT* 7 October 1898.
70. *BT* 21 November 1902.
71. Shakespeare, *Churches* p. 200.
72. For example, see *B* 12 January 1905.
73. *BT* 24 November 1905.
74. *CW* 15 March 1928.
75. According to Charles Brown in his address at Shakespeare's Memorial Service. *BT* 22 March 1928.
76. *BT* 17 October 1902.
77. *BT* 5 June 1908.
78. *Baptist Magazine* vol. 91 (October 1899) p. 462.
79. Arthur Porritt in *CW*, 15 March 1928.
80. *BT* 22 March 1928.
81. Arthur Porritt, *The Best I Remember* (Cassell and Company: London, 1922) pp. 214-5.

82. *BT* 6 May 1910. See pp. 69.
83. J. C. Carlile, *My Life*, p. 163.
84. *St. Mary's Baptist Church Magazine* vol. 3 (November 1898) p. 85.
85. Ian Sellers, 'Edwardians, Anabaptists and the Problem of Baptist Origins' *BQ* vol. 29 (July 1981) pp. 97-112.
86. *Ibid.*, p. 99.
87. J. H. Shakespeare, Baptist and Congregational Pioneers (NCEFC: London, 1906) p. 15.
88. *Ibid.*, p. 17.
89. Sellers, *Edwardians*, pp. 99-105.
90. Shakespeare, *Pioneers* p. 53.
91. *Ibid.*, p. 124.
92. *Ibid.*, p. 125.
93. *Ibid.*, pp. 148-9.
94. *BT* 4 January 1901. In an interesting reflection of Shakespeare's priorities, the correspondent, acknowledging that the churches would be too involved in the simultaneous Mission to be concerned about raising the Twentieth Century Fund, said it would be 'an opportune time' for him to be away.
95. e.g. *BT* 29 June 1900 and 2 November 1906.
96. Charles Keen described the Union of 1904 as ' a colossal organisation, ambitious of ecclesiastical sovereignty in the denomination' (*B* 29 March 1906). The *Baptist* described the programme of the 1906 spring Assembly as 'the customary mechanical list of essays and addresses on pre-arranged topics' (*B* 3 May 1906). 'We have gone back upon the supernatural, soul-quickening faith of our fathers', it wrote two years later (*B* 7 May 1908).
97. Underwood, p. 260.
98. *BT* 6 October 1905. Willis's address is also given in the 1906 *Baptist Handbook* pp. 238-257.
99. *BT* 22 December 1905.
100. *BT* 5 October 1906.
101. *BT* 12 October 1906.
102. *Ibid.*.
103. *BT* 9 November 1906. Shakespeare had first presented a series of proposals outlining such an arrangement to a Union committee in January 1906.
104. *B* 4 October 1906.

CHAPTER 3

The Sustenance of the Ministry

3.1 Union Recognition

Denominational ministerial recognition was a vitally important subject, as well as a controversial one, for Baptists in the pre-war years. For Shakespeare, it was essential to establish clear criteria by which a definitive list of officially recognised Baptist ministers could be drawn up, before other important questions, such as ministerial selection, training, support and pensions could be dealt with. As long as there was uncertainty about who was, and who was not, a Baptist minister, systematic progress in these other areas was impossible. The Union was the only ecclesiastical body capable of offering official recognition on a national level, and had been making gradual steps in that direction since the creation of a Ministerial Recognition Department in 1896.[1] Whether it should be given the authority to decide who should be recognised as a Baptist minister was a fundamental question that lay behind the debates that took place during this period.

Decisions taken at the 1907 spring Assembly and the 1911 autumn Assembly were the two most significant steps in establishing a comprehensive system of ministerial recognition. They set up a clear set of rules by which the Union would operate. The arrangements agreed in 1904 for the new Home Work Fund[2] meant that the Union's assessment of a minister's suitability for office was an important factor in its allocation of grants. The comprehensive scheme of Union recognition agreed in 1907, and subsequently modified in 1911, took this a stage further. These important changes took place against the background of the nineteenth-century approach to ministry.

For most of the nineteenth century, there was no standard practice with regard to ministry among Baptists. Inconsistency in both practice and terminology was an accepted feature of Baptist life. J. H. Y. Briggs, in *The English Baptists of the Nineteenth Century*, opens his section on 'Ordination' with the rather unpromising sentence: 'Ordination practice within the denomination was very varied'.[3] The terms 'ordination ', 'induction', 'recognition' and 'welcome' were often used interchangeably. Some ministers were 'ordained' afresh for each pastorate; others only at the start of their first. Some regarded their call to ministry as life-long; others moved in and out of secular employment. Some were supported full-time; others had part-time secular employment to augment their stipends. The proportion of Baptist ministers who received formal training rose as the century

wore on, but even in 1901, many did not.[4] Frequently, probably in reaction
to the growing strength of Anglo-Catholicism within the Church of England,
the language of ordination was avoided altogether, in spite of the fact that it
was commonly used by Baptists in earlier times. The most prominent example of this was Spurgeon, who was never ordained, and his example was
highly influential.

The gradual rise in prominence of the Union from the 1860's onwards,
leading to the amalgamation of the Particular and the General Baptists in
1891, bringing to an end the most obvious divide within the denomination,
meant that the notion of a national Baptist ministry became meaningful.
Another factor that encouraged the desire for a clearer and more consistent
definition of the ministry was the growing financial resources of the Union.
Denominational fund holders in general found it difficult to evaluate eligi-
bility for support. This is illustrated by the following record from the Devon
and Cornwall Association minute book in 1892:

> We frankly admit the right of the smallest church to choose its pastor, but
> we question the right of any church to say that its electing act, and that
> alone, shall confer full membership to our ministry, and eligibility for
> admission to our funds.[5]

What was true of an association and its funds, with a close knowledge of
churches and ministers, was doubly true of the more distant Union. The
responsibility it had assumed for disbursing money from the Annuity and
the Augmentation Funds since the mid-1870's led to a natural interest in
who had a right to benefit from them. The establishment of the Ministerial
Recognition Committee in 1896 was the first tentative step towards the
acceptance of rules for recognition by the Union that were eventually to
dominate the Baptist perception of the ministry. In the late 1890's, criteria
for acceptance on to the list of recognised ministers were drawn up, local
committees were formed to investigate difficult cases, and steps were taken
to promote the importance of proper training. A list of recognised training
colleges was published, and procedures for the training of non-collegiate
candidates recommended. In 1899 the central committee expressed the
desire that public recognition or ordination services for new ministers
should only take place after it had itself recognised the candidate.[6] The fact
that only a proportion of ministers was recognised by the Union was not a
matter of vital importance to most Baptists, however, unless, of course,
access to Union funds was needed. These were still very limited.

Shakespeare believed that the Union should not only officially recognise
those ministers it believed to be fit for the Baptist ministry, but also exercise
supervision over them. As early as July 1900 he publicly expressed his view
that the Union was the right body 'to guard the door to the ministry'.[7] He
was concerned about the quality of ministry, especially in the smaller

churches. He also felt ashamed because many good ministers were living in real poverty,[8] and was convinced that only a centralised system of regulating the ministry would enable these problems to be properly addressed.

As the Twentieth Century Fund appeal drew to a close in late 1901 and early 1902, the *Baptist Times* printed a series of articles by William Chivers on the need for a Union 'Sustentation Fund' for the support of the ministry, along similar lines to that operated by the United Free Church of Scotland.[9] Chivers was a leading layman in the denomination and a close friend of Shakespeare's. Shakespeare agreed with him that 'there must be more adequate support for, and care for, the ministry'.[10] A prior need, however, was to ensure that only men of the highest quality entered the Baptist ministry. Shakespeare's preference was that no one should be admitted who had not 'matriculated at a recognised University, and subsequently received a satisfactory theological training'.[11] This was a dramatic and unrealistic suggestion at that time, in view of the fact that only a tiny minority then had degrees and a large proportion had never been to a theological college.

The question of Union control of ministerial supply, with a view to raising standards, was raised at the 1903 spring Assembly.[12] The revision of the Union's rules for ministerial recognition became a matter of debate within the denomination from then on, and was discussed by the Ministerial Recognition Committee and the Council. In July 1903 Shakespeare first introduced a series of definite proposals.[13] By then the matter had already attracted controversy, and an atmosphere of confusion and turmoil about the nature and the future of the ministry settled over the denomination for the next four years or so. Members of Union committees, and Assembly delegates, as well as association and college committees, were subject to a series of proposals about ministerial recognition, support, deployment and pensions from Baptist Church House. Readers of the *Baptist* and the *Baptist Times* had to contend with a stream of articles and correspondence. The debate was conducted against a background of unprecedented change on the denominational and wider Free Church stages. A new constitution and headquarters for the Union were quickly followed by the 1905 World Congress, by reports of a dramatic religious revival in Wales, and the 1906 landslide Liberal victory, which tripled the number of Baptist MP's in the House of Commons.[14]

A key figure in steering new rules for ministerial recognition through was Rev. J. G. Greenhough. He was a leading senior minister in the Union, having served as President in 1895. He was minister of Victoria Road Baptist Church, Leicester, and like his ministerial neighbour in that city, Shakespeare's old minister Rev. James Thew, on the liberal wing of the denomination. Like Thew, his name had been mentioned during the controversy of 1887-8 as one of Spurgeon's probable targets during the Downgrade controversy. Greenhough was appointed chairman of the Ministerial Settlement and Sustentation Committee when it was formed early in 1903, which increasingly had joint meetings with the Ministerial Recognition Committee, and he presented many of the key proposals on the ministry at Assembly.

Opposition to the plans of Shakespeare and Greenhough on ministerial recognition came mainly through the pages of the *Baptist*. Its leader writers believed that culture and education were not the main qualities needed for the ministry, in spite of what official Baptist Church House pronouncements suggested.[15] The *Baptist* tended to favour the kind of ministerial preparation provided by Spurgeon's College, where educational qualifications were not insisted upon for ministerial candidates. The newspaper was not slow to point out that Spurgeon's was by far the largest Baptist theological college. Greenhough's address on the need for Union control over the number of men being trained for the ministry provoked an angry response. The *Baptist* thought that there was 'an objectionable vein of Trade Unionism' in what he said, and 'an almost pitiful want of Baptist breadth of belief in spiritual lib-erty'.[16]

After the 1904 spring Assembly, the *Baptist* was once again on the offen-sive. More opportunity should be given to the 'smaller men', and less to those with national reputations and 'glittering talent', to be heard from the Assembly platform, it asserted. In moving towards a 'professional' view of the ministry, the Baptist Union was developing 'a tendency to caste'.[17] The *Baptist* was not, however, altogether against more effective organisation to help ministers, and offered to publish its own lists of those seeking a change of pastorate, together with lists of vacant churches.[18]

During the closing months of 1904, a series of letters from Rev. Walter Wynn, a Baptist minister from Chesham, were published in the *Baptist Times* on the future of the ministry, with the intention of promoting debate about the issues facing the denomination, and preparing the ground for reform in the years ahead. He criticised the lack of a systematic approach to the selection of ministers, and the lack of help given to ministers for exchanging pastorates. He was particularly critical of the independent way the colleges chose and trained candidates, specifically identifying Spurgeon's as a chief culprit.[19] The *Baptist Times* expressed general agree-ment with his views in a leading article at the beginning of 1905, support-ing the need for a more coherent ministerial system.[20] Correspondents in the *Baptist Times* wrote in large numbers throughout 1905 expressing a wide range of views on the subject. In July, a new set of rules for ministerial recognition were due to be presented at the Union session during the World Congress for acceptance by the denomination. Shakespeare said these were necessary 'if a properly organised Sustentation Fund is to operate effec-tively'.[21] In the event they proved too controversial and were not put to the vote, but referred back to the committee for further consideration.

In 1905 a furious row broke out over the distinction made in the forth-coming 1906 *Baptist Handbook* between ministers recognised by the Union and those who were not. The *Baptist* forcibly made its views known on the decision of the Union Council to make this distinction:

> Our pastors, or under-shepherds, complain of hardships and conditions of oppression . . . Their friends whom they had themselves voted to high places have lifted up their heel against them. It was mortification indeed to find the Baptist Union Council refusing to 'recognise' and then seeking power to submerge them, and this not because they were spiritual failures, but by reason of the accident of their non-collegiate training or their unwillingness and possible inability to submit to a test of the schoolmen. And who shall yet deliver them from a form of tyranny so essentially opposed to everything Baptist?[22]

Over 400 non-recognised ministers were clearly identified as such in the *Handbook*, which was published at the close of 1905. It was one thing for Union committees to keep a list of recognised ministers. It was quite another for such a distinction to be made in a publication that long preceded the Union's interest in such matters and was used widely by Baptists in and out of the Union. The fierce response from the *Baptist* resulted from its judgement that by so doing the Union was claiming an unwarranted place of superiority and judgement over the churches and their ministers. The Union's decision led to several angry letters in the *Baptist*, including one from 'J.B.' saying that the time had come for 'those ministers and insulted churches to form a Union of their own'.[23] Judge Willis's defence of 'the Christian pastor and his claims' at the 1905 autumn Assembly, just as the row was brewing, added significant weight to the protests.[24] The rebels against the official line were no doubt encouraged by the knowledge that the Union President for that year agreed with them. Heated correspondence continued to be received by the *Baptist*, as it acknowledged in February 1906. It appealed to leading figures in the denomination by name to deliver the Union from its tendency to 'professionalise' the ministry. Such a step towards hierarchy would be 'not very far removed from priestism'. The cause of this disastrous tendency, it said, was the greater affluence of the Union, and 'the besetting danger of riches'. It was 'unBaptist', 'unChristian' and 'unScriptural'.[25] Nothing could be done about the 1906 *Handbook* once it was published, however, and its identification of 'unrecognised' ministers remained a bone of contention throughout the year.

At the 1906 autumn Assembly Greenhough once again introduced the new ministerial recognition rules, but as had happened in July 1905 opposition resulted in them not being put to the vote. Greenhough said that the object of a thorough set of rules was 'to establish as soon as it was found possible, a Sustentation Fund, to form a guide to the Churches, and to make it known that the candidates who were selected were thoroughly fit for the pastorate'.[26] Critical voices were raised against the scheme, and

Shakespeare found it necessary to defend himself and the Ministerial
Recognition Committee from the attacks they had suffered in the religious
press. In what Shakespeare acknowledged to be 'an educative piece of
work', Principals Henderson and Wheeler Robinson delivered papers on
'The Interpretation of Congregationalism', in which they asserted that 'the
delegation of power to a central or Association body' did not constitute the
abandonment of the Congregational principle.[27]

Sparkes charitably concludes that the reason for the repeated delay in asking the Assembly for a decision on the adoption of ministerial recognition
rules was the 'importance of getting the procedures right'.[28] This may well
have been true, but the fact that the Council feared rejection by the
Assembly, or a damaging split in the denomination, was more to the point.
The *Baptist* ominously claimed that more than half of all Baptist churches
in the country were 'non-Union', and about 20% of the 2,000 ministers were
non-recognised. Feelings were running high in the *Baptist Times* during the
summer and autumn of 1906, but they were mild compared to those that
found their way into the *Baptist*. A leading article in May on 'The Baptist
Union and the Ministry', included the following stinging attack:

> One is fearful to anticipate, but can we detect the Ecclesiastical Baptist
> England, with its Provinces and Bishops, of Bristol, Rawdon, London,
> Manchester and Nottingham, the deeds of the churches in a 'strong room',
> the pastorates filled, adjusted and terminated by a committee and the 'Man
> of God' the puppet of a wire puller![29]

In the light of the strong feeling in the denomination, the Council made
several concessions before the matter was brought back to the Assembly in
spring 1907, this time for a vote. It was announced that the *Handbook*
would in 1907 revert to its earlier practice of listing ministers without distinction.[30] It was also agreed that training received at colleges other than
those recognised by the Union could be accepted as sufficient. Thirdly, it
was made possible for ministers who had entered the pastorate before 1900,
and who received the backing of their association, to be recognised without
submitting themselves to the new procedures, and the rules could be somewhat relaxed for those who entered the ministry between 1900 and 1907.[31]
These concessions were substantial, particularly in making recognition easier for existing unrecognised ministers.

The rules eventually proposed at the 1907 spring Assembly were quite
brief. They provided for the creation of a list of probationer ministers. To
be included on this a candidate needed either to have completed an adequate
college or University training, or to have passed an examination set by the
Union and have had at least two years of experience as a pastor. After at
least two years of acceptable pastoral service, but not more than seven, a
person on the list of probationer ministers could be fully recognised, but

only after passing another Union examination. The original 1898 rules had dealt only with non-collegiate candidates for the ministry, and did not include any provision for a period of probation. The 1907 Scheme was more rigorous and comprehensive, particularly in insisting on the passing of at least one Union examination before any candidate could pass on to the ministerial list. These examinations were its crucial element, as for the first time they gave the Union complete control over entry to the recognised ministry.

The full significance of the changes over ministerial recognition did not lie only in the detailed provisions of the Scheme. Also important was the fact that Union recognition was now seen to matter. The argument over the 1906 *Handbook* had made this clear. It mattered partly because the Union had control over significant funds, and seemed likely to have more in the future. Another important factor was the continuous insistence from Baptist Church House that co-ordination from the centre was the only way that an adequate standard of ministry could only be achieved. The more important the Union's role in ministerial matters became, the less easy it was to see the ministry as rooted primarily in the local church.

The *Baptist*, in its issue immediately before the 1907 spring Assembly, did not directly call on its readers to vote against the Scheme, but made its feelings about the ministry clear. It affirmed that nothing could change the absolute right of a church to choose its own minister, whether he was recognised by the Union or not - a principle that was not, strictly speaking, contravened by the new Scheme, as its advocates were not slow in pointing out. The *Baptist*'s main objection was to the Scheme's reliance on what it called 'technical education and prescribed courses of reading'. Tests of character and work done, which could not be undertaken by 'officials in a London office', were far more valuable in assessing a minister's suitability for office. There was a tendency in the new arrangements to turn the ministry into 'a profession, the qualifications for which are to be purely human and mechanical, instead of divine and spiritual'. The *Baptist* insisted that the Baptist Union should keep its hands off 'the divine prerogative'. Some human agency had to recognise the call of God, if there was to be a ministry at all, of course. The *Baptist* believed that the local church was the right body for this, and that the associations also had a part to play. A major factor underlying these criticisms was the evident lack of trust in the Union and those who were directing it.[32]

The incoming President at the 1907 spring Assembly was William Henderson. He had spoken in favour of a modification of congregationalism the year before and was sympathetic to the new rules. They were proposed by Greenhough, and although an amendment was brought forward opposing the imposition of a 'scholastic examination' on those who wanted to be received onto the list of probationer ministers, this was easily defeated and the proposal was carried 'by a large majority'.[33]

The process leading up to the acceptance of the Scheme for ministerial recognition in 1907 demonstrated that Shakespeare's interest in restructuring the denomination was inseparable from his concern for the ministry. To say that all the denominational reforms of 1898-1907 were undertaken only for the sake of the ministry may be an overstatement, but from the start his sense of the needs of the ministers was a key driving force behind his advocacy of these reforms. He was critical of those who wanted to retain what he called the 'aggressive liberty of the individual congregation'[34] primarily because of its effect on the ministers. They were victims of the 'system', and the system needed changing so that they would not be so frequently 'broken upon the wheel of life'.[35]

It would have been impossible for Shakespeare to have pushed through these changes without substantial support for what he was trying to do, and sympathy for his objectives in the denomination as a whole. He received backing from many of his fellow Baptist leaders. In Greenhough especially, Shakespeare found an able and loyal colleague. The process of decision-making among Baptists was a somewhat tortuous affair. In general, Shakespeare found it relatively easy to win support for his proposals within the committees of the Union. Gaining support at the Assembly was more difficult, especially as decisions had to be carried by a substantial majority if they were to carry any real weight among the churches. The authority of the Assembly was predominantly moral and persuasive, rather than constitutional. It was one thing to win a vote there, but quite another to change practice in the churches. A Union scheme for the national recognition of ministers was in itself relatively meaningless without commitment to it by the churches themselves. That commitment was still not whole-hearted in 1907, but the Scheme did provide a framework for Shakespeare's main objective, which was to put in place a reliable and effective system for supporting and regulating the ministry. To this he could now with more confidence turn. The strains that had been revealed in the denomination were severe, but Shakespeare was nothing if not determined. He continued to apply his many abilities, and his astounding energy, to formulate and then to implement what came to be known as the Ministerial Settlement and Sustentation Scheme.

During the course of this, it became clear that the 1907 Scheme needed to be modified, in order to meet serious objections that arose once it began to be implemented. The account of that modification, which took place in 1911, can best be given as part of the story of the creation of the Ministerial Settlement and Sustentation Scheme.

3.2 The Ministerial Settlement and Sustentation Scheme

3.2.1 Putting the Scheme Together

It was not until the end of 1908 that there was definite progress towards implementing a denominational system for ministerial support. There were, however, signs beforehand that such a system was on its way, and it was often in Shakespeare's mind. From his appointment in 1898, one of his central objectives had been to ease the burden of struggling ministers, and as effective denominational machinery was, step by step, put in place, so the possibility of a scheme for achieving this became more realistic. It was a difficult issue to address because, in spite of the growing denominational consciousness, each local church, and each college, was autonomous. There was no standardised or co-ordinated approach to the acceptance by colleges of ministerial candidates, and the movement of ministers between churches was haphazard.

The churches and ministers received help and advice from a variety of sources, especially the associations and the colleges, in questions of settlement, but there was no co-ordination at a national level. The attempt in 1887 to provide this by the formation of a Union Board of Introduction and Consultation had not been successful, and was only taken up by very few. The ministry was difficult to define even after agreement about rules for Union recognition in 1907. Severe difficulties were faced by some ministers as a result of this lack of precision, particularly over receiving adequate pay and when seeking a move from one church to another. Shakespeare regarded it as a wasteful scandal.

As early as 1901 Shakespeare had published a leading article in the *Baptist Times* on 'itinerant Baptists', in which the lack of method in ministerial settlement was blamed for leading to frequent 'friction and disappointment, and in many instances to weariness and heartbreak, if not to disaster and disgrace'. The article called for 'a system of itineration within a circle, formed by such churches and pastors as voluntarily adopt the system'.[36] During the course of the next seven years, the issue of settlement was frequently addressed. It was soon firmly linked with the question of ministerial sustentation. The need for a Sustentation Fund was raised by William Chivers and W. E. Blomfield in the *Baptist Times* in 1902, and in February 1903 a Union committee was established to explore possible ways in which it might be established, alongside a workable scheme facilitating ministerial moves between churches. At its first meeting Shakespeare stated that his objective was for the Union to assume financial responsibility for all properly recognised ministers.[37]

During the debates on ministerial recognition, concerns about settlement and sustentation were frequently raised. It was not, however, until 1906 that a serious attempt was made to address the issues. In January Shakespeare

brought some ideas to Greenhough's Ministerial Settlement and
Sustentation Committee. He believed they could lay a foundation for securing greater freedom and efficiency for ministers and churches. He made the
following suggestions:

- that the New Testament conception of the visible Church admits of
  there being a common Church in one town or district, consisting of all
  the believers in that town or district.
- that the New Testament conception admits of a number of companies
  of believers, while forming part of a common Church, yet meeting separately for worship and service.
- that there should be one eldership for the common Church, in which
  each company of believers is represented.
- that the common Church should appoint its Pastors and assign to them
  the services they shall respectively render.[38]

The committee felt that the time was 'not ripe' to submit these quite radical ideas to the Assembly. The Council agreed, however, to enquire of the
churches whether or not they would be prepared to accept a system of peri-
odic change of pastorates. This suggestion received the backing of the 1906
spring Assembly, and that summer the churches and ministers of the denomination received a letter from Baptist Church House asking for their views
on this, together with a pamphlet outlining a possible way in which this
could be achieved.[39] This attempt to canvass opinion about the possibility
of an itinerant ministry along Methodist lines was not very successful, as by
January 1907 fewer than 10% of the 1300 churches contacted had replied.[40]
In spite of this, a joint meeting of the Ministerial Recognition and the
Ministerial Settlement and Sustentation Committees recommended that a
scheme be instituted on the basis of a 'voluntary union' of those few
churches (only 83) that had indicated a desire to participate.[41] This failed
because most of the churches could not be persuaded to take the matter any
further.[42] In spite of this disappointment, Shakespeare wrote again, this time
to the associations, in March 1908, asking for their views. Only a quarter of
them replied within six months, and the response was mixed.[43]

1908 had opened with a 'painful surprise' for the readers of the *Baptist*
and the *Baptist Times*. For the first time in living memory, the 1907 membership statistics for the Baptist churches in England and Wales showed a
decline over the previous year. The *Baptist* admitted that 'a note of dis-
couragement' was prevalent in the denomination at the 'depressingly slow'
march of the Kingdom of God.[44] The *Baptist Times* put on a braver face,
interpreting the figures as a 'cutting away of so much dead wood' following
the short-lived increases of the Welsh revival. There had been an increase
in the figures for England, although it was admitted they were very small.[45]

The sense of 'arrested progress' was to be a dominating factor in the various debates in the Union over the next couple of years, and acted as a stimulus to the faltering steps being taken towards a systematic approach to ministerial settlement and sustentation.

It was not only the Baptist denomination that experienced a drop in members. The Wesleyans recorded their greatest decline for 50 years, and it soon became apparent that the whole of Nonconformity had reached something of a peak of membership in 1906. The list of ministers in the 1908 *Handbook* also made interesting reading for Baptists. For the first time, in line with the new rules for Union recognition, a list of probationary ministers was included.

The mood of the *Baptist Times* was very much in favour of continuing change in the denomination's approach to its ministry. Leading articles by W. T. Whitley, a Baptist minister in Preston, and soon to become the inaugural secretary of the Baptist Historical Society, deplored the way in which churches and colleges acted independently in choosing and training ministers. Too many untrained men were entering the ministry (29 out of a total of 70 in 1907, according to Whitley); too little provision was made for retired ministers; there were too many theological colleges and the small number of tutors in each meant they were unable to undertake any serious academic work.[46]

Most of 1908 was relatively uneventful, however, as far as concrete progress towards change was concerned. One significant event in the early part of the year was Shakespeare's speech at the spring Assembly on 'The Arrested Progress of the Church'.[47] In this 'brilliant' and 'epoch making' address (so described by the President[48] and J. H. Rushbrooke[49]) Shakespeare acknowledged that, in spite of more money, more buildings, more societies and more machinery, the Church lacked confidence in itself and its message. He identified two principal causes for this. First, there was 'our defective Denominational system, which fails to use to the best advantage such resources as we do possess'. It was obsolete, he said. It encouraged a spirit of selfishness, made the real advance of the Kingdom of God 'flatly impossible', and degraded the ministry. The second main cause was 'changing conditions of social and national life', illustrated by 'the break-up of the external forms of religion among Christian people themselves' and 'the decay of personal and family piety'.

Shakespeare went on to give a six-fold remedy. First, he said, 'we must return to the Bible'. Secondly, 'there must be more attention to preaching'. Thirdly, 'there must be a more aggressive policy' for denominational life and mission. This should include, among other things, the establishment of one Baptist church in each town, the grouping of village churches, the establishment of 'a special order of ministers at the service of the Union' for church extension and evangelism, the improvement of standards in the colleges, and the better use of denominational literature. Fourthly, there was a

need to lift up the ideal of the church as 'the pure and radiant Bride of
Christ'. Fifthly, he said, 'we must lift up our ideals of the Christian minister', and sixthly, 'we must lift up the ideal of piety'. Shakespeare spoke at
greatest length, and with greatest passion, on the ministry.

> I am deeply conscious that the root and secret of the whole matter is here.
> With so few exceptions as to be insignificant, the Church is what the min-
> ister makes it . . . when he is right, everything is right . . .. To its infinite
> disadvantage, the Baptist Church has lost its sense of the greatness and
> sacredness of the ministerial calling . . .. The call of the risen Lord to this
> office is through the Church as its most solemn function . . .. It is
> absolutely vital that there should be in his speech and bearing a moral and
> spiritual elevation, that there should be about him a suggestion of God and
> eternity . . . What the Church needs more than anything else today is lead-
> ership in its ministry. . (based on) moral earnestness, spiritual power,
> enthusiasm for service, beauty and unselfishness of character, vital and
> pre-eminent goodness, a mastery of the Bible . . .[50]

The *Baptist* expressed broad sympathy with Shakespeare's diagnosis of
the problem, but did not accept his proposed remedy, with its emphasis on
organisation. Its depression about the state of the churches and their future
prospects was not lifted.[51]

For most of that summer, Shakespeare was involved with the European
Baptist Congress in Berlin. In the autumn, the Union President, Charles
Brown, picked up Shakespeare's theme with an address to the Assembly on
'The Christian Ministry and the Baptist Churches', pleading for 'some sort
of vital connexion between each minister and the Baptist Union from the
first to the last'.[52] The *Baptist Times*, in the issue covering the Assembly,
included a leading article by T. E. Ruth asserting, in a markedly unBaptist,
way, that the Christian ministry was 'a Divine ordinance as truly as the
Christian Church'.[53]

From the autumn of 1908, the pace of change began to quicken. The
Ministerial Settlement and Sustentation Committee, under its chairman
Greenhough, disappointed by the poor response from churches and associations to its earlier requests, asked a sub-committee to draft 'a fairly comprehensive scheme'.[54] This was done (probably very largely by Shakespeare
himself) in less than a month, and in November a scheme was agreed by the
committee.[55] It was printed in the *Baptist Times* on 22 January 1909. Its pre-
amble stated that there had been 'for many years an urgent desire in the
Denomination that something should be done to solve the difficult problems
of Ministerial Settlement and to facilitate changes of pastorates'.[56] The committee proposed a 'Federal Union of Recognised Baptist Colleges in Great
Britain' and a 'Federation' of churches that wanted to join the Scheme. It
also proposed fixed terms of appointment for pastors, and the temporary

'stationing' of ministers unable to secure a pastorate. A centrally administered Sustentation Fund for the payment of the stipends of ministers was
envisaged. If the level of stipends was to be improved and guaranteed by
the Union, as was intended, a substantial capital sum would have to be
raised to support this fund.[57] The Scheme was initially designed only for
those churches that specifically chose to join it. In 1909, the indications
were that they would be in the minority.

Shakespeare's impatience to get things moving more quickly is evident in
the way the Scheme emerged between October 1908 and its presentation to
the Assembly in April 1909. Not only was it drafted very quickly, but it was
also published in the *Baptist Times* within three days of the Council having
considered it, and in spite of the Council's view that parts of it needed
redrafting.[58] The Council decided that the section dealing with the colleges
should be referred to the college authorities before wider approval was
sought. The sections dealing with settlement and sustentation were 'provi-
sionally accepted', although some parts were referred back to the committee. A leading article in the same issue of the *Baptist Times* in which the
Council's discussion of the Scheme was reported was clearly intended to
undermine the position of its detractors. Richard Glover, the chief opponent
of Shakespeare and Greenhough's plans at the Council, was described as
'the champion of unbending Independency'. The associations were
described as being in 'general approval' of the earlier version of the Scheme
sent them by Shakespeare during the previous year, in spite of the fact that
most of them had not responded at all. The writer warned that the Scheme,
in spite of being urgently needed and in total accord with the New Testament
teaching on the church, would 'have to encounter the dead-weight of inertia, prejudice and hostility'.[59] A month later Richard Glover wrote to his son,
a student at Cambridge University:

> I have been rather occupied with a wild cat scheme of the Baptist Union
> Council to turn the Baptist denomination into a conference-managed
> denomination like the Methodists: with rotation of ministers: supervision
> of settlements: Sustentation Fund on a mechanical basis etc. I do not think
> there is much likelihood of it being accepted . . . It will do harm to our col-
> leges - associations - churches, by being agitated.[60]

The *Baptist* was similarly pessimistic of its chances of success, describing the Scheme as 'immature and crude'.[61] From the middle of February
until April 1909 there was a scramble to get the Scheme ready for presentation at the spring Assembly. The Settlement and Sustentation Committee
met four times to consider it (on one occasion together with college representatives), and the Council discussed it twice.[62] Spurgeon's College was
uncompromising in its opposition. The trustees of the college declined
Shakespeare's invitation to participate in a united College Board to co-ordi-

nate entry to the ministry, replying that they 'would never agree to any
scheme which would in any way interfere with their absolute and sole
authority in the matter of the choice and training of the students of the
Pastors' College'.[63] Spurgeon's held a sufficiently dominant position in the
training of ministers for their views not to be ignored. Shakespeare revised
the section of the Scheme dealing with the colleges in order to make the
Board's role only 'consultative and advisory'.[64] In the end, however, after a
number of other modifications, the general effect of which was to make the
provisions of the Scheme less prescriptive, the Council agreed to present it
to the Assembly without including the section on collegiate training at all.[65]

Responsibility for presenting and expounding the revised Scheme fell to
Shakespeare. Reports of his speech show him at his most persuasive.
Congregationalism, he assured delegates, would not be threatened by the
proposed changes in procedure, only 'rigid independence' and 'selfish iso-
lation'. Change was needed, both to redeem churches from their inefficiency and to lighten the burden of poverty for many ministers 'The
Wesleyan and Presbyterian systems may not be scriptural', he said, 'but they
do not starve their ministers'. Of the three main elements of the Scheme,
the question of college training was being considered by the colleges themselves, he said. The element dealing with ministerial settlement would
involve the setting up of a 'voluntary union' of participating churches, and
the establishment of fixed seven year terms for ministry. The element concerned with ministerial sustentation would require a substantial central fund
to be raised, to enable the Union to guarantee adequate stipends for recognised ministers. Shakespeare hoped that the Scheme could be launched in
1911, the three hundredth anniversary of the founding of the first 'modern
Baptist church', and he commended it to churches and associations for their
consideration.[66]

The *Baptist Times* described his speech as 'thrilling' and 'magnificent',
and the response from the audience as 'a torrent of applause and cheers'.[67]
The *Baptist* was rather more restrained, drawing attention to the revisions
forced upon the Union because of initial opposition.[68] Richard Glover had
sent a letter to the Assembly regretting his unavoidable absence and expressing his opposition to the Scheme. Several speakers voiced misgivings, but
after the debate the Scheme was unanimously referred to the churches and
the associations for their consideration.[69]

The *Baptist Times* devoted much of its space during the course of the next
twelve months to the debate on the Scheme. One of its most vociferous
opponents, who was given repeated opportunity to express his views, was J.
Moffatt Logan. He urged his readers to be watchful and alert, and warned
them of Shakespeare's ambitions for a national Baptist Church. The proposed voluntary union, or federation, of churches, would, he said, in time
'devour' both Union and associations.[70] Shakespeare replied to criticisms
from Logan and from Glover in leading articles. 'The scheme means that

the Denomination is to take for the first time a common and serious responsibility for its ministers', he said.[71] He was supported in particular by his own minister at Archway Road Baptist Church, Highgate, and a rising figure in the denomination, J. H. Rushbrooke.[72]

At the 1909 autumn Assembly Richard Glover gave his reasons for opposing the Scheme more fully. His address was in reply to Greenhough's warm commendation of it. It could split the denomination, he believed. It also contradicted the scriptural principle that the local church needed neither association with others, nor a minister, to be complete. It involved a wrong exercising of authority by the Union, and would lead to the establishment of cumbersome administrative machinery. Above all, it would not solve the difficulties faced by churches and ministers, and could only lead to disappointment.[73]

1909 ended with the *Baptist Times* confessing to having received 'the keenest and most interesting correspondence ever carried on in our columns'.[74] The *Baptist* ruminated upon 'the far-reaching mischief that a drastic officialism may unconsciously work, by its bestowals of preference, and privileges, towards turning a federation of Christian ministers into something nearly akin to a mere Trade Union organisation'.[75]

The early months of 1910 were taken up with preparation for the spring Assembly. Shakespeare knew that denominational unity was vital, and hoped to gain support from the large majority of churches. Some modifications to the Scheme were made to make it more acceptable to its opponents. Support could not be assumed, particularly as only a small minority of the churches canvassed had sent a response to Baptist Church House by the date requested. Even on the eve of the Assembly the figure was still less than 50%.[76] The proposed time limit on the length of pastorates was relaxed and some of its other provisions, such as the way churches would be expected to contribute to the central fund, were made less prescriptive. Some necessary administrative details were also added. The capital sum that would need raising before the Scheme could be put into operation was fixed as £250,000, and an upper age limit for ministers of 60 was decided upon, above which the Union would not be responsible for finding pastorates.[77] Shakespeare publicised these amendments and additions in the *Baptist Times* two weeks before the Assembly.[78]

Another quite separate development in the spring of 1910 was to play a part in the Union's progress towards adopting the Scheme. In March Shakespeare delivered an address at the annual meetings of the National Free Church Council entitled 'The Free Churches and the National Life'. It was the first significant contribution by Shakespeare to the pursuit of church unity since his appointment in 1898. It led Thomas Phillips, a prominent younger minister who was to be elected Union President in 1916, to report in the *Baptist Times* that 'we all ought to be proud that we have in our Union Secretary the greatest Free Church statesman of the day'.[79]

In this address, Shakespeare spoke of the 'decay of the denominational idea' and argued for much greater co-operation within Nonconformity. To achieve this, he proposed the formation of a United Free Church of England, within which each denomination would act as an autonomous section. 'I would paint', he said, 'the vision of the one Free Church of England in each village, representing one-half of the religious life of the nation, respected and even influential; its minister in some sense the father or the leader of the village'. He also longed to see an influential Free Church at the national, European and colonial level - 'a Free Church in an ampler air and with a vaster service'.[80] The effect of the address, which was greeted with widespread enthusiasm by Free Church leaders, was similar to that of his 1892 address on Church Extension within the Baptist Union. It brought Shakespeare dramatically to the attention of the Free Church constituency as someone with vision and leadership abilities. An article by Shakespeare on 'The United Free Evangelical Church' was shortly afterwards published in the *Christian World*, and reprinted in the *Baptist Times*. In it, Shakespeare expressed the conviction that differences between the Free Churches were 'little more than matters of preference or temperament'. Even with regard to baptism, he was prepared to 'let it go out into the field, and to trust the issue to the individual who has the New Testament in his hand'. The National Council, he believed, could be the 'intermediary' for creating a new United Church.[81]

Within a month of the Free Church meetings, the sudden and tragic death of the National Council's secretary, Thomas Law, was announced. His body was mysteriously recovered from the sea, and the assumption was that he had committed suicide, as he had been suffering with bouts of depression. Before more than a few days had passed, Shakespeare was being spoken of as the right man to succeed Law, by Silvester Horne among others.[82] Exactly what effect this had on Shakespeare it is impossible to know, although it must have been very much in his mind, and in the minds of many of the delegates, throughout the 1910 spring Assembly, which took place soon afterwards. It is conceivable that the possibility of Shakespeare's departure from the Union might have influenced the vote that was taken on the Scheme. Baptists might have risked losing more than just the Scheme if the vote had gone against it. In the event, the Assembly expressed warm support for both Shakespeare and the Scheme. Soon after it was over, Shakespeare sailed to America to help prepare for the 1911 Baptist World Congress in Philadelphia. On his return he told the Council that he had decided not to take up the offer of the Secretariat from the Free Church Council, in spite of the fact that it had been 'strongly pressed upon him'.[83]

The long debate on the Scheme at the 1910 Assembly was reserved for the final session, and after two and a half hours, and eighteen speeches, the following resolution, prepared by the Council, was put to the vote:

That this Assembly of the Baptist Union of Great Britain and Ireland, in commending the Revised Scheme of Ministerial Settlement and Sustentation to the favourable consideration and acceptance of the Associations and Churches expresses its judgement that the adoption of the Scheme would mark a real advance in Denominational usefulness and efficiency, and would tend to mitigate many of the evils of our present system, while at the same time maintaining the unity which so happily prevails in our midst.[84]

The *Baptist Times* gave its usual exhaustive account of the debate. It described as the turning point the speech by Moffat Logan, who had been so vociferous in opposition throughout the previous year. Logan spoke of the great courtesy Shakespeare had extended to him, both in allowing him to express his views in the *Baptist Times* and in personal discussion, and indicated he had changed his mind and would be voting in favour.[85] At least one other speaker who had originally opposed the Scheme also spoke in favour of its acceptance, in view of the amendments that had now been incorporated into it. Most of the contributions to the debate congratulated Shakespeare on his skill and statesmanship. Only Richard Glover spoke against the motion, and he was joined by just eight others in rejecting it when it came to the vote. The *Baptist Times* said the motion pledged the denomination to 'changes of polity and of method of the most vital importance', and 'carried further the movement began by the Twentieth Century Fund'.[86] The Council later expressed its 'gratitude to God for the spirit of unity and love which pervaded the proceedings'.[87] The *Baptist*, in one of its last gestures against what seemed to be an unstoppable movement within the denomination, spoke of the 'weakness' of the Assembly's attitude and policy.

Whereas the 1909 Assembly had merely 'referred' the Scheme to the churches and associations, the 1910 decision wholeheartedly 'commended' it, in its amended form. Whether or not this decision meant the denomination pledged itself to changes of church polity (as the resolution implied) remained to be seen. It was to be nearly six years before a scheme (much altered in the process) actually came into effect. Shakespeare had been successful in achieving a near unanimous vote in the Assembly, but experience had shown that this did not necessarily mean acceptance by the churches. Their response was eagerly awaited. Before the efforts made to try and secure that acceptance are looked at, some observations should be made about the situation in which Baptists found themselves in the light of the decision of 1910.

First, it is important to recognise that the lack of involvement of the colleges in the Scheme, as it was presented to the Assembly, was a serious shortcoming. They were the primary, though not the only, source of candidates for ministry, and all students who completed a college course successfully in the view of the college authorities were automatically entitled to be included on the list of probationary ministers. The proposed Inter-Collegiate Board did not start meeting until 1912, and even then it was not successful in co-ordinating either the selection or the training of candidates for the ministry, partly because Spurgeon's College chose not to be involved.[88] Spurgeon's was not the power it had been in its founder's time, and financial constraints were sometimes severe, but it was still a major national Baptist institution, and its whole ethos and approach to ministry was fundamentally at odds with that of Shakespeare and the Union. Academic examinations were not required for entry, and were not central to the programme of training. The idea of some denominationally pre-deter-mined limit on the number of candidates who could be accepted for minis-terial training would have been abhorrent to its founder. Personal qualities, not denominational requirements, were what mattered.[89] The other colleges were more sympathetic to the Union's aims, and their Principals were some-times among Shakespeare's most ardent supporters, but without co-opera-tion from Spurgeon's, co-ordinated action under the banner of the Union, which was difficult to achieve anyway, was impossible. Unless control over the supply of ministers could be secured, any Union guarantees on ministe-rial settlement and stipend levels were unrealistic.

As Richard Glover had warned, the Scheme also posed a real threat to denominational unity. It gave rise to the possibility that churches would be divided into quite separate groups, at least as far as their relationship with the Union was concerned. One threatened division was between churches receiving aid and those that did not. Churches that relied upon the provision of funds from the Union would be subject to limits being placed on their freedom of action, and pressure to conform to Union policy. On the other hand, churches that were able to meet or exceed the Union's minimum stipend figure, and were net contributors to the Scheme, would be in a posi-tion to preserve their independence. In effect, the distinction was between the smaller and poorer churches on the one hand, and the larger and more affluent ones on the other. The risk was that the Scheme would lead to an ecclesiastical divide, over not only the status of the local church *vis-a-vis* the Union, but also in church polity. The underlying cause of this was the pro-posed imposition of features of a national Church on to a denomination that was fundamentally congregational in ethos.

A second division could result from the establishment of a new and pow-erful Federation of churches within the Union, in which procedures for min-isterial pay and settlement were quite distinct. It was possible that some churches would not join the proposed Federation. In fact Shakespeare assumed, at least initially, that this would be the case. The preservation of denominational unity in the face of such a fundamental difference of polity, where some churches functioned in a Methodist way, accepting a system for regulating the exchange of pastorates and a centrally paid ministry, and oth-ers retained their autonomy, would be a huge challenge. The main task of the next two years (1910-1912) was to gain as wide a consensus among the churches as possible, in order to avoid the threatened denominational divisions becoming a reality. This inevitably involved making significant modifications to the Scheme.

3.2.2 Gaining Support from the Churches

In the summer of 1910, letters were once again sent to the churches and associations with the Assembly's resolution commending the Scheme to them. J. H. Rushbrooke hoped that resolutions from local churches accepting the Scheme would pour into Baptist Church House,[90] but in true Baptist fashion things did not work out in that way. Replies were requested by September, but by November over 1,000 churches had still not done so. Of those who had, 378 were in favour of the Scheme, 93 against and 33 neutral.[91] The Council agreed to promote it more actively, and accepted that its launch would have to be delayed until 1912.[92]

The issue of ministerial recognition reappeared following the 1910 spring Assembly's commendation. This happened once the real impact of the 1907 rules began to be felt.[93] Another reason, perhaps, why the matter was raised at this stage was the prospect of centralised ministerial sustentation, bringing home to many ministers and others the importance of Union recognition. It was debated at the 1910 and 1911 autumn Assemblies, and, in the intervening twelve months, there was considerable controversy over certain aspects of the 1907 agreement.

The need for the matter to be resolved to the denomination's satisfaction was vital. Hugh Brown, a Baptist minister not recognised by the Union, formally raised complaints about the recognition rules at the 1910 autumn Assembly. Brown's opposition to the imposition of academic examinations, or 'man-made tests' as he called them, on ministerial candidates was well known.[94] He moved a resolution deprecating examinations as a condition of enrolment, and there was a sharp exchange between him and Greenhough.[95] His resolution was lost by a large majority, but he was successful in provoking renewed consideration of the matter. The *Baptist Times*, apparently sensing an urgent need to restate the case for the existing arrangements, ran four leading articles on the subject following the Assembly.[96] In November it made the Union's position clear:

> It is not reasonable that the Baptist Union should be expected to put upon its Accredited List any man who is called to the pastorate of a Church, even though he may be deficient in education, in scriptural knowledge, without any theological training, and through his tactlessness a real source of weakness and danger to the Churches. The Union is responsible for great funds.[97]

The rules were in place, the *Baptist Times* said, to protect an exalted view of the ministry, without which no church could 'live and be strong'.[98]

In spite of this spirited defence, criticism continued. Roland J. French, a probationary minister, wrote that many churches were unaware of the Union's rules, and that many probationary ministers bitterly resented the 'coercive measure' of having to sit examinations in order to receive recognition. In spite of the growing disadvantages of remaining officially unrecognised, they preferred this to submission to a system they did not believe in. The 1907 regulations, he said, were both insulting and ineffective, having been drawn up by 'a few men at headquarters'.[99] It became clear that there would be further trouble at the 1911 spring Assembly if they were not looked at again. This would be particularly damaging to the ongoing promotion of the Ministerial Settlement and Sustentation Scheme, as it was planned to make use of this occasion to give the campaign for its acceptance by the churches a major boost.

In January and April 1911, two conferences on the question of recognition were arranged, the April one specifically designed to enable probationary ministers to air their views, and in October the Council agreed to certain amendments to the 1907 regulations. The principal change was that it became possible for probationary ministers to pass on to the Union's full ministerial list without having to take a Union examination, on the basis of evidence of 'spiritual efficiency'. The need for association support before inclusion on either of the Union lists was also made explicit.[100] Brown and those who supported his stand were satisfied with these modifications, and the amended rules were agreed unanimously at the 1911 autumn Assembly. The decisions of 1911 should be regarded as a significant reversal for Shakespeare and Greenhough. The primary means of the Union's control over entry to the ministerial lists was through the examinations it set and marked, and these were now no longer obligatory, except for non-collegiate candidates. The change proved unacceptable to Greenhough, and he resigned from the chairmanship of the Union's Ministerial Recognition Committee in July, a position he had held for fifteen years.

The Union's agreement to review the question of ministerial recognition enabled the supporters of the Settlement and Sustentation Scheme to promote its merits without the fear of a distracting argument at the 1911 spring Assembly. F. G. Benskin, a younger minister from Bristol, gave a stirring appeal for support, emphasising the dire financial needs of many ministers. Their circumstances were 'not only pathetic, they are absolutely tragic', he said, leading to 'one monotonous round of struggle to endure'.[101] In July the *Baptist Times* said that without some kind of unified scheme, under which the rich helped the poor, nearly half the churches were finding it impossible to pay their ministers a decent stipend. It drew attention to the better performance of other denominations over the level of ministerial stipends.[102]

Before the 1912 spring Assembly, in yet another attempt to coax commitment to the Sustentation Scheme by the churches, the Council modified it again. One of the most important changes was that its local administration would no longer be in the hands of special district committees, but would be the responsibility of the associations.[103] Discussion at Baptist Church House turned increasingly to the practical financial implications of the Scheme. In particular, attention was given to raising the required capital fund and to the subsequent annual appeal. A joint conference of the main committee and association officers agreed that it was 'desirable that Associations unite with the Union in making the annual appeal for the Sustentation Fund within their own borders'.[104] Four ministers, including Greenhough and John Clifford, offered to launch the capital fund with donations of £250 each.[105] On the eve of the Assembly, at which adoption of the Scheme and the launch of the appeal was to be proposed, the *Baptist Times* called it 'the most epoch-making event in British Baptist history', and appealed for unanimous support.[106]

The key event at the Assembly was Shakespeare's moving of the Scheme's adoption, and his appeal for the denomination to be 'summoned to make this supreme effort to give expression to the sense of solidarity, which is the crown of the structure of which our fathers laid the foundation'.[107] According to the *Baptist Times*, 'round after round of cheering greeted the Secretary' as he rose to speak. He described the way in which the Scheme had been modified and explained yet again why it was necessary and, in outline, how it would operate. A Federation of those churches in membership of the Union that decided to join it would be created. For the first time the denomination as a whole would accept responsibility for the support of its ministers, both in and out of pastorate. A national sustentation scheme was required, he said, in order to deal with 'a tragic situation, a gigantic problem, and, I fear, with a serious scandal'. He pleaded for the Scheme on the ground of both humanity and efficiency. How can a minister love his people, he asked, 'when all the week he moves about in a dream of helpless wrath that ever he was caught up in the whirling wheels of this denominational system?' He charged the delegates to set their hands to the challenge as 'an undivided host'.[108] John Clifford seconded the motion, and it was passed unanimously.

A second resolution launching the Sustentation Fund and calling upon the churches to devote themselves to the task of raising it was also passed without opposition. F. B. Meyer, who was to play the leading role in raising the money, talked about his plans for doing so. Before the meeting was over, promises and gifts of over £50,000 had been received.

The second major phase in the long struggle to gain support for the Scheme, the raising of the necessary finance to launch it, was now underway. One advantage over the situation thirteen years before, when the Twentieth Century Fund was launched, was that denominational structures and premises were now in place. This made the task of fund raising much more easy to organise. It was soon clear, however, that much of this work would have to be done in Shakespeare's absence. For the first time since 1902 he was forced to take extended sick leave. J. H. Rushbrooke told the readers of the *Baptist Times* on 3 May:

> The Secretary of the Union, to whose magnificent statesmanship more than to any other human cause, the preliminary success is due, is for reasons of ill health compelled to rest for several weeks . . . We shrink from the idea that there should be required from him such a Herculean effort as was demanded in the raising of the Century Fund. It ought to be laid upon the conscience of our people to spare him that.[109]

In the event, Shakespeare was not well enough to resume his duties for almost nine months, and even beyond this, throughout much of 1913, his health was in a fragile state.[110] At the 1912 autumn Assembly Rushbrooke repeated his plea that Shakespeare should not be expected to 'throw himself into fund raising yet again' on his return to health.[111] The women of the denomination played an important role in getting the money in, just as they had for the Twentieth Century Fund. This time they too had an already existing national organisation to help them. This was the Baptist Women's League, which had been formed in 1908, largely due to an initiative by Shakespeare.[112] By the close of 1912, the Fund had received £83,000 in gifts or promises.[113]

By the end of 1913, the appeal had reached over £200,000. The efforts of London Baptists were particularly important. Their 'Sustentation Day' in October of that year alone raised £27,000. The new Baptist Chancellor of the Exchequer, David Lloyd George, lent his support to the campaign, giving a 'great speech' pleading for 'a living wage for the labourer in the village'.[114] A noteworthy incident of 1913 was the appearance of an article in the *Baptist Times* in June by T. R. Glover, Richard Glover's son, entitled 'A Few Words on the Question of Missions', in which he appealed for support for the missionary society to help it reduce its deficit. The missionary society may not be 'a panel of the Baptist Union ', Glover wrote, but 'it is none the less the common concern of every one of us', and lack of support for it showed 'wrong priorities'.[115]

During the early months of 1914, by which time it was fairly clear that the money would be raised in time for the spring Assembly, as planned, the emphasis in committee discussions returned to the administration of the Sustentation Fund once it was in operation. Shakespeare laid stress on the fact that there should be complete co-operation between the Union and the associations in the raising of the required annual collection.[116] At the Assembly, the incoming President, Rev. Charles Joseph, chose as the title of his Presidential address 'Centralisation and Democracy'. He stressed the need for greater centralisation in the denomination. The Sustentation Fund had been inaugurated, he said, 'to help Baptist churches: it has revealed the Baptist Church'. A church aided from central funds could not, he pointed out, be called independent, and there was a duty on the stronger churches not to 'cling to a venerated tradition' of independency when this was denied their weaker brethren. 'We should draw all our churches . . . into genuine and lasting denominational unity'.[117]

The Assembly closed with a 'Great Thanksgiving Rally' in the Albert Hall, chaired by Percy Illingworth MP, the Chief Whip of the Liberal Party, and a Baptist. It was no great surprise when Shakespeare announced the successful achievement of the target. One of the many tributes to him was one to his 'sane and saintly subtlety' in leading the denomination to this outcome.[118] By so doing, he had 'added another monument to his inspired leadership and practical statesmanship', according to Rushbrooke.[119]

3.2.3 Implementing the Scheme

Between the end of the 1914 spring Assembly and the outbreak of war the idea of a national Baptist Church appeared in the *Baptist Times* several times. In May Rushbrooke described how the Sustentation Fund had marked 'the recognition of the minister, not so much as the servant of a local community, but as the representative of a wider fellowship'.[120] A leading article in July entitled 'The Church and Our Churches' appealed for a concept of the whole Church to be held alongside that of individual churches. A week later another wrote that the securing of an efficient ministry was 'the great and all-important problem which the Church has to face'.[121]

The outbreak of war changed everything, of course. Baptists were caught up in the disaster as much as everyone else in the country, and it had a profound effect on their national denominational life, as well as their personal circumstances and the priorities of their churches. It was especially important for church unity, a question that will be considered in the next chapter. The war was an ever-present backdrop to the implementation of the Ministerial Settlement and Sustentation Scheme.

For several months, the Scheme disappeared from view at Baptist Church House. From the opening days of the war, the *Baptist Times* enthusiastically supported the government's stand. On 7 August it said that 'rightly or wrongly we are committed to war, and there can be no drawing back'.[122] By the beginning of September German atrocities in Belgium were being reported, and the war was being increasingly portrayed as a clash between Christ and the Devil. A message agreed by the Council to 'the Baptists of the British Empire' was published in September. It condemned the 'brutal militarism' of German policy, and declared that the call of God had come to Britain 'to spare neither blood nor treasure in the struggle to shatter a great anti-Christian attempt to destroy the fabric of Christian civilisation'.[123]

From then on Shakespeare, in the *Baptist Times*, and Robertson Nicoll, in the *British Weekly*, became the two leading Nonconformist advocates of the war effort. Shakespeare was very quickly involved in discussions with the War Office about the provision of Free Church chaplains for the forces, and about the reception of refugees from Belgium and France.

By November, the Council was able to find room on its agenda for consideration of the Scheme. The main initial anxiety was over whether the money that had been promised to the Sustentation Fund would actually be given. War conditions were already having an impact on people's economic circumstances, and only £165,000 of the £250,000 needed had actually arrived at Baptist Church House.[124] It was decided, however, to start the operation of the Scheme at the beginning of 1916, and steps were put in place for the appointment of an executive committee to run it.

The day after this Council meeting (on 18 November), a conference was held with association secretaries and treasurers to sort out the relationship between the various association funds and the Sustentation Fund, and to clarify the precise responsibilities of the associations to the latter. It was agreed that there should be only one annual appeal for the maintenance of ministers in aided churches, whether or not the Sustentation Fund was involved. It was likely that some of the churches already supported by the associations would either not qualify for central funding, or not wish to join the proposed Federation. This meant that, for them to fulfil their existing commitments, the associations would have to retain some of the money they raised for grants. It was also agreed that the Union would not give a grant without prior association endorsement. As far as the actual payment of stipends from the Fund was concerned, Shakespeare outlined the method that would be used:

> In the case of aided churches, the proportion of stipend provided by the church under the scheme shall be sent by it to the association treasurer, to be forwarded by him to the Baptist Union, which shall pay the full stipend to the minister as it becomes due.[125]

It is clear from this arrangement that the term 'aided churches' is somewhat misleading. The churches would benefit, it is true, but it was the minister who would receive aid rather than the churches themselves. The arrangements for the payment of stipends significantly weakened the relationship between the local church and its minister, at least in terms of financial support, by interposing both association and Union between them. No longer would the churches involved have direct responsibility for providing stipends for their ministers. It was, of course, the churches' perceived failure to fulfil this responsibility that led to the Scheme's formation in the first place.

Another conference was arranged for two months later, in January 1915, at which, the association officers were told, plans for the grouping of churches, and the division of the country into districts under 'General Superintendents ' would be discussed.[126] This was the first time that such appointments had ever been mentioned in the minutes of Union committees. At no time in the years the Scheme had been under discussion had the term General Superintendent been included in any of the proposals brought forward by Shakespeare, or anyone else.

An hour and a half before this second conference took place Shakespeare met with a small sub-committee to prepare the ground. 'After considerable discussion', the minutes record, the six members of this sub-committee agreed to recommend to the association officers that England be divided into ten districts, with a General Superintendent over each.[127] Unfortunately, no details of the discussion that took place are given. At the subsequent conference, the association officers agreed to co-operate with the Union in raising a national total of £15,000 a year. Once the associations' own running expenses had been deducted, this would be used for the support of ministers, both those receiving help under the Scheme and those aided by the associations separately. Shakespeare had calculated that the figure of £15,000 would be required to meet all association and Union commitments. The associations already raised a total of about £10,000 each year. The additional £5,000 would be needed to meet the expected demands made on the Sustentation Fund. This was in addition to the interest earned on the capital raised during the 1912-1914 appeal.

Shakespeare then proposed the division of the country into ten districts, and the appointment of ten General Superintendents, one for each district. Ministers would be appointed to these new posts jointly by the Sustentation Fund's Executive Committee and the associations in each of the districts concerned. Their precise responsibilities were not described at this meeting. Shakespeare also proposed that the Executive Committee's immediate responsibility for administering the Scheme should only be for the districts where there was no whole-time association secretary. This reflected his aim to incorporate associations fully into the working of the Scheme, and, as part of that aim, to see these association secretaries appointed as Superintendents.[128]

The Sustentation Fund sub-committee met again on 16 February and agreed further details about the proposed Superintendents. Final responsibility for their appointment would rest with the Executive Committee, and their stipends would be paid by the Union. The duty of each Superintendent was defined in the following terms:

- Responsibility for the Sustentation Fund for the area in which he is engaged, including the raising of the Common Fund, and dealing with all questions in respect of grants . . .
- That he shall be regarded as the Baptist Union representative in all matters relating to settlement and removal in his particular area.

- That he shall have the charge of bringing before the Association Committee all questions with regard to the grouping of churches.
- That he shall be regarded as the recognised person to whom aided churches may turn in the matter of settlement of differences and disputes.
- That he shall be regarded as the secretary of the association for the above purposes.
- That in cases where a General Superintendent is also appointed as secretary of an association, he shall be provided with an assistant.[129]

The number of districts and Superintendents was reduced from 10 to 9. This was increased to 10 again in July after the English associations in South Wales agreed to co-operate, and were, in effect, incorporated into the Scheme.[130]

At its meeting in March 1915 the full Ministerial Settlement and Sustentation Committee asked the sub-committee to give the matter 'further consideration', and the arrangements were not brought to the Council meeting for endorsement later that month.[131] After a further conference with association secretaries, and a special conference to finalise arrangements for London, however, the main committee was willing to recommended acceptance, and on the 22 April the Council agreed to propose them to the forthcoming Assembly.[132] The description of the Superintendents' duties was amended slightly, and an addition made specifying that:

> It is the intention and hope of the Assembly that a General Superintendent shall not be unduly absorbed in business and financial cares, but that he may be enabled, through the blessing of God, to exercise a spiritual ministry in the Churches of the area and promote their closer union and more effective co-operation.[133]

Sparkes describes the lengthy resolution brought by Shakespeare to the 1915 Assembly as 'in effect, an enabling resolution consequent upon the decision taken at the 1912 Spring Assembly'.[134] It was, in fact, considerably more than that. It introduced some important new elements that would have a major impact on the denomination. The 1915 resolution explicitly stated that there should be 'complete co-operation' between the Union and the associations in carrying out the provisions of the Sustentation Fund, and accepted the principle that there should be 'but one Fund for the maintenance of the ministry in aided Churches'. Shakespeare assumed that grants made by the associations outside of the scope of the Scheme would eventually cease. The 1912 Scheme, on the other hand, had assumed that association grants would continue. The 1915 resolution specified the central payment of ministerial stipends. In 1912 the arrangements for the payment of stipends were not specified, but it is probable that responsibility for payment was assumed to be held by the local churches. The 1915 version of the Scheme included the creation of a national network of districts, normally referred to subsequently as 'areas', district committees and Superintendents. In 1912, it was explicitly stated that the local administration of the Scheme would be in the hands of the associations.[135] These differences are sufficiently important to make the later version a virtually new scheme altogether.

Shakespeare told the Assembly that the appointment of Superintendents was 'a most important and vital element' of the Scheme, and that he could not guarantee to fulfil the hopes realised in the raising of the Sustentation Fund if it were refused. He told them of the custom of the old General Baptists to have 'an officer to supervise the churches', and assured them that it was not an attempt to impose episcopacy. Dr. G. P. Gould, the President of Regent's Park College, in seconding the resolution, made it clear that the Assembly was approving the appointment of 'a new order of ministry'. The resolution was passed and the revised Scheme adopted.[136]

Whether the 1915 proposals would have been accepted had the denomination not been preoccupied with the war is a question impossible now to answer. In view of the radical changes of polity so suddenly introduced, it must be regarded as unlikely. What is clear is that 1915 marks an important stage in the development of Baptist church life in England. It is also apparent that the new elements in the proposals were accepted with remarkably little debate about their significance.

The division of the country into administrative areas was not in itself entirely new. It had been evident before that the associations did not provide very convenient units for national administration. This was partly because there were too many of them, partly because they varied so much in size and wealth, and partly because of their historical independence. They were therefore a hindrance to Shakespeare's attempts to centralise the denomination's structures. Sparkes says the idea of areas was first considered, but not adopted, in 1902 as part of Shakespeare's revision of the Union constitution.[137] In fact a similar arrangement was made in 1896, when, for a short while, the Ministerial Recognition Committee functioned by means of a system of 11 auxiliary committees.[138] Until 1915, however, the associations maintained their position as the only significant Baptist regional bodies. The new areas were created by the Union as an integral part of a national scheme, and therefore marked a significant shift in Baptist corporate life, and of authority, to the Union.

The claim by Shakespeare that the appointment of Superintendents was a return to an old Baptist custom, and was therefore not inconsistent with Baptist principles and history, is one that should be challenged. It is a claim that has been repeated a number of times since. It is true, as Payne says, that the General Baptist Messengers of the late seventeenth and eighteenth century, occasionally called Bishops by the General Baptists themselves, had in some respects a parallel role to that of the new Superintendents.[139] As time went on, Messengers took on an increasingly authoritative and supervisory role among the General Baptists. The primary function of the Messengers when they first appeared in the 1650's, however, was evangelistic, not administrative or supervisory.[140] The Particular Baptists had no such office, in spite of several assertions by Baptist historians to the contrary.[141] B. R. White has convincingly shown that John Collier, who has at times been identified as a seventeenth-century Particular Baptist forerunner to the Superintendents, did not exercise any form of superintendency over the churches that were responsible for his ordination.[142] The New Connexion rejected the eighteenth-century office of Messenger as 'incompatible' with the principle of independency.[143] The General Baptists who did not throw in their lot with the New Connexion rapidly disappeared as a significant force in the denomination in the nineteenth century, together with their Messengers.

The title 'Superintendent' probably originated from the German Lutheran Church. Shakespeare acknowledged this connection in his address to the 1915 spring Assembly.[144] J. H. Rushbrooke later claimed to have suggested it to him because of the similarities in function between the Lutheran Superintendents and the new Baptist officials.[145] As early as March 1914, long before regional ministers of any kind were suggested within Baptist circles, Shakespeare himself used the term in an address to the National Free Church Council, in which he also advocated the division of the country into Free Church Dioceses.[146] On that occasion, the term 'Superintendent' was advocated by Shakespeare as an alternative for Bishop, out of sensitivity for Free Church feelings about episcopacy.

Wherever the title came from, the idea of regional ministers to oversee churches and ministers was linked in Shakespeare's mind with the Anglican Episcopate. He knew that the notion of episcopacy was abhorrent to many Baptists, bringing to mind officialdom, hierarchy and 'worldly pomp', and he was wary of explicitly advocating it in public. On some occasions, however, he overcame this hesitancy to make his feelings clear. In January 1914 an article on the Faith and Order movement appeared in the *Baptist Times* encouraging the discussion of episcopacy as part of a possible move towards church unity.[147] His address at the Free Church meeting in March 1914 was more forthright. On the theme of 'The Contribution of the Free Churches to Christian Unity' he took up the cause he had been pressing in 1910, condemning the waste resulting from the divided state of Nonconformity. He longed to see a reformation of the Free Churches. 'I hope that in this reconstruction', he went on, 'I may live to see England divided into Free Church Dioceses with Free Church Bishops'.[148] It was inevitable, as time went on, that parallels between Superintendency and episcopacy would be drawn. The President of the Western Association, commenting on the new appointments in the spring of 1916, said, 'it is to the credit of us Baptists of these latter days that we have produced an ideal Bench of Bishops'.[149]

It is remarkable how little attention was given at the time, and, indeed, has been given since, to the ecclesiastical implications of the introduction of Superintendents. It is startling that their appointment, and the commencement of their work, was not marked by any kind of ceremony or special service. They took up their posts without any formal induction or public recognition. In commenting on this, and the parallel creation of Moderators by the Congregational Union, Mayor said, 'Congregationalism was becoming episcopal, almost without noticing'.[150] A contemporary Superintendent has described this lack of theological and ecclesiastical definition as 'quite unsatisfactory'.[151] War-time conditions naturally imposed restrictions on any denominational consultation or debate that might have been considered. It is likely, however, that it suited Shakespeare for the whole thing to be done with as little debate and ceremony as possible. Once he had come to the conclusion that this was the right way forward, he was eager to get on with it with the minimum of delay. The unusual circumstances of 1915 and 1916 allowed this to happen.

The lack of attention given to the theological and ecclesiological implications of Superintendency reveals something else about Shakespeare. His interest in the organisation of the church was essentially pragmatic. He was no more committed to episcopacy in principle than he was to congregationalism, or presbyterianism, or any other form of church polity. He was prepared to work with any or all of them as long as they provided the means of achieving his prime objective, which was to secure the Church's progress by means of a highly committed, well trained and adequately supported body of ministers. In his view, as many of his pronouncements demonstrate, the welfare of the churches depended above all on the ministry. His dissatisfaction with Baptist independency arose from its inability, as he saw it, to produce and sustain the ministry the Church required. Insofar as he had an ecclesiology, it was predominantly clerical in its orientation. His apparent blindness to more general ecclesiological implications, and the difficulty of harmonising such an approach with traditional Baptist view of the Church, was bound to result in tensions and ambiguities. Not the least of these was the introduction into Baptist congregational polity of an unacknowledged and undefined form of episcopacy.

However, the lack of a proper theological basis for Superintendency was not in the forefront of Baptists' minds in 1915. The over-riding impression one receives of the appointment of Superintendents, and of the operation of the Scheme as a whole, is that it gained widespread support and met with general approval. After the 1914 Assembly[152] Shakespeare had written to the churches belonging to the Union (the actual number of churches receiving these letters varies in the minutes of the various committees, but it was approximately 1,600) inviting them to join the Federation set up under the Scheme. Within little more than a year over 1,000 had done so,[153] and by the time of the 1917 Assembly this number had risen to over 1,300.[154] The number declining the invitation was less than 2% of the total. This was in marked contrast to the lack of enthusiasm about the Scheme before 1912. Possibly the Union's possession of a large capital fund had something to do with this change of heart.

The Executive Committee was appointed by the Council and the Area Committees set up, in line with the 1915 decision. Arrangements were made to adjust the operation of the Home Work Fund to bring it in line with the new situation. The associations were asked to ensure that their financial year corresponded with that of the Union. The ten Superintendents were duly nominated, and in November 1915 the *Baptist Times* announced their appointment by the Council, upon the Executive Committee's recommendations.[155]

Sparkes gives biographical details of each of the new Superintendents.[156] Five of the ten were full-time association secretaries within their areas at the time of their appointment, and continued in those capacities afterwards, and one other was appointed to the joint post of association secretary and Superintendent. Five had been trained at Spurgeon's College, and four had experience of overseas missionary work. One of their main responsibilities was to ensure that all the federating churches took part in the simultaneous annual collection for the Sustentation Fund. The first of these was in March 1916 (although a similar event took place during the appeal for the capital fund in 1914), and it continued to be held on the second Sunday in that month every year.[157]

Throughout 1916 the Executive Committee hammered out the detailed arrangements for the Scheme's smooth operation, and responded to various difficulties that arose. For ministerial settlement, it decided to ask ministers who wanted to change pastorates to do so in the month of September, and to inform the committee of their desire to do so by the preceding January. A reminder to ministers of this procedure appeared in the *Baptist Times* in January 1917.[158] An original suggestion from a sub-committee, that associations should send all their income to the Union, receiving back an agreed amount to cover their expenses and non-Sustentation Fund grants, was subsequently withdrawn. Instead, it was decided that the associations would keep the agreed sum, and only send the rest.[159]   The Hertfordshire Association exhibited unusual enthusiasm for transferring financial responsibility to the Union, offering to forward all its assets to the Union if the latter agreed to take over all its liabilities.[160] The Kent and Sussex Association was not as amenable, promising only to give the proposed financial arrangements 'a fair trial'.[161] In October 1916, the Executive Committee decided that it could not support any church whose membership roll was not kept up to date.[162] From the beginning of 1917, the Superintendents began meeting at Baptist Church House on a monthly basis to consider requests from ministers for a move, and to make recommendations.

One of the problems that arose was what to do about ministerial grants from Funds that were not under the control of either the Union or the associations. The Council invited representatives of several such Funds to a conference in October 1916, at which Shakespeare asked for co-operation in making a co-ordinated approach to ministerial support, in order to avoid inequality. He proposed that any grants ministers received from other bodies should be taken into account in deciding the level of grant from the Sustentation Fund.[163] Reaction to this request differed, but the largest fund, the Particular Baptist Fund, agreed to co-operate.

It is clear from the pages of the *Baptist Times* that these developments did not all meet with universal approval. The expense of the Scheme was criticised in a number of letters.[164] However, the overall mood was positive. 'The activities of the General Superintendents', the newspaper maintained, 'will prove the best and most fruitful effort we have ever made'.[165] At the 1916 spring Assembly an address by one of the recently appointed Superintendents was approved by the President with the words, 'I have never listened to a bishop with whom I was more satisfied'.[166] In September, the London Superintendent, Rev. John Ewing, announced that 361 grants were being made from the Fund, and appealed for more generous giving from the churches.[167] By February of the following year the number of grants had risen to 462. Readers were reminded that the Fund required an income of £25,000 each year to operate, made up of the £10,000 raised throughout the year by the associations, £5,000 from the annual collection, and the £10,000 interest earned on the capital reserves.[168] The merits of the Scheme were described in glowing terms:

> The anxiety and the penury of the ministers, extending over many years, have been removed by the minimum stipend and by punctuality of payment. The removal and resettlement of ministers, which has hitherto seemed an insoluble problem, is working smoothly and happily.[169]

At the end of 1916, an interview with Shakespeare was printed in the *Christian World* under the heading, 'Creating a Denomination: The Revolution at the Baptist Church House'. The interviewer described the way in which the Baptist Union had become 'a powerful central authority' within the denomination over the previous fifteen years. 'This revolution is the achievement of Rev. J. H. Shakespeare', and its impact is 'not yet fully apprehended' by the churches, he wrote. Shakespeare described the way in which, before the start of 1916, church aid had been mainly a matter for the associations, but was now carried out by the Union through the Sustentation Fund. The interviewer insisted, without being contradicted, on calling the Superintendents 'Bishops'. He asked Shakespeare:

> Then, practically, the Baptist Union takes up a minister as soon as he is ordained according to your regulations, and to the end of his ministerial life, you guarantee him a minimum living wage, and when he retires from ministerial life, or is incapacitated, you guarantee him an annuity?

To this question the answer was simply, 'that is so'.[170] It is impossible to quarrel with the use of the word 'revolution' to describe such a turn-around in Baptist church polity.

3.3 The Union Supreme

By 1916, Shakespeare had succeeded in establishing the Union as an ecclesiastical body exercising authority over the whole denomination. The only Baptist organisation with anything like the same independence and status was the missionary society. The influence of Spurgeon's College had diminished, in spite of the large number of ministers who had received their training there, and it was actually forced to close for eighteen months in 1917 and 1918, largely because of the war.[171] The Council of the Union controlled the Federation of churches it had created under the provisions of the Sustentation Fund, appointing the Executive Committee and having the power to exclude churches that failed to fulfil their obligations.[172] In effect the Union and the Federation soon became practically synonymous because of the very small proportion of churches that did not join the Federation. The Union's financial resources, from which it made contributions, via the Sustentation Fund, to the stipends of at least 25% of all qualifying Baptist ministers, the proportion rising year by year, was something that few churches could ignore, even if they wished to.

The importance of ministerial recognition became increasingly apparent. In November 1915 the Ministerial Recognition Committee received letters from the Southern and Yorkshire Associations expressing concern about the way the Scheme was operating. The Southern Association asked for ministers not accepted by the committee be given the right of appeal to the Council. Yorkshire raised the possibility that ministers who were deleted from the list might take legal action.[173] These letters illustrated how serious a matter recognition had become.

Another more subtle change in the approach to recognition was one of terminology. The procedures agreed in 1907 and 1911 referred to 'ministerial recognition' and 'the ministerial list'. Increasingly, as time went on, however, the term 'accreditation' began to be used, until it became the norm. In 1910 the *Baptist Times* refers to the Union's 'accredited list' of ministers.[174] This was not the first time the term had been used, but it marked the start of its official acceptance. In the 1912 resolution on the Sustentation Scheme, the term accreditation was used as a matter of course. This change in terminology was more than a merely semantic issue. There might have been no practical difference between recognition and accreditation for the minister wanting to get on to the Union's ministerial list, but it did reflect an important change in thinking. Recognition implied a predominantly passive role for the Union, in which it accepted ministerial status granted by others. For the Union to accredit a minister, on the other hand, a more active role in awarding him that status was implied. The language used was a sign of a shift in authority with regard to the ministry.

One of the main constraints on the freedom of action of the Union and its Secretary was the annual Assembly. Wartime circumstances made this constraining influence much less effective, partly because of the difficulties of travel, and partly because of the understandable lack of interest in matters relating to ecclesiastical administration. The autumn Assembly was not held in 1914 and 1915, and in 1916 the decision was taken to discontinue it permanently (partly in the interests of 'efficiency', according to Shakespeare[175]). The reduction in the number of annual Assemblies from two to one, which Shakespeare had pressed for in 1903, had now been made possible by the war. The Assembly did not exercise a very efficient role as the Union's governing body, but it was nonetheless a six monthly check on the Secretariat and the Council. The ability of church representatives to exercise their right to examine and if necessary challenge the Council's decisions was eroded by the reduction in the frequency of Assemblies.

One of the most significant signs of the Union's growing supremacy was the change in its relationship with the associations. Not only was the prime duty for supporting poorer ministers transferred to the Union, but the associations' financial affairs as a whole became subject to Union direction. This was the effect of the agreement that all the money they raised, apart from an amount mutually agreed by them and the Union for their own requirements, was to be sent to help support the Sustentation Fund.[176]

The division of the country into areas and the appointment of the Superintendents were other signs of the decline of the associations in relation to the Union. It was not only the fact that these appointments were made, but also the way they were made, that was important for the associations. Six of the Superintendents also acted as association secretaries in their areas, five having served full-time in that capacity beforehand. Their salaries, which were paid by the associations before 1916, were from that year onwards paid by the Union, and as a result they became accountable, no longer to their association committees, but to the Sustentation Fund's Executive Committee and the Council. This was made clear in their conditions of appointment. The associations' primary officials were in this way transferred at a stroke to the Union.

It is something of a mystery why the associations went along with this reduction of their powers with so little protest. They realised, perhaps, that they could never compete with the Union in terms of its resources and its capacity to organise ministry and mission, and accepted the necessity of a national strategy to meet the needs of the hour. It was the culmination of a long process of centralisation, most of which had occurred with their support. It also reflected Shakespeare's hold on the denomination.

A number of Baptist churches remained outside the Union. McBeth estimates that the proportion was as great as 25% in the early part of the century.[177] Some belonged to associations that were themselves members of the Union. Most were small. The tendency was for churches to join the Union as its importance grew. Those who remained apart were often of a Calvinistic persuasion, and included most notably Spurgeon's Metropolitan Tabernacle. For the most part, they were not organised coherently, some rejecting the idea of associations on principle. Two independent associations were in existence, the Metropolitan Association of Strict Baptist Churches and the Suffolk and Norfolk New Association. Compared to the main body of Baptists in fellowship with the Union, their influence was small, and they made no contribution to the development of the Union. Their existence, however, is a reminder that the Union should not to be identified totally with the denomination. Its dominance by 1916 was nevertheless clear.

1. The primary concern of the department was to decide which names should be included in the list of ministers published each year in the Baptist Handbook. As the status and the financial resources of the Union increased, the significance of this list grew, both for the ministers themselves and the churches they served.
2. See p. 34.
3. Briggs, *English Baptists* p. 86.
4. Briggs gives a figure of 64% ministers having received formal training in 1901 (*English Baptists* p. 84).
5. Devon and Cornwall Association Minute Book, December 1892.
6. BU Minute Book, 17 July 1899.
7. *BT* 20 July 1900.
8. See, for example, *BT* 13 December 1901; 17 January 1902 and 23 January 1903.
9. *BT* 7, 14 and 21 February 1902.
10. *BT* 23 January 1903.
11. *Ibid.*.
12. This was done in an address by J. G. Greenhough. *BT* 8 May 1903.
13. BU Minute Book, 9 July 1903.
14. D. W. Bebbington, 'Baptist Members of Parliament, 1847-1914' *BQ* vol. 29 (April 1981). According to Bebbington, 12 new Baptist MP's joined the 6 existing ones following the 1906 election.
15. *B* 1 May 1903.
16. *B* 8 May 1903.
17. *B* 5 May 1904 and 23 June 1904.
18. *B* 1 and 8 December 1904.
19. Wynn's letters were published in 6 consecutive issues of the *Baptist Times* from 21 October 1904. According to Sparkes, they, and the controversy they provoked, were responsible for increasing the momentum towards change in the denomination (Douglas C. Sparkes, *An Accredited Ministry* (Baptist Historical Society, Didcot: 1996) p. 16).
20. *BT* 6 January 1905.
21. *BT* 16 June 1905.
22. *B* 14 September 1905.

23. *B* 30 November 1905.
24. See p. 48.
25. *B* 8 February 1906.
26. *BT* 5 October 1906.
27. *Ibid.*. See also p. 49.
28. Sparkes, *Ministry* p. 16.
29. *B* 17 May 1906. The cities referred to were the locations of Baptist training colleges in England. With the exception of Spurgeon's College, which did not endorse the Union's plans for ministerial recognition, the colleges were all supportive of Shakespeare's plans.
30. Shakespeare was obviously reluctant to make this concession. As late as June 1906 he and the Ministerial Recognition Committee were refusing to bow to pressure from the associations. In September he acknowledged that 'a strong feeling prevailed throughout the Denomination' and it was decided to discontinue the invidious distinction (see BU Minute Book, 18 June and 17 September 1906).
31. These concessions are summarised in Sparkes, *Ministry* p. 20.
32. *B* 18 April 1907.
33. *BT* 3 May 1907. The Assembly was also memorable for an outspoken address by Rev T. E. Ruth (who was described by the *Baptist Times* as 'unconventional', 'brilliant' and 'audacious') advocating the desirability of a common ministry, a common fund for the support of the ministry and a common church (*BT* 26 April 1907).
34. *BT* 29 June 1900.
35. *BT* 6 January 1905.
36. *BT* 13 January 1901.
37. BU Minute Book, 16 February 1903.
38. BU Minute Book, 29 January 1906. Shakespeare saw these ideas accepted by Hungarian Baptists following his visit there with Clifford and Newton Marshall in 1907 (see p. 40).
39. *BT* 27 April 1906. See also Douglas C. Sparkes, *The Home Mission Story* (BHS, Didcot: 1995) pp. 24-5.
40. BU Minute Book, 14 January 1907.
41. BU Minute Book, 19 February 1907.
42. BU Minute Book, 17 December 1907.
43. BU Minute Book, 17 March 1908 and 20 October 1908.
44. *B* 9 January 1908.
45. *BT* 3 January 1908.
46. *BT* 14 and 21 February 1908.
47. J. H. Shakespeare, *The Arrested Progress of the Church: An Address to the Spring Assembly of the Baptist Union of Great Britain and Ireland* (BUGBI: London, 1908). Shakespeare's address is also printed in *BT* 1 May 1908. The use of the term Church, both in the title and in the address itself, is significant. Without directly claiming that the Union or denomination was a national Church, it implied that this was so. If the title had been 'The Arrested Progress of the Churches' it would have given a truer reflection of normal Baptist usage of these terms.
48. *BT* 1 May 1908.
49. *BT* 8 May 1908.
50. Shakespeare, *Arrested Progress* pp. 21-4.
51. *B* 7 May 1908.

52. *HB* 1909 p. 254.
53. *BT* 2 October 1908.
54. BU Minute Book, 20 October 1908.
55. BU Minute Book, 16 November 1908.
56. *BT* 22 January 1909. The sluggish response from churches and associations to the Union's enquiries over the previous eighteen months did not, however, suggest that everyone shared this urgent desire, by any means.
57. *Ibid.*.
58. BU Minute Book, 19 January 1909; *BT* 22 January 1909.
59. *BT* 22 January 1909.
60. T. R. Glover correspondence (St. John's College Library, University of Cambridge), box 17. Letter from Richard to T. R. dated 21 February 1909.
61. *B* 28 January 1909.
62. BU Minute Book 16 February 1909 - 22 April 1909.
63. Cited from the College Minute Book, 4 March 1909, in Mike Nicholls, *Lights to the World: A History of Spurgeon's College 1856-1992* (Nuprint: Harpenden, 1994) p. 124. The end-notes are wrongly numbered.
64. BU Minute Book 15 March 1909
65. BU Minute Book 21 and 22 April 1909.
66. *HB* 1910 pp. 261-6; *BT* 30 April 1909.
67. *BT* 30 April 1909.
68. *B* 29 April 1909.
69. *BT* 21 May 1909. An interesting aspect of the debate was the presence of the leading Congregationalist, C. Silvester Horne. He spoke briefly, expressing his support for the idea of mutual dependency among the churches that lay at the heart of the scheme. The Congregationalists were due to debate a very similar proposal at their spring Assembly two weeks later. The scheme eventually adopted by the Congregationalists was, in many respects, similar to the Baptist scheme. One significant difference was that college training was an integral part of it.
70. Letters from Logan were printed in *BT* 7 May; 28 May; 4 June; 11 June; 18 June; 2 July and 12 November 1909.
71. *BT* 9 July 1909. Shakespeare also wrote in defence of the scheme on 21 May and 23 July 1909.
72. Leading articles were written by Rushbrooke in *BT* 7 May and 3 September 1909.
73. *BT* 8 October 1909.
74. *BT* 31 December 1909.
75. *B* 2 December 1909.
76. BU Minute Book, 4 October 1909 and 15 February 1910.
77. BU Minute Book 14-15 March 1910.
78. *BT* 8 April 1910.
79. *BT* 18 March 1910.
80. *Free Church Yearbook* 1910 (NCEFC) pp. 66-73. An expanded and revised version of the address, entitled 'The Free Churches and the National Life' was published by the National Council in *A United Free Church of England* (NCEFC: London, 1911) pp. 3-14.
81. *BT* 1 April 1910.
82. *B* 7 and 14 April 1910.
83. BU Minute Book, 19 July 1910.

84. *BT* 6 May 1910.
85. *Ibid..*
86. *Ibid..*
87. BU Minute Book, 27 April 1910.
88. The Inter-Collegiate Board Minute Book (held in the Angus Library, Regent's Park College, Oxford) includes a letter dated 17 May 1911 from Principal McCaig indicating that the college President, Thomas Spurgeon, was 'not inclined to consider the possibility' of meeting with other colleges to discuss any proposed federation.
89. See Nicholls, pp. 60-67 for a description of the college's selection process during Spurgeon's life-time. The criticism that there were not enough churches to support all the men he trained would have seemed irrelevant to Spurgeon, who regarded the establishment of new churches by his students as one of the central objectives of the training.
90. *BT* 6 May 1910.
91. BU Minute Book, 15 November 1910.
92. *Ibid..*
93. See pp. 58-60. The 1907 rules had little immediate impact because they were primarily designed to apply to new, rather than existing, ministers.
94. Letters from Brown on the subject appeared in *BT* 3 and 10 September 1909.
95. *BT* 14 October 1910. Shakespeare also spoke against Brown's motion.
96. *BT* 21 and 28 October, 4 and 11 November 1910.
97. *BT* 4 November 1910.
98. *Ibid..*
99. *BT* 25 November 1910.
100. BU Minute Book, 2 October 1911. Sparkes, *Ministry* gives a description of the 1911 rules and how they differed from those agreed in 1907 (pp. 25-6).
101. *BT* 5 May 1911.
102. *BT* 7 July 1911. Shakespeare himself was in Philadelphia for the second Baptist World Congress in June, playing a leading role in the proceedings as one of the joint secretaries. Newton Marshall credited him with the bulk of the organisation of the Congress, writing in July that 'the whole Alliance project' had faced disaster, and was only rescued by Shakespeare's 'patience, resource, and indomitable will' (*BT* 21 July 1911). He was particularly involved in arranging for delegates from Russia and Eastern Europe to attend, and was officially appointed European Secretary of the Alliance.
103. BU Minute Book, 21 December 1911.
104. *Ibid.*, 20 February 1912.
105. *BT* 12 April 1912.
106. *BT* 19 April 1912.
107. *BT* 26 April 1912.
108. *Ibid..*
109. *BT* 3 May 1912.
110. Although Shakespeare was back to his committee work in January 1913, it was as late as October that we find J. H. Rushbrooke congratulating Shakespeare on his 'thoroughly restored health' (*BT* 10 October 1913).
111. *BT* 11 October 1912.
112. See pp. 139-40.
113. *BT* 20 December 1912.

114. *BT* 31 October 1913.
115. *BT* 27 June 1913.
116. *BT* 17 March 1914.
117. *HB*, 1915 p.249.
118. *BT* 1 May 1914.
119. *BT* 8 May 1914.
120. *Ibid.*.
121. *BT* 10 and 17 July 1914.
122. *BT* 7 August 1914.
123. BU Minute Book, 15 September 1914; *BT* 25 September 1914.
124. BU Minute Book, 17 November 1914.
125. BU Minute Book, 18 November 1914.
126. *Ibid.*.
127. BU Minute Book, 18 January 1915.
128. *Ibid.*.
129. BU Minute Book, 16 February 1915.
130. *Ibid.*.
131 BU Minute Book, 16 March 1915.
132. BU Minute Book, 22 April 1915.
133. *Ibid.*.
134. Sparkes, *Home Mission* p. 59.
135. Sparkes gives the full version of both the 1912 and 1915 resolutions in *Home Mission* pp. 41-5; 59-63.
136. *BT* 30 April 1915.
137. Sparkes *Home Mission* p. 56.
138. Sparkes himself mentions these committees in *Ministry* p. 10.
139. Payne, *Fellowship* p. 43.
140. Underwood, p. 120.
141. For example, A. J. Klaiber, 'The Superintendency in Baptist History' in R. L. Childs (ed.), *The General Superintendency (1915-1965)* (BUGBI: London, 1965) p. 7 B. R. White contends that J. G. Fuller, W. T. Whitley and E. A. Payne all mistakenly follow Joseph Ivimey in seeing John Collier as exercising a kind of general superintendency over the churches of the Western Association in the 1650's (White, *Association Records* p. 109).
142. White, *Association Records* p. 109.
143. Underwood, p. 121.
144. *BT* 30 April 1915.
145. Green, *Tomorrow's Man* p. 138.
146. *BT* 20 March 1914.
147. *BT* 30 January 1914.
148. *BT* 20 March 1914. Shakespeare's discussions with Church of England leaders during the war reveal a surprising readiness to accept episcopacy (see p. 111).
149. Devon and Cornwall Baptist Association Minute Book, 1916. There was a joint Assembly involving the Devon and Cornwall and Western Associations in 1916. The President of the Western Association, W. Hogan, made these remarks in his Presidential address.
150. S. Mayor, 'The Free Church Understanding of the Ministry in the Twentieth Century' in *BQ* vol. 23 (July 1970) p. 297.

151. Geoffrey Reynolds, *First Among Equals: A Study of the Basis of Association and Oversight among Baptist Churches* (Berkshire, Southern and Oxfordshire and East Gloucestershire Baptist Associations: 1993) p. 3.
152. 1913 was the last year when Baptists held two annual Assemblies. The war meant that the 1914 autumn Assembly was abandoned, and it was never resumed.
153. BU Minute Book, 19 July 1915.
154. BU Minute Book, 23 April 1917.
155. *BT* 19 November 1915.
156. Sparkes, *Home Mission* pp. 65-67.
157. When it became clear in 1917 that a few of the federated churches were not taking part, it was recommended by the Superintendents that if they continued to refuse to do so they should be removed from the Federation (BU Minute Book, 22 June 1917).
158. BU Minute Book 16 March 1916; *BT* 12 January 1917.
159. BU Minute Book, 27 April 1916.
160. BU Minute Book, 16 March 1916.
161. BU Minute Book, 17 July 1916.
162. BU Minute Book, 2-3 October 1916. Accurate membership figures were important for various reasons, including as a help to the Superintendents in making recommendations about ministerial moves, and in indicating the amount of money a church could be expected to raise towards its minister's stipend.
163. BU Minute Book, 23 October 1916.
164. *BT* 3 March 1916, for example.
165. *Ibid.*.
166. *BT* 12 May 1916.
167. *BT* 22 September 1916.
168. *BT* 23 February 1917.
169. *BT* 2 March 1917.
170. *CW* 14 December 1916.
171. Nicholls, pp. 116 and 122.
172. The Walton-on-Thames church was apparently the first to be excluded for its failure to participate in the annual collection (BU Minute Book, 22 April 1918).
173. BU Minute Book, 15 November 1915.
174. *BT* 8 April and 4 November 1910.
175. *BT* 5 May 1916.
176. Payne recognises the importance and permanence of this when he says that the principle of the finances of the associations being 'notionally subject to the control of the Union and integrated with its own finances' has remained ever since (Payne, *Baptist Union* p. 184).
177. McBeth, p. 521.

CHAPTER FOUR

The Search for Unity

Shakespeare's pursuit of church unity during and after the war became an obsession. Although he became increasingly isolated over the issue, his standing among Baptists means that it is an important part of their twentieth-century story. Through him, Baptists made a significant contribution to ecumenism. His search for unity also had a long-term influence in the denomination. In part this was a negative one, seen in the reaction against Shakespeare's ecumenical adventures after his departure. There has also, however, been a continuing Baptist interest in the search for unity ever since his pioneering involvement, and his successors at Baptist Church House have played a leading part in the twentieth-century ecumenical movement. Contact with other traditions under Shakespeare also helped Baptists develop a clearer understanding of their own ecclesiological principles.

4.1 The National Council of the Evangelical Free Churches

The years leading up to the Great War were difficult ones for the Free Church movement. It had begun with such high hopes in the 1890's, and mobilised to such great effect during the struggle against the 1902 Education Act and in the 1906 election campaign, but ever since the Liberal victory of that year a growing unease had developed about the way things were going. It became clearer as each year passed, and as each Education Bill presented to Parliament failed, usually as a result of opposition from the House of Lords, that the campaign over education was unlikely to be successful. There was a vast gulf between the issues on which the Free Churches had campaigned in 1906 and the central challenges facing the country after the 1910 elections. The Nonconformist values that had given the Free Churches such confidence a few years before were incapable of providing answers to the constitutional, economic and social problems faced by the Government they had helped bring to power.

The Free Churches were also increasingly uneasy about their lack of progress in the religious sphere. Anglo-Catholicism, the chief threat to the Gospel according to many Nonconformists, continued to advance within the Church of England. The missionary challenge of the cities remained just as daunting as ever. In fact, the slow fall in membership statistics across all the main Free Church denominations, which began in 1906, showed no signs of reversing in the years that followed.

The chief embodiment of the Free Church movement was the National Council, with its more than 1,000 local Councils. The Council did not represent the Nonconformist denominations in any official sense. Its membership was made up of individuals, rather than churches. It was, therefore, more of a popular movement than an ecclesiastical body. For much of its early life, it was both a political pressure group and an evangelistic organisation. These two functions were not always easily harmonised.

Before 1914, Shakespeare was for the most part either indifferent to, or critical of the National Council, although as Secretary of one the largest Free Church denominations, he could not escape involvement altogether.[1] His interest in inter-church co-operation, however, which he had displayed during his years in Norwich, was re-awakened from 1910 onwards, when he quite suddenly emerged as a leading figure among the Free Churches. His address of 1910 at the annual meetings in Hull, in which he advocated a United Free Church of England, was his first major contribution. It was, by implication at least, a condemnation of the Council's previous approach to co-operative action. 'The depressing fact of the present situation', he said, 'is that the public can afford to ignore us . . . A united church would tend to alter all this'.[2]

Interest in the question of church unity was given a boost in the summer of 1910 by the Edinburgh World Missionary Conference. Shakespeare was not involved personally in that event, but he made another contribution to the unity debate later in the year. He was one of the speakers at a conference on Christian unity organised by the Congregational Union in October, and called for 'an immediate and practical policy of reunion', starting with 'a federation of the Baptists and Congregationalists'.[3] At the National Council's spring meetings in 1912 he pleaded again for a United Free Church, in order to prevent 'so much of our weakness and waste', but confessed he felt like 'a voice in the wilderness' in doing so.[4] The National Council did, however, agree later that year to set up a commission to investigate the possibility of union.[5]

In January 1914, representatives of the Nonconformist denominations, including Shakespeare, met a deputation from some American churches in London. The Americans were from various denominations, and they came to meet church leaders in Britain about a proposed World Conference on Faith and Order, first suggested by the General Convention of the Protestant Episcopal Church of America after the 1910 Edinburgh Conference.[6] Before the meeting, the *Baptist Times* was enthusiastic about the prospect, boldly asserting that 'British Baptists are most heartily in sympathy with the objects in view'.[7] At the same time it severely criticised the National Council's attempts to provide a platform for united action. Unless it could come up with a more constructive policy, the Council's usefulness was over, the newspaper said, and it had better call a halt to 'the waste entailed by its elaborate machinery'. It was 'frittering away its resources' as a 'useless middleman' in the search for unity. Real progress could only come from the denominations acting 'through their appointed organs'.[8] In spite of this negative assessment of the role of the Council, Shakespeare spoke again on unity at its spring meetings that year - the third time he had done so in four years. He advocated that its role should be that of a mediator between the denominations, enabling them to confer on the best way of achieving greater unity.[9]

Shakespeare's criticisms of the National Council are similar to his attitude towards the lack of unity and organisation within his own denomination earlier in the century. In both cases, he saw a greater degree of centralisation as the solution. The local Free Church Councils, linked through a loosely structured network to the National Council, were, in his mind, like the independently minded Baptist churches, wasteful and ineffective.

It was probably inevitable that Shakespeare would be drawn on to the wider church stage sooner or later. After twelve years in office at the Baptist Union, during which time he had won attention and admiration for himself, both inside and outside his own denomination, he was, whether he wanted it or not, a respected leader within Nonconformity as a whole. He was not the sort of man to have a position like that without making use of it. His instinct was to try and mould the disparate elements of the different denominations into a more effective ecclesiastical organisation, just as it had been, and still was, among the Baptists. This was to become a passion that increasingly dominated the rest of his life, and within a few years widened its scope to include the Church of England as well as the Free Churches.

Quite how things would have developed had the war not intervened is impossible to know. In June 1914 Shakespeare attended an interdenominational conference connected with the Faith and Order movement at Westminster Abbey, and it is difficult to imagine anything other than his active involvement in the increasing momentum towards unity. Morris West believes that, were it not for the war, the proposed interdenominational Faith and Order Conference would probably have been held in London in 1917, and that Shakespeare would have become 'a pioneer Baptist ecumenist on the world stage'.[10] Even as it was, his contribution to the early stages of the movement was considerable. However, the onset of war gave him the opportunity to pursue his vision of Free Church co-operation in a very different direction. This was through the United Army Board, an organisation that owed its formation very largely to his initiative, and has played a significant role in service life to this day.

4.2 The Impact of the War

4.2.1 The United Chaplaincy Board

The need for Baptist chaplains in the armed services had been discussed in Union committees before 1914. The only Free Church chaplains officially recognised until that year were Wesleyans and Presbyterians.[11] The issue was really part of the wider one of how to secure proper recognition of the denominational affiliation of soldiers and sailors who came from Nonconformist backgrounds. In 1901 the Union Council resolved to make an approach to the Secretary of State for War,[12] and later that year a joint committee was set up with the Congregationalists to discuss the matter. Over two years later this committee agreed to nominate a number of chaplains.[13] Nothing, however, seems to have come of this initiative. In 1905, Shakespeare, following a visit to the War Office, obtained, according to Frederic Spurr, 'a certain slight recognition of the existence of Baptists and Congregationalists in the army', but this had virtually no effect on the organisation of the army's chaplaincy provision, and little effect on the registering of recruits.[14] The established church was firmly entrenched in the army, and the large majority of recruits were registered as Church of England, unless they professed membership of one of the few other religious groups acceptable to the recruiting officer. Difficulties were inevitable when huge numbers of volunteers, many of them from Nonconformist backgrounds, came forward in 1914. When their professed denominations were rejected as 'fancy religions',[15] and the published religious affiliation of the new recruits showed an overwhelming bias towards the Church of England, resentment was a natural consequence.

Within a few days of the outbreak of war, Shakespeare and R. J. Wells, Secretary of the Congregational Union, wrote to the War Office asking that Baptist and Congregationalist chaplains be permitted to accompany the Expeditionary Force being assembled for service in Belgium and France. They received a reply regretting that circumstances would not allow this, although the appointment of 'officiating clergymen' at army bases in England would be permitted. The reason given was that the numbers of recruits did not justify such appointments.[16] This was unacceptable to Shakespeare and Wells, and with the help of two prominent Baptists MP's, Percy Illingworth and Lloyd George, they managed to achieve a change of policy, in spite of Kitchener's vociferous objections.[17] Following a meeting between Shakespeare and Kitchener to discuss the organisation of the chaplaincy service for the non-Wesleyan English Free Churches, and three inter-denominational conferences in November and December 1914, the United Army Board was set up, with Shakespeare and Wells as joint secretaries. Its main task was to nominate chaplains from the participating denominations, their work to be done on a united, rather than a denominational, basis. Following the inclusion of the navy in these arrangements in March 1915, it became the United Navy and Army Board.

Apart from the Baptists and Congregationalists, the two main non-Wesleyan Methodist Churches in England, the United and Primitive Methodists, also participated in the Board's work. The Wesleyans, who already had their own honorary chaplains in place, decided not to join with this new co-operative venture. Shakespeare became the Board's first chairman, and following the inability of the War Office to provide office accommodation, Baptist Church House became the headquarters of the new organisation. During the war, 320 United Board chaplains were appointed, of whom 10 were killed in action.[18] It was a remarkable achievement in co-operation, as well as bringing comfort and help to many, whose spiritual and personal needs at times of great crisis might not otherwise have been adequately met.

As well as nominating chaplains, the Board's other main task was to ensure that neither Free Church chaplains nor recruits were treated less favourably than those of the established church. Shakespeare himself was always eager to protest at what he regarded as unfair discrimination. The correct registering of recruits was a regular concern,[19] and when the military subordination of the senior United Board chaplain to Bishop Gwynne, the senior Anglican chaplain, came to light, it was viewed as a serious infringement of religious liberty.[20] Lloyd George's establishment of the Interdenominational Advisory Committee on Chaplaincy Services in 1916 was largely an attempt to meet complaints from the United Board about the unequal treatment of its chaplains. It included not only representatives of the Church of England and the Free Churches, but also the Roman Catholic Church. Agreement was reached about such disputed matters as the number of chaplains that should be appointed from different denominations for particular divisions of the army.[21] The distribution of medals caused a further argument in 1918 when Shakespeare complained that too high a proportion had gone to Church of England chaplains. According to Mews, 'so strongly did he feel about the matter that a special supplementary honours list had to be produced'.[22]

The creation of the United Board was an important event for Shakespeare and the Baptist denomination in several ways. The first, and most obvious, was its contribution to attitudes about Free Church co-operation, and church unity in general. Secondly, it played a significant role in reflecting the fuller integration of Baptists, along with Nonconformity as a whole, into national life during the war. Thirdly, the existence of Baptist ministers in the service of the Crown was an important step in the development of Baptist thinking about ministry.

One of the most powerful consequences of the Board's creation and success was the way it showed how the Nonconformist denominations could work together harmoniously. As far as the War Office was concerned, the Board was treated as a separate and single denomination. This had clear administrative advantages for the War Office. T. R. Glover described it, with unnecessary cynicism, as 'a dodge to let the War Office dispose of people it does not want to be bothered with'.[23] It was nevertheless an important ecclesiastical development. The Wesleyans and the English Presbyterians, although not officially part of the Board, also co-operated in the appointment and deployment of chaplains. For Shakespeare, the significance was obvious. He wrote in 1916, 'we have seen the working in miniature and for a specific purpose of a partially United Free Church of England. It has worked well'.[24] Chaplains from different denominations led undivided military Nonconformist congregations, and he viewed this as a model upon which a fully united Church could be based.

Not only within Nonconformity, but also more widely, contacts were built that inspired a greater ecumenical spirit. In spite of a rivalry with the Church of England that became quite intense at times, the issue of chaplaincy provision forced the two sections of English Protestant Christianity to acknowledge each other and work together in unprecedented ways. This largely came about after the Government's Interdenominational Advisory Committee was established in 1916. The chairman, Lord Derby, was not prepared to let either Nonconformist sensitivities, or traditional Church of England privileges, threaten the practical co-operation that was needed for the efficient deployment of chaplains. Shakespeare and the Wesleyan representative, J. H. Bateson, were the two leading Free Churchmen on this committee, and according to Thompson it represented a 'coming of age' for Nonconformists, with Shakespeare and Bateson its 'pillars'.[25]

On a personal level, as chaplains worked together more closely than ever before, co-operation and respect grew between them, and denominational ties frequently seemed irrelevant. As the 1919 report on The Army and Religion expressed it, 'seen against the vast and terrible background of the trenches and the battlefield, ecclesiastical divisions look spectral and unreal'.[26] F. C. Spurr, in his 1916 account of the work of the United Board chaplains, describes a Roman Catholic soldier, about to entrain for the front, requesting a prayer of blessing from a Baptist chaplain. 'It is a sign of the new time and of the new spirit', he wrote.[27] In 1917, the United Board agreed to the production of a joint Church of England/Free Church hymnbook for use by the forces.[28]

The second important aspect of the United Board's contribution to Baptist church life was to draw Shakespeare, and other leading Nonconformists, closer to the Government of the day. The absolute need of the nation for men from every section of society to serve in the armed services meant that, within one of the strongest bastions of privilege of the established church, the Free Churches could no longer be ignored or marginalised. Through the Board, this incorporation into national life was institutionalised. Lloyd

George's influence was vital in guaranteeing this process of integration, especially once he was appointed Secretary of State for War, and subsequently Prime Minister, in 1916. His advocacy was crucial in 1914 in the creation of the Board, and he consistently championed the Free Churches in their disputes with the Church of England. In 1915, he strongly associated himself with the temperance cause, one always popular among Nonconformists. With characteristic enthusiasm, he described alcohol as a national threat as great as German submarines. The sincerity of some of his pronouncements may have been questionable, but there is no doubt of his personal affinity with the Free Churches, and that he genuinely valued their support, both for his own political ambitions and for the war effort.[29]

The close war-time relationship between Lloyd George and the Free Churches was important in shaping the post-war fortunes of Nonconformity, and of Shakespeare personally in particular. It proved a mixed blessing, and in the long run, probably did more harm than good. When Lloyd George became Prime Minister at the end of 1916, increasing numbers of Nonconformists began to express concern about the direction of his policies. Many viewed with alarm the shelving of Welsh Disestablishment, agreed shortly before the war. The Military Service Act of June 1916, which introduced conscription, had struck at the heart of Nonconformist political ideology, and provoked repeated expressions of concern about the treatment of conscientious objectors. It was, however, generally accepted as a regrettable necessity. More worrying to many was Lloyd George's political alliance with the Conservatives and suspicions about his role in the downfall of Asquith. Opposition to Lloyd George and the Government was naturally muted, with the nation at war, but nonetheless increased steadily as time went on. It was one of the main factors involved in the political disintegration of Nonconformity, which probably became irretrievable by the beginning of 1917. Some, like F. B. Meyer, remained loyal to Asquith. Others, like John Clifford, saw hope for the future only in the Labour Party.[30]

Not only was the political unity of Nonconformity broken, but also its spirit. Step by step its values were being abandoned, and its ability to provide moral leadership diminished. Claims that the conflict was a 'holy war' in defence of Christian civilisation seemed increasingly hollow as the years of slaughter went by, and when news emerged of the army's regulation of brothels in France early in 1918, there seemed little room left for idealism. The Nonconformist Conscience, which, according to Bebbington, had ceased to be politically significant in 1910,[31] could play little further part in the war effort, despite Lloyd George's attempts to persuade Nonconformists otherwise.

Shakespeare, however, together with Robertson Nicoll at the *British Weekly* and Joseph Compton-Rickett MP, the leading spokesman of the Free Church Council in Parliament, remained staunchly loyal to Lloyd George. The *Baptist Times* expressed its total confidence in him during and after the government crisis at the end of 1916.[32] The Prime Minister's Baptist background secured him Shakespeare's personal support, which was of some importance for him politically. Not only was Shakespeare the leader of one of the main Nonconformist denominations, but he was also, in 1916, President of the Free Church Council, and editor of a major denominational newspaper. The relationship was naturally advantageous to Shakespeare as well. His sense of pride, and that of most Baptists, at Lloyd George's rise to high office was accompanied by the kind of access to the corridors of power that no Nonconformist had ever dreamt of before.

Shakespeare was, of course, aware of Nonconformist ambivalence, and used his influence throughout 1917 and 1918 to boost support for Lloyd George. In May 1917 he wrote to Christopher Addison, then Minister of Munitions, who had been given responsibility for canvassing Free Church support for the Prime Minister. 'The Free Churches', he said, 'upon whose support Mr. Lloyd George must depend so much in a General Election, are generally speaking, in a state of perplexity or suspicion towards him'. He urged the Government, among other things, not to tamper with Welsh Disestablishment and to deal with the 'Drink Traffic' Shakespeare advocated wartime prohibition - if it wanted to secure their allegiance. He also suggested that the Prime Minister meet Free Church leaders so that they could hear a statement from him.[33] Such a meeting took place in October of that year. One of the participants was Arthur Porritt, the editor of the *Christian World*. Later, Porritt described the relationship between Shakespeare and Lloyd George in the following terms:

> When Mr. Lloyd George became Prime Minister, Dr. Shakespeare exerted every ounce of his power to bring the Free Churches wholly over to Mr. Lloyd George's banner, and he was indefatigable in devising means to that end. Between Mr. Lloyd George and Dr. Shakespeare there was so close a friendship that it used to be said that Dr. Shakespeare had a latch key to 10 Downing Street.[34]

Lloyd George himself wrote to Shakespeare in March 1918 thanking him for his 'loyal friendship' and asking him to continue sending 'any information in the political line which you think may be useful'.[35] Shakespeare helped draw up a programme acceptable to Lloyd George's supporters in the Liberal Party during the course of 1918, and when the time came for the General Election at the end of the war, Shakespeare was a member of the committee that met daily in Downing Street to oversee the campaign.[36] For the Secretary of the Baptist Union to be an enthusiastic and respected supporter of a Government that included Edward Carson, A. J. Balfour and Bonar Law, not only in war, but also in the peace that followed, was a bewildering turnaround, politically and socially. A close personal attachment to Lloyd George was risky, as the post-war years would demonstrate, but amid the exhilaration of his access to the highest echelons of power in 1918, it is not perhaps altogether surprising that Shakespeare was blind to any such considerations.

Shakespeare's involvement in Government and politics, and with the Prime Minister in particular, was one element in the apparent acceptance of Nonconformity's role in national life. Before the war, in spite of a strong Nonconformist presence in the Liberal Government, and its vigour in the nation as a whole, it was still frequently regarded as a peripheral element in English society, as Kitchener's assessment of 1914 illustrates. One effect of the war was to bring many previously marginal sections of society, such as the Nonconformists, closer to the mainstream. Lloyd George, and, in his own more limited sphere, Shakespeare, played their part in bringing this about. It was symbolised most dramatically by the Free Churches' Albert Hall Thanksgiving Service on 16 November 1918, attended by the King and Queen Mary. The *Baptist Times*' report of the occasion reflects its overall significance, as well as Shakespeare's personal involvement:

> It was a historic occasion, this first meeting of Royalty and Nonconformity for Divine worship . . .. At the presentation, when the King arrived and spoke individually to the ministers present, it was a matter of some surprise to discover the extent of his acquaintance with Free Church personalities. To Mr. Shakespeare, both before and after the service, he expressed the strongest sympathy with his work for the unity of the Churches, as did also Queen Mary.[37]

Three weeks later, on the eve of the General Election, the newspaper printed a letter from Lloyd George thanking Baptists for their support during the war and 'inviting their co-operation and assistance' in the tasks that lay ahead.[38]

The United Board was only one factor among many in the long process of the integration of Nonconformity into national life, but it made a significant contribution to the process, and is illustrative of how it occurred. It was an ambivalent development, for it seemed to contradict the very essence of Nonconformity.[39] It provided part of the background to the changes occurring in Baptist church polity at this time.

The United Board, then, was important ecumenically and politically for Baptists. It also had an ecclesiological significance. Two fundamental aspects of traditional Baptist ecclesiology were challenged by its creation: the congregational foundation for ministry, already under serious threat as a result of Shakespeare's denominational reforms, and the principle of the separation of Church and State.

The demands of war resulted in accredited Baptist ministers joining the armed services as commissioned officers, and submitting themselves to the armed services' discipline and command structures. They worked outside the context of local congregations, and their ministry was defined in an entirely new way. Some unprecedented suggestions were made, and initiatives taken, as a result of this. One was the Baptist Union's proposal to form a 'Baptist Navy and Army Church', in which baptism could be deferred for new members, an idea that was dropped as a result of protests from the other denominations in the United Board.[40] Another was the publication of a joint Baptist and Congregationalist liturgy.[41] Such novelties were attempts to meet the enormous challenge presented to the chaplains by the young men at the Front. They also showed that Baptist ministers were venturing on radically new ground.

Clergy of all denominations faced enormous challenges in serving as chaplains in the Armed services both pastorally and theologically. Particular anomalies were created for ministers who understood their ministry in the context of a local congregation, however. The centralisation of denominational life that was occurring under Shakespeare, leading towards an acceptance of a separated denominational order of ministry, meant that the existence of Baptist ministers serving the Crown in the armed services was not quite as much of a radical departure as it might have been a generation before. It nevertheless resulted in a significant shift in how the ministry was perceived. The chaplaincy services provided examples of Baptist ministers exercising a ministry quite unconnected with any particular Baptist church. In this respect it has a connection with the 1916 Ministerial Settlement and Sustentation Scheme, one effect of which was to reduce the importance of a minister's relationship with the local church.

The United Board also obscured the distinction of Church and the State. The chaplains were servants of the State as well as ministers of the Church. Although Baptist ministers had engaged in political campaigning in the pre-war years, notably John Clifford, such an official and open combination of secular and church duties was entirely new. There were no ministers, for example, among the Baptists who became Members of Parliament in the 1906 and 1910 elections.[42] Not only did the ministers who were appointed chaplains become servants of the State, so too did the members of the Board themselves, including Shakespeare as its chairman. They acted on behalf of the War Office in the administration of the chaplaincy service.

The circumstances of war were, of course, exceptional. The new pattern of ministry, however, outlived the war years. The existence of Baptist ministers in the service of the State was something that became, from 1918 onwards, an integral feature of denominational life. Not only did the Board continue to nominate chaplains for commission within the armed services, but also a similar kind of chaplaincy provision was extended into the civilian sphere. Already, during the war, chaplains were attached to military hospitals, and, as the war drew to a close, agreement was reached among the four main denominations on the Board to co-operate in nominating chaplains for ministry in State hospitals, work-houses, asylums etc..[43] There is no record of any consideration being given to the principles involved in this development within the Baptist Union, as occurred among the Wesleyan Methodists after the war.[44] It seems that the ecclesiological issues at stake were of no interest. This lack of concern is itself significant, and illustrates how changes in church polity were taking place, not only without any consensus about the ecclesiological principles involved, but also without any real consideration of what they might be.[45]

In the autumn of 1916 there were 61 Baptist ministers appointed chaplains through the United Board, out of the Board's total establishment of 174.[46] Their significance for the development of Baptist church polity was considerable. Their ministry marked an unprecedented contribution by Baptists to national life. It also both reflected and reinforced important changes that were taking place elsewhere in the denomination. The Board introduced practices that outlasted the war, and helped shape Baptists' understanding of themselves and their place in society. As the leading figure on the Board, and one of the leading figures on the Interdenominational Advisory Committee, Shakespeare played the central role in this. It was a decisive development in his increasing pre-occupation with the search for church unity. His first ambition on the wider ecumenical stage was to make progress towards the fulfilment of his pre-war vision of a United Free Church of England.

4.2.2 The Federal Council of the Evangelical Free Churches

The Free Church Federal Council first met in September 1919, but its genesis lay in the war years. Shakespeare, whose appeals for a United Free Church of England and criticisms of the National Council as moribund had become a familiar feature of the National Council's meetings between 1910 and 1914, was elected President of the Council in the spring of 1916. This was a clear endorsement of his views, and, in effect, an authorisation to make his vision a reality if he could.

Shakespeare outlined his proposals in his Presidential address at the annual meetings of the Council in March 1916.[47] He began by reminding the audience of his appeals for unity over the previous six years. He described what he considered to be the essential unity of Nonconformity. The denominations were divided by forms of church polity, but these, he believed, were not essential to the character and validity of a Church. His overall theme was that 'the principle of division has spent its force and the era of union must begin'.[48] He argued that denominationalism was 'a decaying idea', and that unless the competitive and wasteful divisions among the Free Churches could be brought to an end, their decline would continue until they slowly bled to death. Shakespeare said that the heart and centre of the problem was the disastrous effect of division on the ministry. The most gifted young men were not offering themselves for the Nonconformist ministry, and this was because of the 'fatal system' and 'impossible conditions' under which it operated. A national network of Free Church parishes needed to be created, in his view, so that the skills and abilities of ministers could be more effectively utilised. Division not only damaged the ministry; it also prevented the Free Churches exercising the influence they should at a national level. 'The extraordinary thing to day', Shakespeare said, 'is that our numbers are so enormous and our powers so comparatively small'.[49] The United Board's success, he believed, had shown the way ahead.

> If we will only work together, by constant pressure and sleepless vigilance, by entering every door which is open to us and forcing open every door that is closed to us, we could rapidly change the entire situation and compel something more than lip service from our rulers and governors, our Members of Parliament and those who are jealously safeguarding their monopoly in the life of the nation.[50]

Shakespeare urged the Free Church denominations not to allow themselves to be 'forever cowed and dominated by its smallest and narrowest people and by timorous counsels',[51] and proposed the formation of a federation, advised by a board of leading Nonconformists. He concluded with a ringing appeal: 'Today I raise upon the battle field the standard of the United Free Church of England. Let all who are ready to do battle for the cause gather beneath its folds'.[52]

The speech is typical of Shakespeare in its bold width of vision, passionate rhetoric and call to action. The twin themes of the need to unite for effective national mission, and the central importance of the ministry, were familiar. His impatient dismissal of those who might hesitate about taking the steps he proposed, as narrow minded and backward looking, is also something his own denomination had got used to. The principles that Shakespeare outlined as the basis of unity, namely, that the church is composed of those who have been 'born again', that the church's internal life is 'a spiritual fellowship' and that the authority of the church is vested in the people of God and not 'a clerical order or a sacerdotal hierarchy',[53] were not entirely clear and uncontentious for Nonconformists themselves. Other important matters were not addressed by him at all. Differences in church polity, for example, were more than just pragmatic questions of organisation and government. They reflected a Church's character and history, and so often expressed important ecclesiological principles. Diverging views of baptism and the ministry, which Shakespeare wanted to be left on one side as secondary, were actually central to the whole task of achieving unity.

During the course of the next few months, the Nonconformist denominations were asked to send representatives to a committee that would consider how closer co-operation could be achieved. In September 1916 and in March and September 1917, conferences were held in Oxford, Cambridge and London, with Shakespeare presiding. The *Baptist Times* kept its readers informed of the progress made. The report from the conferences was sent to the participating denominations, eleven in all, for their approval. It included a 'declaratory statement' of common faith, which was, the report emphasised, not a comprehensive creed, but 'a declaration of such truths as, in the circumstances, it seems proper to rehearse and emphasise'.[54] The report also included a suggested constitution for a proposed denominational federation. Its ruling body would be a Federal Council, whose powers would be merely 'advisory', unless, as Shakespeare no doubt hoped would happen, the denominations decided to entrust it with executive powers. A recommendation was made that all the ministers of the participating denominations be mutually recognised, as there was, the report controversially affirmed, a common basis of understanding of the ministry.[55] The report spoke of the Christian Ministry as an 'order' or 'office' in the Church, and as a divine institution.

The movement towards federation received an additional boost from the Congregationalist theologian, and Principal of Hackney College, P. T. Forsyth. His book *The Church and the Sacraments*, the essence of which was reproduced in a *Baptist Times* article in January 1917,[56] argued for a federal approach to church unity on the basis of the Gospel.[57] Forsyth warned, however, that there was a need to provide such an approach with 'a positive idea' of the church, and not to rely merely on 'sheer insistence', or fear of decline. In 1917, he feared, the movement lacked 'the inspiration of a positive idea of the Church, a formative core of ecclesiastical principle'.[58] Forsyth's book attempted to meet that need, by providing a theological basis for the unity of the church, and a justification for the federal approach to demonstrating that unity. It contained much that was positive and helpful in this regard, although whether it carried much weight with Baptists is uncertain. The importance of Forsyth's theological work in general was not widely acknowledged until years later.

The Baptist Union's General Purposes Committee agreed to recommend to the 1918 Assembly that the Union join the federation on the terms suggested,[59] a decision later endorsed by the Council. In February, however, notice was received from James Mountain, a minister from Tunbridge Wells and outspoken opponent of Shakespeare, of his intention to oppose this step, on the grounds of the inadequacy of the Declaration of Faith.[60] The Baptist group at the conferences of 1916 and 1917 (including Shakespeare) issued a statement in response, published in the *Baptist Times* in March, clarifying what it believed to be misconceptions about the proposed federation.[61] The group was especially concerned to reassure Baptists that the Declaration was not intended to be comprehensive, or to have the authority of a creed. It also emphasised that the proposed union was not a corporate one, but a federal one, in which each denomination would retain its autonomy. In April, there was a need to issue another word of 'clarification', to counter a

move intended to delay the decision to federate. Shakespeare had heard that
an amendment proposing the referral of the matter to the associations and
churches was to be brought to the Assembly. The *Baptist Times* stated that
the Assembly was competent to make the decision without reference to the
churches, as the federation proposed was one of 'Unions, Conferences and
Synods', not of individual churches.[62]

Shakespeare presented the report on the suggested federation at the
Assembly. The Baptists were the first denomination to be asked to decide
whether or not to join. He admitted that the proposal did not go as far as he
would have liked. 'This tiny shoot, this tender plant, lifts its little head
timidly above the ground after the long winter of sectarianism', he said, 'but
it has the promise of spring'.[63] He reminded the Assembly of the historic
times they were living through, and admitted his personal commitment to
the cause of union:

> For years I have watched this Baptist Union. It is not small, or narrow, or
> bitter, and it will not look on this little promise of Christian unity with dis-
> trust or suspicion. We have come to a great hour in human history, and
> nothing will ever be the same again. Let us not so completely mistake the
> temper of the men at the Front as to wait for their return before we prepare
> for united action . . .. This movement of Christian Unity is sweeping
> through the world like a breath of God . . .. It is unthinkable that the
> Baptists should wreck the movement or even look at it with distrust or hes-
> itation. Such a course would wreck the Baptist Union. I cannot pretend
> that I bring these proposals to you with a merely impersonal or academic
> interest. I have given far too much of my life, my strength and my labour
> to them . . . the Churches must unite or perish, and I take my stand with
> all those who desire to rally the Evangelical Churches for the salvation of
> our fellow-countrymen.[64]

The Union President, Rev. J. E. Roberts, moved the acceptance of the
report and agreement to federate. In seconding, Dr. Charles Brown referred
to a pamphlet entitled 'Shall Baptists Forfeit their Honour?' which had been
circulated by the resolution's opponents. He declared that it was not the
time of day for 'splitting straws on theology'.[65] Two amendments were lost
and the resolution was carried quite easily, much to the relief of its supporters, who had expected greater difficulty in getting it through. The Union
treasurer, Herbert Marnham, moved a vote of thanks to Shakespeare,
couched in the warmest and most appreciative language. It was 'carried by
an upstanding vote'.[66]

The decision of the 1918 Assembly to join a Federation of Free Churches
raised important ecclesiological and constitutional questions. It implied, at
least, that the Union could be considered a Church for this purpose, and that
the Assembly was a competent body to make such a decision on its behalf.

This was highly controversial, in spite of assurances from the *Baptist Times*. The significance of the decision was diminished, however, by the fact that the status and authority of the Federation was still unclear. It was an expression of support for the new body, but it actually did not commit local churches to anything. Its main practical effect was to give authority to the Union to continue its involvement in discussions with the other Free Churches.

Seven months later, in November 1918, Shakespeare's views on church unity were published in his most famous work, *The Churches at the Cross Roads*. Most of its content repeated or expanded on views he had already expressed in addresses on Free Church unity since 1910. Hastings regards the book as 'in principle one of the most important books of twentieth-century English Christianity because it sets out so clearly the logic of the forthcoming ecumenical movement'.[67] It did not have the intellectual weight of Forsyth's work, as Shakespeare was an organiser and leader rather than a theologian. It nevertheless showed him, according to one leading Baptist contemporary, to be 'the most distinguished prophet and apostle of church unity among the Free Churches'.[68]

The book began with a review of English society at the end of the war, and how Shakespeare believed circumstances for the churches had changed since the beginning of the century. Values that had been clung to passionately twenty years before were now of little significance, he wrote, and there was a general determination not to allow a return to the pre-war state of affairs, either in society or in the churches. He particularly drew attention to the 'new place of woman in the social order' as one of the most hopeful features of the new post-war society.[69] He pleaded for the churches to understand and respond to the new rational and scientific temper of the time. This change of attitude was impatient with the inefficiency of the denominational system of church organisation. When this was taken together with the fact that the major Nonconformist denominations shared all the most important Christian affirmations, and were moving towards each other in terms of church polity, the case for unity became overwhelming.

Shakespeare went on to describe the decline in membership within Nonconformity between 1906 and 1916, which amounted to 'a very serious call to set our house in order'.[70] 'Sectarian distinctions and rivalries' were a major hindrance to mission, and were of no interest to those outside the church, he wrote. He compared the inability of Nonconformists to organise major national initiatives with the achievement of the Church of England in organising the 1916 National Mission of Repentance and Hope. That mission was an example of what could be done by united activity. Only the unity of the Free Churches, he believed, would capture the imagination and commitment of the youth of the day, and would do justice to their sacrifices during the war. The best young people would only be attracted to the ministry of a united church, and only a united church could nurture the kind of ministry required. In a description that is almost priestly in its language, Shakespeare emphasised the absolute importance of the ministry for the future of the church:

> With so few exceptions as to be insignificant, the church is what the minister makes it. To a great extent he determines the measure of its activity and usefulness. The spiritual life of the church will not rise higher than his own; the care of souls must fall chiefly on him . . .. He must be apt to teach, one who is instinct with sacrifice and moral earnestness, who suggests by his bearing the unseen and the eternal, who has healing in his touch and who mediates the mystical and the divine. It is essential that the ministry should supply a leadership, not merely official, but based upon spiritual power, unselfishness, vital and transparent goodness. [71]

For Shakespeare, the way of federation was the best method of translating vision into reality. His preferred title for such a federation was 'The United Free Church of England', a title that would constitute a rallying point for those who valued the ideal of union. It would supplement, rather than supplant, denominational titles. The time was not ripe for corporate union, he admitted. Federation would enable each denomination to keep its own identity and name within the wider body. It would enable small local churches to amalgamate, by means of reciprocal arrangements between denominations, and so create the possibility of more effective mission. A single Free Church in a community would provide 'the centre and symbol of the modern religious spirit of welcome and fellowship'.[72] Larger churches in the cities would offer opportunities for a more varied ministry, and especially the ministry of women.[73]

A federation of churches would be a much more effective vehicle for unity than the old National Council, Shakespeare argued, because the latter was not answerable to the central authorities of the churches. It would not run the risk of becoming a predominantly political pressure group, like the National Council. The fact that the large majority of Baptist churches had agreed to federate under the Ministerial Settlement and Sustentation Scheme, and accept the system of General Superintendents, indicated that congregational church government was not necessarily an obstacle to co-operative action of this kind.[74] Shakespeare believed that if the Free Churches would only 'come together and bend their resources in unity to the one end, they would usher in a day of national religious awakening such as no living man has ever seen'.[75]

For those who had heard Shakespeare's appeals at the National Council meetings, and were familiar with the progress towards unity among the Free Church denominations, most of this, which occupied the bulk of the book, was not particularly remarkable. After dealing with the question of Free Church unity, however, his ideas unexpectedly became much more wide-ranging and ambitious. They were not as well developed. It was as if a new theme had been introduced as an afterthought. The thrust of Shakespeare's argument in this later section of the book was the need for union between the Free Churches and the Church of England - a theme absent from its first 165 pages. Shakespeare advocated a corporate union,[76] a concept he had earlier avoided in relation to the Free Church denominations, to bring to an end the cleavage of 1662. He acknowledged his conviction that this would only come about on the basis of episcopacy. He also recognised that differences over the ministry, and especially the question of the validity of Free Church ordination, would be a major difficulty. He finished this part of the book with a remarkable appeal for the accredited representatives of the churches of Great Britain and her overseas dominions to meet in London for council when the war was over to 'lay the foundation of a United Evangelical Church of the Empire'.[77]

The book closed with an autobiographical chapter in which Shakespeare referred to some of the main personal influences on his career. He reflected on his strict Baptist upbringing and the example of his grandfather, a village pastor. Any thought of church unity 'lay beyond the horizon' at that time.[78] Even his experience at St. Mary's in Norwich had not included any meaningful fellowship with members of the Church of England, although the influence of men such as Joseph Parker and Hugh Price Hughes had opened his mind to the possibility of co-operation among the Nonconformist denominations. He recounted how in more recent years he had met leaders of the Church of England on several different occasions, and had been impressed with the level of agreement and cordiality that had been achieved. Any progress after the war would depend on 'whether the churches attempt to carry the lumber of the past with them into the new time'.[79] They owed it to the soldiers who had fought and died, however, 'to face things courageously and with idealism'.[80]

Reaction to *The Churches at the Cross Roads* was mixed. The *Baptist Times* was predictably positive, reviewing it in a series of issues throughout November 1918. The response of others was not always as congenial. Robertson Nicoll's denunciation of Shakespeare's call for union with the Church of England in the *British Weekly* was particularly fierce. He published his views under the headline 'Mr. Shakespeare at the Crossroads', accusing him of falling under the spell of the Anglican Communion, and failing to realise that 'some things are more valuable than unity'.[81] The book's advocacy of union with the Church of England was indeed shocking to many, and in the years after its publication overshadowed efforts to secure Free Church union. It was the opinion of some that the book imperilled the latter, without bringing union between the Anglicans and the Free Churches any nearer.[82] Nicoll went as far as to say that Shakespeare's obsession with the unrealistic goal of wider union made him 'the worst enemy of Church Unity' he had known, and resulted in the failure of the movement for feder-

ation.[83] An assessment of the validity of these opinions, and of the significance of Shakespeare's commitment to unity for his own denomination,
must await consideration of his dealings with the Anglicans during the war,
and the story of post-war church unity discussions.

4.2.3 Conversations with the Church of England

The possibility of some form of reconciliation between the Free Churches
and the Church of England had been raised early in 1914 as a consequence
of the Faith and Order movement. For Shakespeare, this possibility
received a significant boost as a result of his experiences during the war.
The gulf between them was deep, however, and had a long history.
Suspicion and hostility characterised the relationship on both sides.

Before the war, links were established in settings where the need to
resolve differences was not pressing, such as among student groups, or at the
Grindelwald holiday conferences in Switzerland organised by Henry Lunn
in the 1890's. Intercommunion was the issue that gave rise to the greatest
difficulties on the Anglican side. It provoked a dangerous crisis for the
whole Anglican Communion in 1913, when Frank Weston, the Bishop of
Zanzibar, accused some of his fellow bishops of heresy when they participated in an interdenominational communion service at the Kikuyu
Conference in British East Africa. From the Free Church side, a common
rallying point for opposition to closer links was any suggestion of associating with Anglo-Catholicism. The Romewards tendency of some sections of
the Church of England was regarded with horror, and as a betrayal of the
essential Protestantism of England. The controversy provoked by the proposed procession of the Blessed Sacrament, which was to have been the cli-
max of the 1908 Eucharistic Congress in London, illustrates the heat that
opposition to Catholicism could still generate.[84]

Confrontation between church and chapel was a central feature of English
politics during much of the nineteenth century, and although by 1900 its relevance had diminished, it was revitalised by the controversy over the 1902
Education Act. Most Nonconformists believed that the Act unfairly discrim-
inated against them by allowing public money to be used in support of church
schools. They expressed their opposition at large protest meetings and
through the campaign of Passive Resistance led by John Clifford. Feelings
about the matter remained high until the war. Historically, calls for the disestablishment of the Anglican Church had been another highly contentious
issue. Free Church calls for disestablishment in England, mainly from the
Liberation Society, were only occasionally heard after 1900, but the cause of
Welsh disestablishment was vigorously pursued in both Wales and England.[85]

The most contentious issues dividing church and chapel (especially education) became more marginal in national politics as the Edwardian period
progressed. The 1910 Edinburgh Missionary Conference, and the resulting

proposal for an ecumenical conference on Church Faith and Order, opened the door to the possibility of more positive relations. Randall Davidson, the Archbishop of Canterbury, was broadly sympathetic to the cause of church unity, and took initiatives to enable conversations with Free Church representatives to take place.[86] In 1912 he invited Rev. Tissington Tatlow, General Secretary of the Student Christian Movement, to take responsibility for co-ordinating the Church of England's response to the Faith and Order initiative from the American Episcopalians. This included establishing contact with the Free Churches, and in April 1914 letters were exchanged between Tatlow and F. B. Meyer, the secretary of the Free Church Council.[87]

In May 1915, a few weeks after Shakespeare had been appointed President elect of the Free Church Council, he sent Tatlow a lengthy letter in which he outlined some of his ideas on the desirability of moving towards church unity. It contained no positive suggestions, raising a number of questions about such things as the Episcopate and inter-communion, but it does express the view that 'it is worth while making an effort to bridge the chasm which through many blunders came about in 1662'.[88] Tatlow organised a number of conferences during the war involving representatives of the Church of England and the Free Churches. In February 1916 an interim report, entitled 'Towards Christian Unity', was issued by a sub-committee appointed at those conferences, outlining areas of agreement and difference.[89] Shakespeare was one of the members of this sub-committee.

Davidson's own papers include several articles from the religious press about Shakespeare's proposals for a United Free Church of England in 1916. They also include a note of a 'long conversation' about it between Davidson, Shakespeare and Cosmo Gordon Lang, Archbishop of York, at Lambeth Palace in March of that year. According to Davidson's note, Shakespeare expressed views about episcopacy that are surprisingly frank:

> He is dead against Disestablishment, as always, saying, as he has often said before, 'I am at heart an Episcopalian'. He expanded this by saying that he has now arranged for nine Dioceses in England for the Baptist community, 'only we call the man Superintendent and not Bishop, but he is a bishop for all that'. He vaguely hinted, and I purposely did not press him further, that a movement in the direction of union such as he is inaugurating will not ultimately stop there, 'especially', he said, 'when our Superintendents become really bishops'.[90]

Interdenominational meetings and correspondence occurred with increasing frequency as the war progressed. Although the Church of England's National Mission in the autumn of 1916 did not officially involve the Free Churches, they were sometimes drawn into it, such as when Shakespeare, together with other Free Church leaders, was invited to address a meeting in Oxford.[91] In March 1918 Tatlow's Anglican/Free Church committee issued its second interim report. A major topic of discussion at its meetings since 1916 had been episcopacy, and specifically the difficulties involved in bringing episcopal and non-episcopal Churches together. The report outlined the conditions of reunion that the committee believed to be necessary. These included the preservation of continuity with the 'historic Episcopate' on the one hand, and the assumption by the Episcopate of 'a constitutional form', both for the election of bishops and their method of government, on the other. The committee believed that agreement on the precise character and function of the Episcopate was not necessary as a precondition of reunion, and that acceptance of episcopacy in principle need not involve any of the Free Churches disowning its past.[92] The Baptist Union Council immediately accepted this report as 'valuable'.[93]

During 1918 the *Baptist Times* reported several important initiatives involving the Free Churches and the Church of England, including a joint Good Friday Service of Intercession in Hyde Park[94] and an interdenominational Parade Service on the Western Front.[95] It also published an article by the leading Baptist historian W. T. Whitley claiming that episcopacy could become a bond of church union if it were re-interpreted.[96] Impetus towards union was maintained in November by the publication of *The Churches at the Cross Roads,* and by the Albert Hall Service of Thanksgiving in the presence of the King and Queen.

Reunion was given a further boost in January 1919 with the publication of the report of a joint Anglican/Free Church conference at Mansfield College, Oxford. It was signed by more than sixty church leaders, including Shakespeare, Rev. J. E. Roberts, President of the Baptist Union, and several other prominent Baptists. The signatories asserted that they were 'in entire accord' in their mutual recognition of each other's communions as Christian Churches. They accepted that 'a reformed Episcopacy' would have to be included in a reunited Church, and believed that the essential values of Presbyterian, Congregational and Methodist church polity could be preserved within it. The report called for the exchange of pulpits and other forms of joint action.[97]

Papers given at the various Anglican/Free Church meetings and conferences during and immediately after the war, together with the resolutions agreed by those attending, were published in 1919 in a volume entitled *Towards Reunion: being contributions to mutual understanding by Church of England and Free Church writers.* The four editors were the Anglicans A. J. Carlyle and Stuart H. Clark, J. Scott Lidgett, representing the Wesleyans, and Shakespeare. Their preface was confident and forthright in tone.

Earnest men have seen a vision, with ever-growing distinctiveness, of a great spiritual and visible unity, which gives glad recognition and welcome to every variety of spiritual form that has proved its value to the world . . . the world is right in asking, as a condition of its faith, that it may be able to see and appreciate the links which unite all Christian people. An invisible unity, that only be spiritually discerned, is of little service to a non-believing world.[98]

Scott Lidgett and Shakespeare were the two most prominent Free Church advocates of union in the immediate post-war years. Shakespeare was the more representative figure in the sense that he was more obviously associated with the Free Churches as a whole. The Wesleyans had always been ambivalent about Nonconformity, and believed they occupied a distinct position within the Free Church movement, as seen in their refusal to join the United Board and their delay in agreeing to participate in the Federal Council. They were historically closer to the Church of England, and bilateral discussions about reunion running parallel to the more general conversations were held during the war. Shakespeare regarded these with disapproval.[99]

Serious conversations about the possibility of church reunion, both among the Free Churches and between them and the Church of England, were not simply a product of the war. In both cases, significant developments took place before 1914. Indeed, in some respects, the war hindered the cause of unity by disrupting the progress being made in connection with the Faith and Order movement. Overall, however, the war increased the sense of urgency about the need for reunion, and opened up new opportunities for expressing it. This was so for Shakespeare, who was deeply involved with the United Board, with the Free Church movement towards federation, and with the Church of England. The United Board was a practical and successful experiment in co-operation. Its effect was primarily felt by the non-Wesleyan English Free Churches, but, in the second half of the war, it also had an impact on all the other Churches. The creation of the Free Church Federal Council was, potentially at least, a first step towards the organic union of the Free Churches. This was Shakespeare's explicit ambition for it. The Mansfield Conference of January 1919 was the culmination of the efforts during the war to grasp the biggest prize of all, reunion between the Church of England and the Free Churches.

The real test of the lasting value of these events, however, came once the war had ended. Could the rapid, and somewhat opportunistic, progress during the exceptional circumstances of the 1914-1918 years be consolidated into genuine and more stable expressions of unity in peace-time? Or would the apparent victories won prove illusory? The remaining five years of Shakespeare's active ministry at Baptist Church House were, in the event, to prove a substantial disappointment in his campaign for unity. The mood among the churches, including the Baptists, swung increasingly against him, and his lack of realism was increasingly evident as the issues were explored in greater depth. His own commitment to the wider unity he sought did not waver, and the conversations between the churches went on as long as they did largely because of the energy and time he was prepared to invest in them.

The central event for reunion in the immediate post-war years was the Lambeth Appeal issued by the Anglican bishops following their 1920 conference. This can be regarded as the chief monument to the ten years of progress following the Edinburgh Conference. The fact that it was made at all is substantial evidence of how far church relations had changed. It also demonstrated, however, how long a journey still had to be made if reunion was to be achieved.

4.3 The Lambeth Appeal

At the end of 1918, Shakespeare's health deteriorated, and it remained fragile for the next two and a half years. He was able to continue working for most of that time, but was unable to attend committee meetings between December 1918 and February 1919 and between December 1920 and February 1921.[100] His poor state of health was an important limiting factor in what he achieved in the post-war years.

Shakespeare's chief antagonist within his own denomination over reunion was the classicist, and fellow of St. John's College, Cambridge, T. R. Glover. Glover's father Richard had been the only leading Baptist to stand out against Shakespeare's scheme for ministerial settlement and sustentation before the war, and from 1919, following the death of his father, he became the chief spokesman for Baptist doubts over church unity.[101] Glover had spent most of the war overseas, in India and America. His lectures in India, on behalf of the Baptist Missionary Society, were published as *The Jesus of History* in 1917. Early in 1919 he made it clear to the Union Council, of which he was a member, that he intended to bring a resolution to the May Assembly opposing any steps towards unity that implied irregularity about the Baptist ministry, or suggested the need for Baptist ministers to be episcopally ordained.[102] The prospect of such a resolution, and how it was to be worded, gave rise to considerable anxiety on Shakespeare's part,[103] and there were evidently some heated exchanges between the two men.[104]

Glover was supported in his views by the veteran John Clifford, who had made his feelings clear in a letter to Robertson Nicoll in February 1919. 'Now under the influence in part of this war', wrote Clifford, 'we are in danger, it seems to me, of sacrificing sincerity, liberty, and the truth of the Gospel for the sake of obtaining an external and mechanical uniformity'.[105] As the business of the 1919 Assembly was being prepared, Clifford wrote to Glover himself, thanking him for bringing the subject forward. 'It was necessary. It has done good, great good', he said. He also subsequently warned him that Shakespeare would do all he could to prevent the matter coming up for debate, and said he was glad not to be bound up with any suggestions of association with the 'historic Episcopate'.[106] Clifford and Glover were not alone among leading Baptists in their opposition to the course Shakespeare was taking. Thomas Phillips, Union President in 1916, and Superintendent of Bloomsbury Baptist Church in London, was another.[107]

In April 1919, about three weeks before the Assembly was due to convene, Shakespeare responded to the unease in sections of his own denomination in an address at Kingsway Hall, London. He expressed again his own personal commitment to the search for unity. He was looking forward to the forthcoming inaugural meetings of the Free Church Federal Council in September, and repeated his view that reunion would only be possible on the basis of episcopacy. Episcopacy could be consistent with the priesthood of all believers, he believed, if it were 'constitutional' in form, rather than 'prelatical' or 'monarchical', and if it were not subject to political appointment. In fact, he said he 'should regard it as unChristian to refuse an episcopal order of this kind if it is the price of Reunion'. He appealed to the Anglican bishops to accept the Free Churches as ' a true part of the Catholic Church'. Many of the most contentious matters, such as ordination procedures, Church-State relations and baptismal practice were subsidiary questions, he believed, that could be decided upon at a later stage, after the commitment to unity had been made. He also expressed his frustration with the delays in progress towards unity.

> The real enemies of Church unity are those who have a fervent passion for it so long as it is in the air, but the moment it takes any tangible form, the moment it comes out of the abstract or begins to descend from the skies, they cry out with alarm and oppose it with all the force with which they are capable.[108]

The 1919 Assembly was a difficult one for Shakespeare. In 1918 he had seen his proposals for membership of the new Free Church Federation accepted enthusiastically, and his standing among Baptists had been as high as ever. Twelve months later, the mood of the denomination was quite different. In its report of the Assembly, the *Baptist Times* records a complaint made by one speaker about the 'ill informed detraction' of Shakespeare evident in some quarters.[109] A motion was carried critical of his editorial policy at the *Baptist Times*, particularly in its partisan support of Lloyd George in the 1918 General Election.[110] Glover proposed his motion on Free Church/Anglican relations. It included a welcome for better relations between the Christian Churches, but also rejected 'any basis of union which implies the irregularity of its (i.e. the Baptist) ministry long blessed by God, or is inconsistent with the priesthood of all believers'.[111] In his address he raised the thorny issue of re-ordination. Shakespeare's response was vigorous:

> We . . . have no intention of stampeding the Baptist denomination, or doing anything dishonourable. It is almost incredible that anyone should have thought it necessary to bring forward a resolution . . . Most of what

Dr. Glover has said seemed . . . entirely irrelevant. I am not at the cross-
roads; I have chosen my path, and I shall follow it.[112]

Clifford seconded Glover's resolution, expressing total rejection of any
move towards either 'the government of a Church by the State' or 'baptismal
regeneration'.[113] It was impossible for Baptists to resist expressing their support for a resolution couched and supported in such terms, and it was carried
unanimously. It had little if any effect on Shakespeare's involvement in discussions with the Church of England, but it injected an important note of
caution into the process.

From the summer of 1919 onwards, debate within the Church of England
over church unity intensified. Shakespeare suffered from intermittent poor
health during this period, and was unable to attend the 250th anniversary cel-
ebrations at his old church of St. Mary's in Norwich, in June. These meetings were notable because they were reportedly the first occasion an
Anglican bishop had spoken at a Nonconformist service. In the same
month, a group of High Churchmen, led by Dr. Gore, the Bishop of Oxford,
presented a petition to the Upper House of the Convocation of Canterbury,
opposing the increasingly frequent calls coming from some sections of the
Church for the exchange of pulpits. 'There are no circumstances', the petition uncompromisingly said, 'in which we can invite members of non-episcopal bodies to minister or preach in our Churches'.[114] A committee set up
by the Convocation attempted to resolve the question of the conditions
under which such preaching could be regarded as acceptable, but no consensus could be arrived at.[115]

Church of England conferences in Cheltenham in 1919 and joint Free
Church/Anglican conferences in Swanwick (1919) and in Oxford (the second Mansfield Conference of January 1920) urged faster progress towards
unity. It was suggested that this should be done by allowing intercommunion and authorising ministers to serve across denominational boundaries.[116]
In April, 88 Anglican clergy and leading laymen who could not accept the
validity of Nonconformist ministries issued a reply to the resolutions of the
Second Mansfield Conference. They asserted that to take the proposed steps
without proper regard for 'the Catholic principle of the episcopal succession' would be a disaster, and would in fact result in the Church of England
losing its status as part of the Catholic Church.[117] The reason for much of this
lobbying was the forthcoming Lambeth Conference of 1920. Davidson
himself was determined to wait until the bishops from the whole Anglican
Communion had considered the question of unity at before making any public pronouncements on the subject.

During the autumn of 1919 Shakespeare was involved in two other significant events related to the search for church unity. One was the first meeting of the Free Church Federal Council in September. All the main
Nonconformist denominations had agreed to participate and were repre-

sented, with the exception of the Wesleyans, who were to join in 1920. Shakespeare was appointed Moderator, and continued in that office for the Council's first two years. The official record of the proceedings gives the impression that they did not match the high expectations of 1918. This may have been partly because Shakespeare's illness prevented him from contributing with his usual energy. The fact that his attention, as well as that of many others, had largely passed away from Free Church unity to the prospect of unity with the Church of England no doubt played its part as well.

One of the Council's first priorities was to sort out its relationship with the older National Council.[118] The compatibility of the two bodies was to be an important theme of the Federal Council's business in its early years, and a matter of some confusion among the churches. It is ironic that an organisation described by Shakespeare as ineffective and virtually obsolete should intrude so much into the business of the new body. The two Councils, which were eventually to merge, though not until 1941, were constitutionally different, although representative of the same people. A conference of representatives from the two Councils was held in November, and the outcome was the setting up of a joint 'Nexus Committee', which became, over the course of the next few years, an important Free Church body in itself.[119]

Other decisions at the Federal Council's first meeting included a recommendation for a Day of Rededication for the churches of all the participating denominations, the urging of joint meetings of ministers and others at the local level to organise united action, and the request that a common minimum ministerial stipend be set.[120] The prospect of the hoped-for United Free Church of England does not seem to have been officially discussed at all.

The second event in the autumn of 1919 was of a more personal nature. Since 1918, preparations had been going on for a presentation to Shakespeare in recognition of his promotion of the cause of church unity, mainly at the initiative of the leading Nonconformist Member of Parliament, Sir Joseph Compton-Rickett.[121] At the end of October, Shakespeare, together with the presentation committee, met at Baptist Church House for the unveiling of a portrait of Shakespeare by John Collier, and the presentation of a handsomely bound illuminated address. Appreciative letters were read from the Archbishops of Canterbury and York, the Bishop of London, the Prime Minister and the Secretary of the War Office.[122] Several speeches were made, including one reviewing Shakespeare's achievements within the denomination, as well as those for church unity, by Herbert Marnham, the Treasurer of the Baptist Union. The personal cost borne by Shakespeare for the work involved in terms of his health was acknowledged.

In his response, Shakespeare repeated his conviction that reunion, by means of the incorporation of the Free Churches into a United Church upon the basis of episcopacy, was a vital necessity. He referred to his sittings with Collier, at which he was often 'prostrate and broken, and on the eve of collapse'. 'I feel I am completing a period of my life in which I have done most imperfect work, and I wish I could think that I should have the strength to enter upon a period in which I could do good work', he said.[123]

The address itself was signed by over 160 people, including four archbishops, 33 bishops, the Prime Minister, several Members of Parliament, leading figures of other denominations and leading lay and ordained Baptists. It began with these words:

> For a long time we and many others in the Christian Churches on the European and American Continents have followed with keen interest and grateful appreciation your able and zealous advocacy of the cause of Christian unity, to us one of the most important and promising movements of the age. Your untiring labours, your willingness to understand and meet difficulties, the wisdom of your proposals, and the eloquence of your appeals, have been enhanced and reinforced by the absolute sincerity of your motives and the manifest intensity of your convictions.[124]

It was a warm tribute, and perhaps reflected the sense of some of the subscribers that Shakespeare's active work might be drawing to an end. Although he was only 62, he had driven himself to the point of exhaustion in several of his projects, and was throughout most of 1919 in poor health. Other tributes, of a more political nature, were pressed upon him at around this time, but he steadfastly refused them, according to his personal secretary William Ball.[125] He was, however, prepared to accept an honorary Doctor of Divinity from Glasgow University, given in recognition of his services to Christian unity.[126]

The Free Churches' response to the Lambeth Appeal dominated their collective activity for two or three years. The *Baptist Times* published the Appeal in full on 13 August 1920. It was similar in outline to the Lambeth Quadrilateral of 1888, and affirmed that its four articles were the only proper basis of unity.[127] There were however, differences, both in content and tone, between the statements of 1888 and 1920. The fourth article was modified, so that the explicit reference to the Historic Episcopate in the earlier document was replaced by a reference to 'a ministry acknowledged in every part of the Church as possessing not only the inward call of the Spirit, but also the commission of Christ and the authority of the whole Body'. The first three articles were left substantially unchanged. These related to the Holy Scriptures as the rule and standard of faith, the Nicene and Apostolic Creeds, the former being 'the sufficient statement of the Christian faith', and the sacraments of Baptism and Holy Communion. The different tone of the Appeal was evident from its opening paragraph, in which the bishops explicitly accepted that all believing and baptised Christians were members of the universal Church of Christ, deplored the divisions among Christian people, and committed the Church of England to the pursuit of visible unity.

The crux of the matter was the ministry. The Appeal acknowledged divine blessing on non-episcopal ministries, but claimed that the Episcopate was the best way of maintaining the unity and continuity of the Church. It expressed the desire that 'the office of a Bishop should be everywhere exercised in a representative and constitutional manner', and hoped that, for the sake of unity, ministers of non-episcopal churches would accept 'a commission through episcopal ordination' for ministry within the Church of England. In return, and once the terms of union had been 'otherwise satisfactorily adjusted', Anglican clergy would accept a commission from the appropriate authorities in other churches.[128]

There had been considerable apprehension on all sides about the Lambeth Conference's deliberation of the question of reunion, and relief, afterwards, that a statement had been agreed that met with general approval among the bishops. The Appeal was a major step forward in its positive statements about other church bodies and their ministries, and its commitment to the pursuit of unity, but it did not resolve the major areas of difference, nor did it claim to. The *Baptist Times* immediately welcomed it as going further than had been hoped, and called for a generous and sacrificial response.[129] The Federal Council, under the chairmanship of Shakespeare, met for its second annual meeting during September 1920. It issued a 'provisional statement' on the Appeal, 'thanking God for moves towards unity, committing itself to do what it could to further these, while at the same time recognising difficulties in the Lambeth proposals'.[130] The Nexus Committee was asked to appoint a special committee to examine the Appeal, which it did in October.[131] A week later Shakespeare told Randall Davidson that this committee was 'very jealous for its prerogative', and 'would not like anything even to appear to be taken out of its hands' on the Free Church side during any negotiations over reunion. This reflected his eagerness to discourage any bilateral conversations, such as had occurred between the Wesleyans and the Church of England during the war.[132] Davidson asked Shakespeare for a 'conference of elucidation' with the committee. He also gained his support for copies of the Appeal to be sent to the 'eight chief Denominations' for their individual responses.[133]

In December 1920 and January 1921 Shakespeare was prevented by ill health from attending the conference that Davidson had requested. Nor was he able to take the chair at the preparatory meeting of the Free Church representatives.[134] He was back at work in February, however, and chaired the meeting that agreed on the wording of a progress report for distribution to the denominations. Approval for this from the Federal Council was achieved at a special meeting called a fortnight later,[135] and the report was published under the title *The Free Churches and the Lambeth Appeal*.

This report welcomed the Appeal. The Council acknowledged that they could not reply to it formally, as only the denominational bodies had authority to do that. It identified three matters that needed further clarification.

The first was the need for a full and unambiguous recognition of the Free Churches as corporate parts of the Church of Christ by the Church of England. This was complicated by the close ties between the Free Church denominations in England and their 'sister-churches' in other countries. This meant that recognition could not easily be limited to the Churches in England alone. The second problem was the meaning of the phrase in the Appeal, 'commission through episcopal ordination'. Did this involve 're-ordination', or not? A denial of the validity of Free Church ordination would be unacceptable to the Free Church denominations, the Council believed. While they were prepared to accept episcopacy, they could not accept it as the only right form of church polity, and as necessary for a valid ordination to the Christian ministry. The third concern of the Council was over what it called 'spiritual freedom'. This had two elements. One was uncertainty over the precise authority of the Creeds in any united Church. The other related to the Church's relationship with the State. The report declared that 'Free Churchmen cannot be asked to consent that the civil power . . . has any authority over the spiritual affairs of the Church'. It concluded with an endorsement of the vision behind the Appeal, and called for definite acts to demonstrate Church unity, such as intercommunion and the exchange of pulpits. It maintained that such steps were more important than agreement over matters of church polity.[136]

In April 1921 the Baptist Union Council agreed to recommend that the Free Church report be endorsed at the forthcoming Assembly, and that the Free Church committee responsible for handling discussions with the Anglicans be asked to continue their work.[137] This was supported unanimously by the Assembly a few days later.[138] This Assembly was also notable for two other events. After two and a half years of poor health, Shakespeare announced his intention of retiring twelve months later. He would by then, he told the meeting, have reached the age of 65, and felt he had achieved the main objectives he had set himself when appointed in 1898.[139]

The second notable event of the 1921 Assembly was the visit of Cosmo Gordon Lang, the Archbishop of York, who gave an address on the Lambeth Appeal. Lang was closely associated with the Appeal, having chaired the committee that drafted it at the 1920 Conference, and being directly involved in the conversations with the Free Churches following its publication. He spoke at the General Assembly of the Presbyterian Church in England as well as the Baptist Assembly in the spring of 1921, and was in regular contact with Scott Lidgett, by then Secretary of the Free Church National Council, and other leading Nonconformist ministers. In his address, Lang outlined the content of the Appeal, emphasising that it was not a definitive scheme to be rejected or accepted, but 'simply an invitation to all Christian people to come together, to pray together, to think together, and to confer together', and 'a contribution toward the cause of fellowship'.[140] Lang professed penitence for the part played by the Church of

England in creating past divisions, and denied that re-ordination was being demanded as the price of reunion. Shakespeare was deeply moved by the occasion, writing to Lang shortly afterwards, 'your address was so persuasive that I said afterwards that if someone had risen and moved that we accept episcopal ordination, it would have been carried. I think perhaps this is an exaggeration, but something very near it would have been reached'.[141] Lang himself was not as sanguine about the prospects of achieving common ground:

> ...the reception was very cordial to me personally, but I do not think these good people have any real care about a visible Church at all. I am afraid that they are still content if only they can preach at St. Paul's and communicate at our altars. A great deal of thinking about the meaning of the Church must come before any union worth having is at all possible.[142]

In general, the responses of the individual Free Church denominations to the Lambeth Appeal were positive, paving the way for a series of conferences at Lambeth Palace that began in November 1921.[143]

In March 1921 one of Shakespeare's most valued and able supporters in the denomination, George Pearce Gould, died. Gould, who had known Shakespeare in Norwich, was President of the Union in 1913, during the campaign to raise the Sustentation Fund, and had subsequently served as chairman both of the Fund's Executive Committee and the Superintendents' Board. He was also committed to the search for reunion, having been a member of the committee organising the Anglican/Free Church Mansfield Conferences during the war and involved in the Faith and Order discussions. He had served as tutor and then Principal of Shakespeare's old college at Regent's Park. Shakespeare was deeply affected by his death, as his address at Gould's memorial service showed. 'Now he has gone', he said. 'The company is getting smaller - the world is cold and grey; we shiver in the chill wind of the early evening hour, and we think of the burdens which he helped us to carry'.[144]

In the same month as Gould's death, T. R. Glover's booklet *The Free Churches and Re-Union* was published. It was based on articles previously printed in the *British Weekly*, and amounted to a warning about the dangers involved in pursuing church unity without proper consideration for other important principles involved. Co-operation and the search for a more friendly spirit between churches were laudable objectives, Glover maintained, but reunion was not something that could be pushed through quickly and easily. He wrote:

> The fatigue of the War, the emotionalism that it induced, the general decline of interest in religious truth, even the practical man's restless wish to 'get things done', may conspire with higher motives to produce a desire

to settle the matter, to achieve re-union, and to be done with it. But Truth is not served by decisions reached in fatigue.[145]

It is hard to avoid the conclusion that Glover had Shakespeare in mind when he wrote this, especially in view of the latter's indisposition, due at least in part to nervous exhaustion, in the post-war period. John Clifford endorsed his views as representing Baptist convictions, and Glover quoted him to this effect in the book's preface.[146]

The Free Churches and Re-Union was not the only publication from Glover's pen in 1921. His more substantial *Jesus in the Experience of Men* was also published that year. Shakespeare, or at least the approach to church life that Shakespeare represented, appears to have been in his sights in sections of that book as well. In his account of the early history of the Church, Glover regretted the victory of 'organisation and the sacramental interpretation of Christianity' in the third century, which led to the Gospel being 'refused to the laity'.[147] Salvation, in his view, became a matter not of personal conviction but of association with the Church. The result was a standardisation of doctrine and organisation under the direction of 'an official priesthood', rather than the freedom and openness of thought that he believed characterised the ministry of Jesus. This spirit, Glover wrote, had dominated the Church from the time of Constantine until the Reformation. In language that must have seemed remarkably pertinent to the contemporary debates within the Baptist denomination, particularly on church unity, Glover described what he considered to be a fundamental weakness of the Church's organisation during this period:

> A great organisation, in proportion as it is successful and means to be more successful, must have practical men to manage it, whether it is a railway company or a church; and it tends to choose leaders of the strenuous successful type, who can speak for it with the Government and command the support of ordinary people . . . The type is familiar to us, not too subtle, not too intellectual, not too spiritual, but quick, drastic and effective.[148]

Unfortunately, he wrote, practical businessmen are not good at discerning spiritual truth. Such discernment required an openness to the unexpected and freedom of thought. Diversity was not necessarily a bad thing. 'At Pentecost, we are told, every man heard in his own tongue; at Nicaea the language was Greek'.[149] 'We must unlearn some of our talk about 'unhappy division', he went on, directly confronting the church unity question, 'Divisions are only unhappy when tempers are sharp and awkward; otherwise, they may be very profitable, and very happy'.[150]

Glover's contribution to the reunion debate in the immediate post-war years was important because he was the most outspoken and able of Shakespeare's opponents among the Baptists, and because of his ability to win popular support. As Public Orator of Cambridge University he had impressive intellectual and communication skills, as well as a high national status in academic circles. Added to these qualities were his Baptist family background and his proven commitment to the work of the Baptist Missionary Society. He was more than capable of leading the challenge to the official Baptist establishment in London.[151]

In spite of Glover, the talks on reunion continued apace. Davidson and Lang were handicapped in their attempt to engage in meaningful conversations with the Free Churches by uncertainty over the extent to which they were united about reunion at all, and who, if anyone, had the authority to speak on their behalf. Of the two Free Church Councils, the Federal Council officially represented the denominations, but it had only recently been created, and had no executive power to act. Shakespeare, as Moderator from 1919 until 1921, was eager to emphasise the importance of its role, and his personal standing among the Free Churches was undoubted, but his passion for unity meant that the objectivity of his judgement could not always be relied upon. He was doggedly optimistic, insisting from the start that 'the Free Churches had no difficulty about the future Ministry being Episcopal'.[152] His later assessment that Glover's views on reunion were 'not generally representative' of Baptists as a whole, and 'reflected a tradition left by Dr. Spurgeon'[153] was expressed a month or so before Glover was elected Vice-President of the Union, and seemed more a matter of wishful thinking than objective judgement.

The difficulties involved in the negotiations with the Free Churches are reflected in a memorandum in Davidson's papers, written shortly before their commencement, stating that the Federal Council had 'received explicit authority of a kind' from most of the Free Church bodies, and 'implicit' authority from the Wesleyans for the forthcoming joint conference in November. At the same time, the Presbyterian, Wesleyan and United Methodist Churches had also proposed bilateral conferences with the Anglicans.[154]

The Baptists left discussions with the Anglicans to Shakespeare and others involved with him in the Federal Council. The question of Anglican/Free Church reunion only very occasionally appeared in the Baptist Union Minute Book, or in the pages of the *Baptist Times*, between the 1921 and 1924 Assemblies. It does not seem to have been a matter of any pressing importance for most Baptists.

In September 1921 Shakespeare concluded his two-year period in office as Moderator of the Federal Council. The Secretary of the Congregational Union, J. D. Jones, was elected for the following two years. Shakespeare was, however, appointed one of three Secretaries of the Council, and continued to be the main correspondent with Lambeth Palace on unity matters, and involved in the conferences and committee meetings during that time. The rather tortuous progress of these is recorded in the Lambeth Palace library archives. Between November 1921, when the first conference at Lambeth took place, and November 1923, three major conferences and ten committee meetings took place.

At the 1922 Baptist Assembly Shakespeare reiterated his convictions about the importance of the search for unity.[155] A few weeks later, following the second conference at Lambeth Palace, an interim report was issued, outlining the stage that the discussions had reached. It included a number of agreed statements about the most contentious subjects: the ministry, ordination, the Episcopate and the Nicene and Apostles' Creeds. The Ministry of the Word and Sacrament was described as 'a Divine ordinance for the Church', the commission for which was given through ordination, in which 'Divine Grace is given'. The Episcopate 'ought to be accepted', the report stated, as the means whereby the authority of the whole church is expressed in the act of ordination, and should be a permanent element in the order and life of a united church. The Nicene Creed should be accepted as the sufficient statement of faith, and the Apostles' Creed used at baptism.[156] This report was signed by the two Archbishops and the Moderator of the Federal Council, and was enthusiastically supported by Shakespeare.[157]

The report provoked an immediate response from Glover. In a letter printed in the *British Weekly* on 8 June 1922 he made his feelings clear.

> To a plain man of ordinary intelligence it seems hard to understand what our leaders are doing. Are they giving away everything which we have learnt to believe of moment, or do they think that convinced Churchmen are prepared to make a corresponding sacrifice, or do they suppose that neither of us will see that unity was reached in these proposals by studied ambiguity?

Describing Baptist Church House as 'that palace of dissolving views', Glover raised some crucial questions over which the report was ambiguous. 'Is infant baptism baptism?' he asked. 'What is Episcopacy?' and did it include Baptist superintendency? he wanted to know, and 'What does authority mean?' 'If the Churches accept this concordat of ecclesiastical politicians', he concluded, 'I do not know how anybody is to commend the Church to the sincere'.[158]

At the next Baptist Union Council meeting Glover wanted to discuss the implications of the report, but was persuaded by Shakespeare to wait until the Federal Council had discussed the matter at its meeting in the following September. Glover gave notice that he intended to move a resolution on the subject at the 1923 Assembly. Several of the larger associations had also written to Shakespeare opposing the contents of the report.[159]

The fourth annual meeting of the Federal Council was held at Baptist Church House in September 1922. The Council agreed a number of responses to the interim report. Firstly it made clear that it was up to the

individual denominations, rather than the Federal Council itself, to respond
to any official approach about reunion by the Church of England. The
responsibility the Council believed it had been given was simply 'to inquire
into the conditions antecedent' to any such reunion. Having made this clear,
the Council referred to five remaining practical difficulties, insisting that
there were a number of specific questions needing a clear answer:

What was meant by a 'representative and constitutional' episcopate, and
how were the elements of presbyterial and congregational order to be combined with it? What would be the status of the existing Free Church ministry within a united church? What would be the nature of the relations of
the Free Churches to communions with which they are in fellowship in other
parts of the world? How were the problems connected with the union
between Church and State to be addressed? How could the evangelical principles of the Reformation be safeguarded?[160]

The Council expressed its resolve not to imperil the inherited freedom of
the churches it represented. It reaffirmed its convictions that an unambiguous recognition of the Free Churches as part of the one Church of Christ was
the primary question in the negotiations, and that discussion about union
'should be increasingly accompanied by acts of unity'. Shakespeare and six
others were asked to continue their work on the joint Anglican/Free Church
sub-committee meeting at Lambeth Palace, and urged to seek a 'clear understanding on these points'.

The spirit of this response was not encouraging for the prospects of
reunion, as it showed that the gap between the two sides was as wide as ever.
From the autumn of 1922 onwards the joint discussions at Lambeth Palace
became increasingly difficult. An air of unreality seemed to pervade the
proceedings, with the Free Church representatives keen to try and press on
towards unity despite increasing hesitations from sections of both their own
denominations and the Church of England.[161] Lang expressed his disappointment at the way things were going.[162]

At the Baptist Union Council meeting in November 1922 Glover proposed the resolution about which he had given notice in July, but was once
again frustrated by an amendment adjourning discussion.[163] Shakespeare
was desperate to give the negotiations about reunion every possible chance
of success. 'It would be tragic indeed, if this dawn is clouded over', he said
in a lecture in December. 'Many of us who are older will have no heart to
speak of unity again'.[164] He hoped that the next joint Free Church/Anglican
conference, which was due to take place in the summer of 1923, would
resolve the outstanding issues, and he was successful in persuading Glover
not to speak on the subject at the Assembly until this had happened.[165] He
could not prevent him expressing his views in the press, however, and in
April 1923 an article by Glover appeared in the *Daily News* headed
'Compromise and Truth'. 'Why should it be so constantly dinned into us
that a divided Church militates against the world's acceptance of Christ?' he

asked. Division might actually be a sign of health, and compromise simply gave the impression that truth did not matter. The attempt to muffle differences was in his view 'ludicrous and pathetic'.[166]

The conference upon which Shakespeare pinned his remaining hopes was eventually held in July 1923.[167] It was dominated by a memorandum from the Church of England representatives on the committee entitled 'The Status of the Existing Free Church Ministry'. The sensitivity of this memorandum is clear from the fact that it was headed 'Very Confidential'.[168] The Anglicans attempted a clarification of the conditions under which existing Free Church ministries could be regarded as 'real ministries of Christ's Word and Sacraments in the Universal Church'. They believed that those that had been confirmed by a 'solemn and authoritative act implying ordination to the ministry of the Universal Church . . . and which are regarded as involving a life-long vocation . . . and which imply a sincere intention to preach Christ's Word and administer the sacraments' could be so regarded. They might nevertheless be 'irregular or defective' without episcopal ordination, which was indispensable for all recognised ministries within the Church of England.[169]

This memorandum was a fatal blow to the unity negotiations. It was an admission that episcopal re-ordination would be necessary if existing Free Church ministers were to be fully accepted within a united church. The issue of ordination had at last been confronted, and the gulf this revealed between the two parties proved too great to be bridged. The Federal Council, at its annual meetings two months later, expressed disappointment that re-ordination was apparently being insisted upon.[170] Although it gave renewed authorisation to its committee members to continue discussions, it admitted in a letter to Davidson about the memorandum that 'the way of reunion is not yet clear to any one of us'.[171]

Davidson himself regarded these developments in the summer and autumn of 1923 as the end of the search for unity with the Federal Council. In a letter to Lang he wondered whether formal negotiations with 'a definite Church' such as the Wesleyans or the Presbyterians might be the best next step. 'I think the Baptists are pretty hopeless', he wrote.[172] He may have read the letter published in the *Times* on 27 September from W. E. Blomfield, the President of the Baptist Union, written with the support of Glover, now Vice-President. In it, Blomfield referred indirectly to Shakespeare and other leading Baptists in the reunion discussions, writing, 'the Baptist denomination is wholly uncommitted by any of the proceedings which have followed the Lambeth Conference. Highly esteemed Baptists represent themselves, they do not commit the denomination to anything'.[173] It was also at about this time that the conversations about reunion between representatives of the Church of England and Cardinal Mercier at Malines that had taken place during the previous March came to light. The news caused widespread dismay and anxiety among the Free Churches.[174] The conferences at Lambeth

Palace continued until 1925, but no substantial further progress was made. They had to continue without Shakespeare, whose health suddenly and decisively broke down in October 1923.

Few developments of any great significance among the Free Churches took place after the formation of the Federal Council in the autumn of 1919. Hopes for a united 'Rededication Sunday', planned for October 1920 and involving all the participating denominations seem to have come to nothing.[175] At the second annual meeting, in September 1920, it was agreed by the Federal Council that 'united meetings of ministers and office bearers be held in each district, to be convened by the local representatives of the Free Church Council', i.e. the National Council.[176] The response to this resolution was 'disappointing', according to the Nexus Committee meeting of the following April. At the local level there was apparently 'considerable misapprehension regarding the function of the Federal Council and its relations to the National Free Church Council'.[177] The amalgamation of the two Councils was discussed but the prospects of this being achieved seemed remote in view of their incompatible constitutions. The third annual meeting of the Council in 1921 received reports saying that the subjects suggested for discussion at local meetings had already been dealt with by the local Free Church Councils.[178]

An issue that lay at the heart of the purpose behind the creation of the Federal Council was the need to eliminate unnecessary overlapping between the denominations. Attempts were made during 1921 to investigate the extent of this overlapping. A report on the situation in Lincolnshire concluded that most of the overlapping that did occur was among the Methodist churches.[179] At the 1921 annual meeting the importance of co-ordinating church extension in new districts was emphasised. It was agreed that the Federal Council would not seek to form interdenominational Free Churches, but rather aim to enable the denominations to co-operate in establishing new causes.[180] To this end, a United Church Extension Board, which included representatives of all the denominations, was set up. This first met in November 1922 to discuss specific areas, but did little other than urge the holding of conferences at the local level. It was unfortunate that one of its first decisions was a negative one, in refusing to recognise the new Independent Free Church at Welwyn Garden City as 'being within its federation', because of the Council's policy of only establishing churches associated with particular denominations.[181] In 1923 it was agreed that the Federal Council should act on behalf of the denominations in preparing for the proposed 1925 world conference on Faith and Order, but this decision was reversed as 'inadvisable' in 1924.[182]

Apart from its work for reunion, the Federal Council organised two major conferences during this period. One was at Mansfield College, Oxford, in January 1922, to consider 'The Evangelical Faith and Modern Views of Scripture', and the other was a remarkable meeting to discuss world peace held at Baptist Church House in October of the same year. The latter was unusual in that it included representatives not only of the federating Free Churches and the Church of England, but also the Greek Orthodox Church and the Quakers, as well as various non-denominational bodies. The Roman Catholic Church was invited to participate but sent no representatives. The conference recommended that Christmas Eve 1922 be observed as a day of prayer for world peace.

The Federal Council's crucial failure was in its inability to make any progress towards the realisation of Shakespeare's vision of a United Free Church of England. This was partly a consequence of its lack of authority to act on behalf of the denominations it represented. Confusion about the nature of its relationship with the National Council, which had an already well-developed network of Councils at the local level, was also a hindrance to any decisive action. More basically, there was no strong desire to achieve further unity, and no sense of direction about how it should be done. The Council did not tackle any of the issues of principle and practice that divided the federating denominations. The conviction that, on the most important matters, the Free Churches were united, was not enough to create any real sense of unity out of the nebulous idea of federation.

An important contributory factor in the failure of the Federal Council to fulfil its potential was the lack of leadership provided by Shakespeare himself. He had been the dominant figure in the Free Church movement during the war, and his vision and organising ability had provided the inspiration behind the Council's creation. From 1919 onwards, however, the combination of his poor health and the diversion of his energies towards Anglican/Free Church unity diminished his ability to take the project forward. Those who shared the leadership of the new movement with him, such as J. D. Jones and J. Scott Lidgett, did not possess either his passion for unity or his organising ability. They were therefore not able to make Free Church unity anything more than a distant ideal.

The Federal Council suffered because it neither had popular support at the local level, the kind of support that gave the National Council its strength, nor the confidence of the denominational authorities. To have developed into an effective ecclesiological body, more attention should have been given in its early years to establishing a real sense of unity and common purpose among its member Churches. Shakespeare did not bear responsibility for this failure alone, and many of the factors hindering the Council's success, including his own poor health, were clearly beyond his control. However, as the one whose vision brought it to birth, and who was entrusted with its leadership for its first two years, his contribution, or lack of it, was always bound to be crucial to the success of the whole enterprise.

4.4 Shakespeare and Reunion

Some of Shakespeare's achievements for church unity were substantial and lasting. Baptist Church House, the venue for many of the discussions between church leaders, was itself principally his responsibility. As an alternative venue to Lambeth Palace it had considerable value, not only practically, but also symbolically, as a substantial Free Church centre in London.

The importance of Shakespeare's bold vision of unity in the opening stages of the modern ecumenical movement has rarely been acknowledged. The Lambeth Appeal is rightly regarded as one of the milestones in the journey towards better inter-church relations in the twentieth century. It expressed the conviction that had been growing for many years, but came to the fore powerfully during the war, that a disunited Church could no longer be accepted with equanimity. In England, relations between representatives of the Free Churches and the Church of England were the central feature of the discussions in connection with the Appeal. Shakespeare's contribution to this process, both before and after the issuing of the Appeal, was vitally important, and makes him one of the most significant figures of early ecumenism.

Shakespeare's earliest, and arguably most concrete and practical achievement in the cause of church unity was the creation of the United Chaplaincy Board. It has proved its value ever since as a co-operative venture in providing pastoral and spiritual care for the armed services. The Baptist and the Congregationalist Unions have been its primary constituent denominations, both at its beginning, when leadership was provided by the two denominational secretaries, Shakespeare and Jones, and later, when Methodist involvement ceased after the unification of Methodism in 1932.

The establishment of the Federal Council, disappointing as it may have been in terms of the original vision, was nevertheless an important and permanent development in English church life. It provided an institutional framework within which the Free Church denominations could confer and, at times, act together. When the two Free Church Councils were united in 1941, the Federal Council was the model for the amalgamated body. It provided a necessary complement to the earlier National Council, whose informal and locally based structure was inadequate for the pursuit of any meaningful discussions about co-operation at the denominational level.

The discussions between the Federal Council and the Church of England following the Lambeth Appeal also had some positive value. Lockhart came to the conclusion that 'their importance perhaps lay not so much in anything that was said or in the measure of agreement discovered, as in the fact that they were held at all'.[183] The fact that the two Archbishops and Free Church leaders were able to meet and debate at such length, and in such depth, after two hundred and fifty years of official alienation and hostility, was, by any measure, a welcome development. The talks did also result in some concrete gains for future church relations. Areas of significant difference in ecclesiology, particularly in relation to the ministry, were identified and clarified. The issues the participants addressed have dominated inter-church discussions ever since. Considerable courage was shown by their willingness to seek a resolution of these differences, in view of the sometimes fierce opposition from their own churches. It is surprising, and to their credit, that they continued to try for as long as they did.

Apart from official negotiations at Lambeth Palace, personal contact between church leaders was established during the war, in a way that would have been inconceivable before 1914. The result was a deepening of understanding about the life and mission of the Church in England as a whole. For the first time, Anglican bishops and Nonconformist ministers were invited to participate in each other's services, albeit in a limited way. Many, even among those most aware of the obstacles to reunion were able to acknowledge a sense of fellowship between churches in the Church's mission to the nation.

Shakespeare's contribution to the cause of reunion was not altogether positive, however. Apart from the consequences within his own denomination, Shakespeare is chiefly vulnerable to criticism over the failure of the Federal Council to foster a greater sense of unity among the Free Churches. This was his central ambition before 1918, but few, if any, steps were taken towards it once the Council had been formed. Shakespeare's pre-occupation with the pursuit of wider unity with the Church of England was partly responsible for this. His goal was never a realistic one, facing insuperable difficulties over a range of questions, especially the ministry. What might have been achieved among the Free Churches was sacrificed for the sake of what proved to be impossible on the wider stage.

In the end, this dogged pursuit of the unachievable also damaged relations with the Church of England. Davidson and Lang were misled by Shakespeare's unjustified optimism about the prospects of reunion. Shakespeare portrayed the Federal Council as a reliable barometer of Free Church opinion as a whole, when its members were more favourably disposed towards reunion than most. When even the Council expressed reservations, he minimised their importance. He cherished every sign of hope for reunion, and was blind to any indications to the contrary. The result was inevitable disappointment, and a sense of waste about the time spent searching for a way forward, when the path turned out to be so comprehensively blocked.

Shakespeare's personal popularity and status, both within his own denomination and among the Free Churches generally, nevertheless remained high throughout the post war period. He had a track record of achieving what seemed to be impossible, and winning over sceptics by his powers of persuasion and willingness to compromise. He was by nature a man of action rather than thought, believing that courageous acts were more important in achieving change than theological debate. These factors seem to have driven him to persist in his pursuit of reunion beyond the point when most reasonable people would have recognised its impossibility.

Broader discussion on the search for church unity in the light of eighty years of ecumenical debate since the end of the Great War, and Shakespeare's place in that debate, cannot be undertaken here. The experience of those years would, perhaps, suggest that the pursuit of a deeper sense of Christian unity by means of the reform of church institutions at a national level is much more difficult than Shakespeare realised. Possibly the older National Free Church Council, with its local, unofficial character, might have been a more fruitful model for progress towards genuine unity than the Federal Council. There has, during the later years of this century, been a renewed emphasis on local and unofficial steps towards unity. In 1919, however, when a strong united effort at a national level seemed essential to meet the challenges facing the churches, the emphasis was placed elsewhere.

Shakespeare's legacy for church unity is therefore a mixed one. He was to a large degree responsible for getting church unity onto the churches' agendas, building on the opportunities created by the war. He was also, on the other hand, responsible for hindering progress towards deeper mutual understanding, as a result of his lack of realism about what unity really entailed.

1. Shakespeare was on the Council's committee from at least 1903 (*Free Church Yearbook* 1903 and 1908).
2. *BT* 18 March 1910. It was following the 1910 meeting that the Council Secretary, Thomas Law, died, and Shakespeare was approached about taking his place. See p. 68.
3. *BT* 14 October 1910. This was not by any means the first call for Baptist/Congregationalist union. The Congregationalist Joseph Parker had made one at a joint Assembly in 1901.
4. *BT* 8 March 1912.
5. *BT* 19 April 1912.
6. According to W. M. S. West, Shakespeare had been in correspondence with the Secretary of the Faith and Order Movement in America (Robert Gardiner) since 1910 (W. M. S West, 'The Reverend Secretary Aubrey (part 3)' *BQ* vol. 34 (July 1992) p. 320.
7. *BT* 9 January 1914.
8. *BT* 2 January 1914.
9. *BT* 20 March 1914.
10. West, 'Aubrey' p. 321. When the Faith and Order Conference did finally take place, in 1927, it was held in Lausanne. Shakespeare had retired from office by then and the English Baptists were either indifferent or antipathetic. No official Baptist Union delegates were sent.
11. According to John Thompson, there were 117 commissioned chaplains in the armed services in 1914. These consisted of 94 from the Church of England, 16 Roman Catholics and 7 Scottish Presbyterians. There were also 40 non-commissioned acting and honorary chaplains, including 18 Wesleyans and 3 English

Presbyterians. (see John Handby Thompson, 'The Free Church Army Chaplain 1830-1930' (*PhD* thesis, University of Sheffield: 1990) pp. 276-9).

12. BU Minute Book, 20 November 1900 and 15 January 1901.

13. BU Minute Book 16 July 1901 and 26 November 1903.

14. Frederic C. Spurr, *Some Chaplains in Khaki: An account of the work of Chaplains of the United Navy and Army Board* (second edition) (H. R. Allinson Ltd. and the Kingsgate Press: London, 1916) p. 23.

15. *Ibid.*, p. 26.

16. *Ibid.*, pp. 24-5. See also Thompson, *Chaplain* p. 293.

17. Mews and Thompson both cite Lloyd George's correspondence in referring to the row that took place in the Cabinet over the issue. Kitchener apparently viewed Nonconformists as 'superfluous and eccentric sects'. Cabinet approval was granted on 28 September 1914 (Stuart Paul Mews, 'Religion and English Society in the First World War' (*DPhil* thesis, University of Cambridge: 1973) p. 182; Thompson, 'Chaplain' p. 294-5.

18. *BT* 17 January 1919.

19. See, for example, BU Minute Book, 17 December 1915, 10 February 1916 and 25 July 1916 (N.B. the minutes of the United Board meetings are in the BU Minute Book).

20. BU Minute Book, 22 September 1915.

21. BU Minute Book, 18 August 1916.

22. Mews, 'Religion' p. 193.

23. Cited in Thompson, 'Chaplain' p. 280.

24. Spurr, p. 8.

25. Thompson, 'Chaplain' pp. 367-8.

26. D. S. Cairns, *The Army and Religion: An Enquiry and its Bearing on the Religious Life of the Nation* (MacMillan and Co. Ltd.: London, 1919) p. 419.

27. Spurr, p. 1.

28. BU Minute Book, 17 May 1917.

29. Mews, 'Religion' pp. 116-128.

30. *Ibid.*, pp. 318-321.

31. D. W. Bebbington, *The Nonconformist Conscience: Chapel and Politics: 1870-1914* (George Allen and Unwin: London, 1982) p. 160.

32. *BT* 8 and 15 December 1916.

33. Letter from Shakespeare to Addison dated 1 May 1917 (in the Lloyd George Papers, House of Lord's Record Office: ref. F/1/3/17)

34. *CW* 15 March 1928.

35. Letter from Lloyd George to Shakespeare dated 19 March 1918 (Lloyd George papers: ref. F/94/3/33).

36. Letter from Captain Frederick Guest to Lloyd George dated 13 July 1918, and a memorandum dated 29 November 1918 (Lloyd George papers: ref. F/21/2/27 and F/21/2/49).

37. *BT* 22 November 1918.

38. *BT* 13 December 1918.

39. There have been many studies of the changing role of Nonconformity in national life which describe this pattern of gradual integration, and the challenges it posed for the churches. These can be found, for example, in Bebbington, *Conscience*; Clyde Binfield, 'Hebrews'; Robert F. Cox, *English Churches*; Alan D. Gilbert,

Religion and Society in Industrial England: Church Chapel and Social Change 1740-1914 (Longman: London, 1976) and *The Making of Post-Christian Britain: A History of the Secularisation of Modern Society* (Longman: London, 1980); John Grant, *Free Churchmanship in England: 1870-1940 (with special reference to Congregationalism)* (Independent Press: London, no date); Robert F. Horton, *The Dissolution of Dissent* (Arthur H Stockwell: London, 1902); Mark D. Johnson, *Dissolution*; Stephen Koss, *Nonconformity in Modern British Politics* (B. T. Batsford: London, 1975); James Munson, 'A Study in Nonconformity'. See pp. 169-175.

40. Thompson, 'Chaplain' pp. 374-5.
41. BU Minute Book, 16 July 1918.
42. See Bebbington, 'Baptist Members of Parliament'.
43. BU Minute Book 21 November 1918 and 18 November 1920.
44. Thompson, 'Chaplain' pp. 440-1.
45. The *Baptist Times* did briefly raise the issue in August 1915, stating rather unconvincingly that, although being paid by the State, chaplains were placed under no direction and conditions with regard to their ministry, and that their appointment therefore contravened no Baptist principles (*BT* 20 August 1915).
46. Thompson, 'Chaplain' p. 348.
47. The Council published this in the same year (J. H. Shakespeare, *The Free Churches at the Cross Roads* (NCEFC: London, 1916)).
48. *Ibid.*, p. 7.
49. *Ibid.*, p. 11.
50. *Ibid.*.
51. *Ibid.*, p. 13.
52. *Ibid.*, p. 16.
53. *Ibid.*, p. 5.
54. *The Report of the Representatives appointed by the Evangelical Free Churches of England to consider the closer co-operation of the Free Churches* (NCEFC: 1917) p. 5. The authority and adequacy of this statement was to prove one of the most controversial aspects of the whole movement towards federation for Baptists.
55. *Ibid.*. pp. 20-1. This common basis included: the acceptance of the office of the Christian Ministry as a gift of Christ to his Church, and therefore divinely instituted; the duty of the Church to examine a person's call to Ministry; and recognition or ordination (by 'that branch of the Church in which the ministry is to be exercised') as a necessary condition of regarding a minister as duly appointed. There are a number of issues raised by this section of the Report, not least what is understood by the terms 'Church' and 'branch of the Church'. The implication is that the latter means 'denomination'. No reference is made to any specifically congregational basis for ministry.
56. *BT* 26 January 1917.
57. P. T. Forsyth, *The Church and the Sacraments* (Longmans, Green and Co.: London, 1917). See especially pp. 26-47.
58. *Ibid.*, p. 49.
59. BU Minute Book, 20 November 1917.
60. BU Minute Book, 14 February 1918.
61. *BT* 8 March 1918.
62. *BT* 12 April 1918.

63. *BT* 3 May 1918.
64. *Ibid.*.
65. *Ibid.*.
66. *HB* 1919 p. 22.
67. Adrian Hastings, *A History of English Christianity 1920-1985* (Collins: London, 1986) p. 98. Hastings describes Shakespeare as 'the most deeply and consistently ecumenical of all the Church leaders of the time'.
68. The view of H. Wheeler Robinson (*BT* 8 November 1918).
69. Shakespeare, *Churches* p. 9.
70. *Ibid.*, p. 72.
71. *Ibid.*, pp. 91-2.
72. *Ibid.*, p. 140.
73. *Ibid.*, pp. 143-4. Shakespeare says, 'the ordained ministry of women will, it is to be hoped, take its place in our churches in the near future' (p. 143).
74. *Ibid.*, p. 155.
75. *Ibid.*, p. 165.
76. *Ibid.*, p. 166.
77. *Ibld.*, p. 199.
78. *Ibid.*, p. 202.
79. *Ibid.*, p. 210.
80. *Ibid.*, p. 211.
81. *BW* 5 December 1918. A remarkable omission from *The Churches at the Cross Roads* was the lack of any consideration of how the divide between Baptists and most other churches over the legitimacy of infant baptism might be bridged. Cross writes that to enter into such a debate would "have been contrary to the stated irenic nature of the book" (*Baptism and the Baptists*, p. 49)
82. For example, see Henry Townsend, *The Claims of the Free Churches* (Hodder and Stoughton: London, 1949) p. 313.
83. In a letter to the Congregationalist J. D. Jones dated 11 January 1919 (see J. D. Jones, *Three Score Years and Ten* (Hodder and Stoughton: London, 1940) pp. 209-11).
84. See Carol A Devlin, 'The Eucharistic Procession of 1908: The Dilemma of the Liberal Government', *Church History* vol. 63 (September 1994) pp. 407-25.
85. See, for example, *BT* 5 January 1912. Disestablishment of the Church in Wales was agreed by Parliament in 1914, and came into effect in 1920.
86. One of these was a conference of church leaders (including Shakespeare) at Lambeth Palace in October 1914 to consider the implications of the outbreak of war (G. K. A. Bell, *Randall Davidson: Archbishop of Canterbury* (Oxford University Press: London, 1952) p. 744).
87. Tissington Tatlow Correspondence, Lambeth Palace Manuscripts vol. 1794.
88. *Ibid.*. Shakespeare's letter is dated 7 May 1915.
89. 'Towards Christian Unity - Interim Report', in SPCK, *Documents bearing on the Problem of Christian Unity and Fellowship 1916-1920* (The MacMillan Company: London, 1920) pp. 5-8.
90. Davidson Papers vol. 261 (LPL) pp. 69-72. The conversation took place on 23 March 1916. There is little doubt that the contents of such a conversation would have horrified even the most ecumenically minded of Shakespeare's Baptist colleagues.
91. *BT* 27 October 1916.

92. 'Towards Christian Unity - Second Interim Report', in SPCK, *Documents 1916-1920* pp. 9-14.
93. BU Minute Book, 22-5 April 1918.
94. *BT* 5 April 1918.
95. *BT* 23 August 1918.
96. *BT* 11 October 1918.
97. Resolutions from the First Mansfield Conference, in SPCK, *Documents 1916-1920* pp. 54-5.
98. A. J. Carlyle *et al* (eds.), *Towards Reunion: being contributions to mutual understanding by Church of England and Free Church writers* (Macmillan and Co.: London, 1919) pp. xiv-xv.
99. See 'Proposals for Reunion between the Church of England and the Wesleyan Methodist Church' in SPCK *Documents 1916-20* pp. 48-50, in which Winnington Ingram, the Bishop of London, in an address in February 1919, presents quite detailed suggestions for the union of the two churches, following two years of informal discussion. The *Baptist Times*, commenting on this, undoubtedly reflects Shakespeare's view in speaking against such a 'piecemeal' approach to reunion (*BT* 14 March 1919).
100. See BU Minute Book for those periods.
101. Richard Glover died on 26 March 1919.
102. BU Minute Book, 18 March 1919. It was at the meeting of the Council on this day that the resolutions agreed at the January Mansfield Conference were received (see p. 112). It seems likely that Glover's decision to move a resolution at the Assembly was in response to the conference. He received support in his stand from at least one other leading Baptist, the ex-President of the Union, Charles Brown. Brown appears to have modified his position to some extent after the March Council meeting, and to have acted as an intermediary between Shakespeare and Glover (see the letters from Brown to Glover dated 26 February and 18 March 1919 in the T. R. Glover correspondence (box 5)).
103. See the letter from Charles Brown to Glover dated 18 March 1919, in which Brown says Shakespeare was 'deeply moved' by Glover's notice of his resolution (T. R. Glover correspondence (box 5)).
104. See Shakespeare's letter to Glover dated 4 April 1919 (T. R. Glover correspondence (box 5)). According to Shakespeare, Glover had accused the committee appointed to look at the unity proposals of 'sedition' and spoke of the need to 'fight it out'.
105. T. H. Darlow, *Robertson Nicoll: Life and Letters* (Hodder and Stoughton: London, 1925) pp. 390-393. Clifford's letter is dated 22 February 1919. He says that he had avoided any open attack on Shakespeare out of respect for their friendship.
106. T. R. Glover correspondence (box 5). The letters from Clifford are dated 26 March and 14 April 1919.
107. T. R. Glover correspondence (box 5). Phillips wrote to Glover on 3 May 1919, after the Assembly.
108. *BT* 17 April 1919.
109. *BT* 2 May 1919.
110. *Ibid..*
111. *BT* 9 May 1919.
112. *Ibid..*
113. *Ibid..*

114. SPCK, *Documents 1916-1920* pp. 59-60.
115. *Ibid.* pp. 62-64.
116. *Ibid.* pp. 73-84.
117. *Ibid.* pp. 88-90.
118. Federal Council Minute Book, 30 May 1919.
119. The first meeting of the Nexus Committee took place in April 1920 (Federal Council Minute Book, 15 April 1920).
120. *Report of the First Federal Council of the Evangelical Free Churches of England* (FCEFC: London, 1919).
121. A meeting between James Marchant and Randall Davidson on 22 November 1918 was concerned with the presentation, which was originally to have been made in February 1919 (Davidson Papers vol. 261 (LPL) p. 164).
122. *BT* 7 November 1919.
123. *Ibid.*.
124. Randall Davidson *et al*, *Illuminated Address Presented to John Howard Shakespeare* (1919). (Shakespeare family private papers).
125. 'The Rev. John Howard Shakespeare, MA, DD, LlD. - A Retrospect by Mr. W. H. Ball MBE' p. 8, in the E. A. Payne papers (box A/3) (Angus library, Regent's Park College, Oxford).
126. The honour done to Shakespeare by Glasgow University was announced at the 1920 Assembly (*BT* 14 May 1920), and he was formally presented with a gown, hood and cap at the Council meeting in July (BU Minute Book, 13 July 1920).
127. The four articles of the Quadrilateral were the Holy Scriptures as 'the rule and ultimate standard of faith', the Apostles' and Nicene Creeds as statements of faith, the sacraments of baptism and the Lord's Supper and the Historic Episcopate. The Baptist Union regarded them at the time as an unpromising basis for discussion about reunion (see Payne, *Union* pp. 272-4).
128. *BT* 13 August 1920.
129. *BT* 20 August 1920.
130. Federal Council Minute Book, 21-3 September 1920.
131. Federal Council Minute Book, 21 October 1920.
132. Davidson papers vol. 261 pp. 381-2. The Wesleyans joined the Federal Council in the autumn of 1920. It is arguable that Shakespeare's insistence on a joint approach actually hindered progress that might have been made had the individual denominations been free to engage in conversations separately. One of the difficulties that dogged the conversations from this point on was the uncertainty (particularly from the Anglican side) about the nature of the relationship between the Free Church denominations and the committee actually conducting the negotiations.
133. Davidson papers vol. 261 p. 382.
134. Federal Council Minute Book, 8 December 1920 and 3-5 January 1921.
135. Federal Council Minute Book, 21 February 1921.
136. FCEFC, *The Free Churches and the Lambeth Appeal* (Religious Tract Society: London, 1921).
137. BU Minute Book, 21 April 1921.
138. *BT* 29 April 1921.
139. In fact, this intention never materialised. An improvement in health, and repeated requests that he reconsider, caused him to withdraw his notice of retirement in November (BU Minute Book, 15 November 1921). He remained in good health until the autumn of 1923 (see p. 153).

140. *BT* 29 April 1921.
141. J. G. Lockhart, *Cosmo Gordon Lang* (Hodder and Stoughton: London, 1949) p. 274.
142. *Ibid.*.
143. See G. K. A. Bell, *Documents on Christian Unity 1920-1924* (Oxford University Press: London, 1924) for the responses from the Baptist Union (p. 104), the Congregational Union (pp. 105-6) and the Methodist Churches (pp. 138-9) in 1921.
144. *BT* 1 April 1921.
145. T. R. Glover, *The Free Churches and Re-Union* (W. Heffer and Sons Ltd.: Cambridge, 1921) p. 51.
146. *Ibid.* (preface).
147. T. R. Glover, *Jesus in the Experience of Man* (Student Christian Movement: London, 1921) p. 164.
148. *Ibid.* p. 167.
149. *Ibid.* p. 170.
150. *Ibid.* p. 250.
151. His standing among Baptists was confirmed when he was elected to the Presidency of the Union in 1923.
152. He said this during a discussion on Episcopacy at the November 1921 conference (Headlam papers (Lambeth Palace MS 2628) pp. 230-40).
153. Davidson papers vol. 263 p. 235. Shakespeare expressed these opinions at a meeting on 23 March 1923.
154. Davidson papers vol. 262 p. 167. The memorandum is dated 3 October 1921.
155. *BT* 5 May 1922.
156. Bell, *Documents* pp. 143-151.
157. Shakespeare wrote to Davidson on 26 May 1922 giving his approval of the report (Davidson papers vol. 263 p. 107).
158. *BW* 8 June 1922.
159. BU Minute Book, 11 July 1922. The Yorkshire, East Midlands and Lancashire and Cheshire Associations had sent resolutions in opposition to various aspects of the interim report, including the proposed use of creeds, the continuing links between Church and State and the exclusion of the Salvation Army and the Quakers.
160. Bell, *Documents* pp. 151-155.
161. This sense of unreality is reflected in the agreement of the joint committee that the Federal Council's response to the interim report demonstrated 'general approval' of its contents. This was an optimistic, if not misleading, interpretation of events (Davidson papers vol. 263 p. 142).
162. Davidson papers vol. 263 p. 163f.
163. BU Minute Book 21 November 1922.
164. *BT* 22 December 1922.
165. The minutes of the Council Meeting that was held immediately prior to the 1923 Assembly record that Glover 'kindly consented' not to proceed with his motion on reunion (BU Minute Book, 20 March 1923).
166. *Daily News* 21 April 1923.
167. There is some confusion about the date that was originally planned for this (the third) conference at Lambeth Palace. There are earlier references in the BU Minute Book to plans for it to be held in December 1922 and March 1923.
168. Davidson papers vol. 263 p. 375.

169. Bell, *Documents* pp. 156-63.
170. *Ibid*. pp. 164-8.
171. Davidson papers vol. 264, p. 47.
172. *Ibid*. p. 60. The letter was written on 12 October 1923.
173. *Times* 27 September 1923.
174. The Malines conversations began on an informal basis in 1921, but did not receive Davidson's blessing until 1923. He did not want to make them public, but there was correspondence in the *Times* about them in October 1923. The matter was first raised at the Free Church/Anglican negotiations as a matter of concern at a committee meeting on 11 January 1924 (See Bell, *Davidson* pp. 1255-1299; Davidson papers vol. 264 pp. 90ff; Headlam papers (Lambeth Palace MS 2630) pp. 89ff).
175. According to the Minute Book of the Federal Council, Rededication Sunday was discussed at length in its first few months, but there is no reference to it after the meeting on 15 July 1920. It seems to have been eclipsed by the need to respond to the Lambeth Appeal.
176. Federal Council Minute Book, 21 September 1920.
177. *Ibid*., 22 April 1921.
178. *Ibid*., 26-8 September 1921.
179. *Ibid*., 3 November 1921.
180. *Ibid*., 26-8 September 1921.
181. *Ibid*., 24 November 1922.
182. *Ibid*., 17-19 September 1923 and 15-17 September 1924.
183. Lockhart, p. 274.

CHAPTER FIVE

Final Years at the Baptist Union

5.1 The Ministry

5.1.1 The Ministry of Women

The search for reunion was not Shakespeare's only concern during the post-war years. He was active in promoting other important developments within his own denomination. One of the most important of these was the move towards the acceptance of the ministry of women among Baptists, a cause Shakespeare had consistently supported from the start. A leading article appeared in the *Baptist Times* within a year of its acquisition by the Baptist Union headed 'Brains: Male and Female', supporting the growing pressure in some quarters for a wider recognition of the role of women in public and church affairs. 'Little by little', it said, in a remarkably contemporary manner, 'it is being recognised that civil rights and civil duties are not a question of sex'.[1] Shakespeare's motives were no doubt partly pragmatic. He saw women as a wasted resource within the church, and was particularly keen that they should be recruited for his fund-raising activities, during both the Twentieth Century Fund and the Sustentation Fund campaigns. His interest in the women question was, however, more than merely a device for raising money more effectively. Another *Baptist Times* leading article, in May 1901, in which the work of the Baptist Women's Century Fund League was commended, described the importance of the contribution women could make in the following terms:

> The world would be a very different place today if its recognition of this great factor in the progress of humanity had not been so tardy. That women are not as yet permitted to take their proper share in the life and work of our churches is, to our thinking, a relic of barbarism.[2]

In 1908 the Baptist Women's Home Work Auxiliary was formed, largely as a result of an initiative by Shakespeare. He invited Mrs. Russell James, the daughter of a friend of his, and who subsequently became national President of the organisation, to call a meeting of women with a view to starting its first branch in that year. In 1910 it was renamed the Baptist Women's League. Its object was 'the development and unification of women's work, both at home and abroad, throughout the Baptist denomina-

tion'.[3] Also in 1910, the Union agreed to allow the election of up to ten additional women to serve on the Union Council, over and above any elected
according to the provisions of the 1904 constitution.[4] The League was frequently called upon to help raise denominational funds. In an interview in
the *Baptist Times* in 1912, Mrs. James said that it had accepted the task of
raising £50,000 for the Sustentation Fund.[5] In January 1914, in order to meet
this objective, the League decided to visit 'all the members of the churches
and congregations throughout the Baptist Union' to promote the simultaneous collection in aid of the Fund planned for March that year.[6]

A Baptist Deaconesses' Home and Mission had been founded in London
in 1890, under the auspices of the London Baptist Association, following the
example of other denominations, and particularly inspired by the example of
women officers in the Salvation Army.[7] It became independent in 1894. Its
work in central London was mainly with needy women and children. Its
Superintendent was F. B. Meyer, whose national reputation enabled him to
raise the funds it needed. In the years immediately before the war its work
expanded beyond the capital by means of the Caravan Mission, which was
supported by the Baptist Union's Home Work Fund. As the work spread, the
idea of a national organisation of Baptist deaconesses, supported by the
whole denomination grew.[8] In January 1917 a report of the work of 'The
Baptist Sisters' appeared in the *Baptist Times*, commending their ministry in
slums and hospitals as well as their own Home, and appealing both for
financial support and for young women to join the movement. At that time
there were 48 deaconesses attached to various churches.[9]

During 1918 the possibility of the Deaconesses' Home and Mission being
formally adopted by the Union was raised at a meeting at Baptist Church
House. Representatives of the Baptist Women's League, as well as the deaconesses and the Union, attended the meeting. One of the objectives of this
proposal was to enable women to be properly trained for 'the home service
of the Baptist Denomination'.[10] In April 1919 the same committee resolved
that 'a Department of the Baptist Union, including the Baptist Women's
League, to be known as the Baptist Sisterhood, be established for the selection and training of women for various forms of service in the Churches and
organisations affiliated with the Baptist Union and especially for work
among the poor'. Responsibility for the existing work of the Deaconesses'
Home and Mission would be taken over by the new department. A
'Settlement' would be created whose function would primarily be to provide
training. Miss Kathleen Dunn was recommended as the Lady Warden of the
Settlement.[11]

These suggestions were approved by the Union Council a month later and
the decisions announced at that year's Assembly. The Sisterhood
Committee first met in June 1919, and in July the Union agreed to buy a
house in Hampstead to be used as a 'Sisterhood Training College'.[12] The
Sisterhood functioned in a way that was quite distinct from the regular pas-

toral ministry, mainly because of its close links with the Union, and its formation amounted to a new form of ministry within the denomination. There is no record of any debate over the significance of this, nor of the change in title from Deaconess to Sister. The Home and Mission was now no longer an independent Baptist organisation for women church workers based in London, but had become an official Baptist Sisterhood, functioning under the authority of the Union.

In *The Churches at the Cross Roads*, Shakespeare had expressed the hope that 'the ordained ministry of women will . . . take its place in our churches in the near future'.[13] He personally took up the cause of the new Baptist Sisterhood in two of a series of articles in the *Baptist Times* in the autumn of 1919. He referred to the increasing pressure from the women themselves to make the Deaconesses' Mission a denominational enterprise, and the need to find a way of enabling girls and women to 'realise their vocation' within the denomination. He specifically - and characteristically - cited the example of the Wesleyans and the Church of Scotland, both of which had established Orders of Deaconesses. A two year training course would be undertaken by the women who were accepted as Sisters, partly at the Sisterhood's own Settlement, and partly at Regent's Park College. A variety of work would be undertaken by the Sisters, he wrote, but a special priority would be given to putting 'Christ-like women in slums and poor areas'. 'Those who devote themselves entirely to the work of the Churches', he went on, 'will be set apart as Sisters at a session of the Baptist Union, and will then wear the uniform of the Sisterhood, dark navy blue with a white cross'. He appealed for gifts towards the £25,000 capital sum needed to fund the new venture.[14]

In October 1919 Regent's Park College and the two London Congregational colleges (New College and Hackney College) were re-opened after the war in a joint ceremony. For the first time women appeared on the list of students. The *Baptist Times* reported that 'the war-time service of womanhood had made previous restrictions impossible, and the colleges now throw their doors open without distinction to all who are truly qualified to hold positions of influence and leadership in Christian service'.[15] It was not practicable to fulfil this statement of intent immediately, and it was not until 1924 that a woman's name appears on the list of students at the college seeking settlement in a church.[16]

The Union needed to raise money for the Sisterhood if it was to be a success. The opportunity came in 1920, when a joint appeal to the denomination for £250,000 was made with the Baptist Missionary Society. This 'Baptist United Fund' was launched at the 1920 Assembly and successfully raised by the end of the year. The Council approved a proposal from the Sisterhood Committee that £20,000 of the Union's 50% share of the total would be designated for the equipment and maintenance of the Baptist Women's Training College and the Sisterhood.[17] With the assurance of financial backing from the Union, the Sisterhood Committee met frequently during the course of 1920 to agree procedures for the engagement of Sisters by churches and arrangements for the opening of Havelock Hall, the new training college in Hampstead. It was officially opened in October.

In 1921 the development of the Sisterhood received a setback when the Principal of the newly opened Havelock Hall, Kathleen Dunn, resigned. This was, according to the Minute Book, on health grounds, and there is no definite evidence of any other reason.[18] However, it seems likely that other factors influenced her decision to go. Dunn's resignation took place just six months after the college's opening and only two years after her initial appointment. There were no prior suggestions of ill health. Most significantly of all, Dunn's letter of resignation was written just six days after the Council had decided to implement a new scheme for the Union's administration of the college and Sisterhood and reconstitute the Sisterhood Committee.[19] Whatever the real reasons for Dunn's resignation, it was not until over two years later, in June 1923, after a long and difficult search for a successor, that another Principal, J. J. Arthur, was appointed.[20] During the intervening months, in which the Sisterhood Committee's time was inevitably spent largely in the search for a suitable candidate, little progress in developing the Sisterhood itself was possible.

The principle that women could exercise an acceptable and recognised ministry among Baptists was rarely challenged. The value of the work of deaconesses had been acknowledged for many years, and the service of women missionaries, especially under the auspices of the Baptist Zenana Mission since its formation in 1866,[21] but also within the general work of the missionary society, was widely appreciated. The recognition of the ministry of women as equal to that of men was more difficult to achieve, however. Their inclusion on the Union's ministerial list raised administrative and financial complications for the Union over issues such as sustentation and pensions. More importantly, most churches would not consider inviting a woman to be their minister, and it was unrealistic for the Union to recognise and support those who were very unlikely to secure a pastorate.

A Union committee to look into accepting women for general ministerial training had been set up by the Council in 1918.[22] The question was also part of the remit of a Commission of Enquiry on the Ministry that first met at the end of 1919.[23] In May 1920 the *Baptist Times* reported an event that marked 'a new epoch in our Denominational history' and set 'a seal upon the labours of our women' when Margaret Hardy was invited to preach at the Regent's Park Church in London.[24] It was probably more the status of this particular church than the fact of a woman preaching that made it a significant event. In 1922 the first woman, Edith Gates, was accepted on the list of probationer ministers, having served as a minister in Oxfordshire since 1918, and having fulfilled the conditions of admission as a non-collegiate candidate. By 1925 there were two other women on the Union's lists of ministers, one other probationer and one on the full ministerial list, and in 1926 the Council formally gave official support to their accreditation, issuing a statement declaring that gender should not be a bar to admission to the Baptist pastoral ministry. This support was qualified by the acknowledgement that the difficulties of securing an invitation from a church were very considerable.[25]

Shakespeare was keen that the ministry of women should be accepted by his fellow Baptists, and officially recognised by the Union. He played a decisive role in creating the Baptist Women's League and the Sisterhood, and promoted both organisations through the pages of the *Baptist Times*. He saw in the Sisterhood an opportunity to found a new order of ministry for women not primarily linked with the local churches, but with the Union. He arranged for them to be 'stationed' in local churches under the overall direction of the Union's Sisterhood Committee. In the two years leading up to the spring of 1921 the matter received frequent and urgent attention in the committee rooms of Baptist Church House, and in the pages of the *Baptist Times*. After that, however, the impetus slackened. It is possible that Shakespeare realised, following the publication of the Lambeth Appeal in the summer of 1920, that the ordination of women to the ministry would create an insuperable obstacle to reunion with the Church of England, although there is no evidence that the issue was raised by either side in the Lambeth Palace conversations. It is also possible that insistence on the close control of the Sisterhood by the Union had a part in Kathleen Dunn's resignation and the stifling of its development.

Both the Deaconess movement[26] and the Baptist Women's League have played an important role in Baptist life throughout most of the twentieth century. Whether the creation of the Sisterhood helped or hindered the cause of women's ordination to the Baptist ministry, Shakespeare's professed objective in *The Churches at the Cross Roads*, however, is not easy to assess. Its very different character from the rest of the recognised Baptist ministry tended to mark women out as exercising a ministry that was quite distinct from that of men. It represented a pattern of ministry that Shakespeare would have liked to have seen adopted throughout the denomination, for men as well as women. He argued, with only limited success, for Union control of the selection, training, deployment and support of all recognised ministers before the war. His plans for the Sisterhood were an attempt to put this into effect among women. It was an unrealistic ambition, even within the limited sphere of the Sisterhood, and the attempt to achieve it may well have done as much harm as good to his objective of the general acceptance of women in ministry. The development of the Sisterhood in 1919 and 1920 was nevertheless a significant part of Shakespeare's contribution to the denomination and its ministry. His advocacy of the place of women in ministry shows him as a visionary in an area, which, like the pursuit of church unity, was to become increasingly important as the century progressed. The fact that he was probably misguided in the way he sought to realise this vision should not obscure the importance of the vision itself.[27]

5.1.2 Ministerial Support

The demands on the Union's Sustentation Fund grew rapidly in the immediate post-war period. This was mainly because of the increasing number of
churches applying to the Union for help with their ministers' stipends: by
1921 583 were grant-aided.[28] The Sustentation Scheme was based on the
principle that the Union was ultimately responsible for ensuring at least a
minimum stipend level for all accredited ministers. In 1917 this minimum
was fixed at £130 a year.[29] To qualify for a grant, churches had to meet certain conditions set by the Union, including the provision of a minimum proportion of the stipend. Another source of pressure on the Fund was infla-
tion, which after 1919 rapidly eroded the levels of stipend as well as its capital resources.

In July 1919 the Fund's Executive Committee asked a specially formed
committee to explore ways in which the minimum stipend allowed under the
Scheme could be raised to a more realistic level, following an appeal from a
number of associations.[30] Comparisons elsewhere usually showed that, of the
main Free Church denominations, the Baptist minimum stipend was significantly lower than the rest.[31] Frequent letters appeared in the *Baptist Times* on
the subject of ministerial support, including one in September 1919 from
Shakespeare himself and Herbert Marnham, the Union President, a copy of
which was also sent to every church secretary. They asked churches to
devote the proceeds of their harvest thanksgiving services as a special gift to
the ministry. The letter referred to the 'grinding poverty' in many manses,
where there was often 'not enough to eat'.[32] It was becoming increasingly
clear that the Scheme was not succeeding in meeting the needs of the poor-
est ministers, and the appeals for adequate payment seemed no less urgent
than before the Scheme had come into operation. The low level of the official minimum meant that the problem of widely differing stipend levels,
depending on the affluence of a minister's church, was as great as ever.

The Fund's income came from three sources: interest on its capital, money
forwarded to the Union each year by the associations, and the annual simultaneous collection. It had been estimated in 1915 that this should provide
about £25,000 a year in total, sufficient to meet the expected demands on the
Fund. It soon proved inadequate, however. Appeals for more generous giving to the simultaneous collection became more urgent from 1918 onwards,
and the amount raised in this way substantially improved in 1919 and 1920,[33]
but it was still not enough to meet the growing demand. Minimum stipend
levels were felt to be shamefully low, but it seemed impossible to raise them.
Another matter of concern was the totally inadequate financial provision for
retired ministers through the Union's Annuity Fund, although this was something that would have to be dealt with separately.

Apart from appealing for more generous giving to the simultaneous collection, the Union's response to this crisis of ministerial pay was two-fold.

First, a Commission of Enquiry on the Ministry was set up at the end of 1919 with a wide ranging brief to look at the recruitment, training and recognition of ministers, and the ministry of lay people and women.[34] Secondly, and with more immediate effect, there was a joint financial appeal with the Baptist Missionary Society for the primary purpose, as far as the Union was concerned, of raising an extra £100,000 for the Sustentation Scheme's capital fund. The joint appeal, given the title 'The Baptist United Fund', was first announced in the *Baptist Times* in April 1920. The hope was expressed that the money raised, along with proposed new regulations for the operation of the Scheme, could make a virtual doubling of the minimum annual stipend level possible.[35] A goal of a £250 minimum stipend was accepted by the Assembly that year, and the appeal officially launched. Marnham warned the Assembly that if the commitment to raising stipends were to be realised, it would require the grouping of churches. Individual churches not able to meet their financial obligations under the Scheme should not issue an invitation to a minister, he said.[36]

The money raised by the Baptist United Fund was to be divided equally between the Union and the missionary society, with £125,000 going to each. It was a novel experiment in co-operation, and met a critical need of both organisations at that time for more money. Baptist giving to support overseas missionaries had traditionally been generous, and the Union probably stood to gain most by such a link. The Union's share would be divided three ways - £100,000 for the Sustentation Fund, £20,000 for the Sisterhood's Havelock Hall, and £5,000 to support Baptist work on the continent of Europe. In July 1920, Shakespeare wrote in the *Baptist Times* that raising the money was not to be undertaken over the same time scale as for previous appeals. The aim was to raise it quickly, mainly during the course of a single week in November. This was achieved, and before the end of the year, the *Baptist Times* could announce that over £260,000 had been given or promised.[37] The official minimum stipend could not, however, be raised to £250, as had been hoped. The figure eventually agreed was just £160.[38]

5.1.3 Lay Ministry

As well as its involvement with the ordained ministry, the Union took on greater responsibility for the supervision of lay ministers after the war. In October 1919 the question of the 'recognition of lay pastors' was raised at the Union's Ministerial Recognition Committee by J. C. Carlile.[39] This became an increasingly important matter over the next few years, partly because of the difficulty of smaller churches in affording the required contribution towards the stipend of an accredited minister. Although a Local Preachers' Federation had existed in the Union for some time, the question of official Union recognition or accreditation had never been raised before. In April 1920 Carlile, writing in the *Baptist Times*, explained why the

Sustentation Scheme made the formal recognition of lay preachers an urgent matter. The grouping of churches, he said, and 'to some extent the adoption of a circuit system', was an inevitable consequence of the raising of stipends under the Scheme, and would lead in turn to a greater need for lay preachers to support the fully accredited ministers. He pleaded for a new Lay Preachers' Department of the Union, to supervise a proper scheme of training and recognition.[40] The question of lay ministry was one of the matters that had been referred to the Commission on the Ministry in 1919. It was not until late in 1921, however, that there was any real progress over the question of Union recognition of lay ministers. The Local Preachers' Federation agreed with the suggestion then brought to it that it should be 'strengthened and developed' and that an accredited list of Baptist local preachers be drawn up.[41]

In 1922 it was decided that, in order to achieve this objective of strengthening the organisation of local preachers, the Local Preachers' Federation should be made a more integral part of the Union's direction of the ministry as a whole. A list of recognised lay pastors, together with evangelists, would be published each year in the *Baptist Handbook*.[42] Union recognition of local preachers would depend, among other things, on the successful completion of an examination. An effort would be made to bring all the associations' local preachers' organisations under the umbrella of the central federation.[43] In 1923 consideration turned to how the recognition of local preachers should be marked by the churches, associations and Union. It was recommended that after services of 'dedication and recognition' in their home church, newly qualified lay preachers should be solemnly commended 'to the grace of God for the work to which they have been called and given themselves', at association and Union Assemblies.[44]

Discussion in the Union in and around 1922 over non-ordained ministries reflected changes in the approach to the ministry generally. One noteworthy feature was the unexplained variation in the use of the terms 'local' and 'lay'. The 'Local Preachers' Federation' had been listed in the annual Handbook as a department of the Union since 1905.[45] The term 'local preacher' continued to be used until 1921, but by the summer of 1922, the Union's committees had abandoned it in favour of 'lay preacher'.[46] This change was not accompanied by any debate about the distinction between ordained and other ministers, but it is significant in the light of the whole thrust of ministerial reforms within the denomination under Shakespeare. The use of 'local' implies a distinction between the two types of ministry that is primarily geographical. 'Lay', on the other hand, is explicitly ecclesiological, heightening the significance of ordination and creating a clear lay-clerical divide in ministry. Such a distinction was alien to traditional Baptist understandings of ministry, which emphasised the priesthood of all believers and the non-sacramental character of ordination. This change in terminology, then, reflected an increasingly clerical understanding of the ordained ministry.

The replacement of the term 'local' by 'lay' also revealed a tendency towards centralised control and direction of non-ordained ministers, as had largely happened in the case of ordained ministers. The Union sought to raise the status and quality of local preachers by means of a national scheme of training and recognition, much as had been done for the ordained ministry. Their ministry might be limited to a particular geographical area, as indeed, in practice, was that of many ordained ministers, but the new arrangements were an attempt to assert that proper authority to minister within the denomination could only be given by the Union. The local character of their ministry was no longer so clear under these circumstances. It is difficult to avoid the impression of a national hierarchy of officially recognised ministers, centred on Baptist Church House, involving the ten Area Superintendents, whose main task was to supervise the deployment of the ordained ministers, the ordained and accredited ministers themselves, and the recognised lay preachers. There was in practice no fundamental ecclesiastical or functional distinction between lay and ordained ministers, nor between services of 'dedication and recognition' for lay preachers and ordination. Apart from the fact that they were given different titles and appeared on different Union lists, the main differences between them were administrative, such as the length and rigour of training required, the recognition procedures and the provision of financial support, rather than ones based on ecclesiological principle.

Two features of the traditional understanding of the church among Baptists meant that the attempt to give formal Union recognition to lay ministers was bound to be fraught with difficulty. One was the emphasis on the priesthood of all believers, according to which ministry was the possession of the whole church, rather than of any particular group within it. Giving those who had been ordained and accredited for ministry a distinct status within the denomination was difficult enough to achieve. Extending the same practice to those who ministered in a lay capacity was even more difficult, for it could imply that only certain authorised church members were able to exercise an acceptable ministry. The other was the still strong congregational understanding of the church, according to which judgement about the acceptability of any particular ministry lay, in the end, with the local church. Where questions of financial support and settlement were not relevant, the Union's ability to intervene was severely limited.

5.1.4 Accreditation

Significant though the moves towards a formalisation of a Baptist lay ministry were, the accreditation of ordained ministers was a more pressing concern. In November 1920 the Ministerial Recognition Committee began looking at the possibility of tightening up conditions for accreditation, motivated partly by the Union's increasing difficulty of meeting the demands put on the Sustentation Fund. One of the greatest difficulties resulted from the unwillingness of the colleges to allow the Union any control over the number of ministerial candidates they admitted for training. The committee took steps to try and ensure that all ministerial candidates accepted the Union's rules at the start of their training, and wrote to the colleges to that effect.[47]

In July 1921 H. Wheeler Robinson, recently appointed Principal of Regent's Park College, responding to what he saw as the decline in the quality of suitable candidates, pleaded for 'a new emphasis on the dignity and status of the home ministry'. He proposed an annual Induction Service at the Assembly, along similar lines to the missionary society's Valediction Service.[48] The Commission of Enquiry on the Ministry took up Wheeler Robinson's suggestion, and at its meeting in November recommended that ministers joining the accredited list should be presented to the Assembly and 'commended to God'. The Commission also made a number of other recommendations, including the adoption by the Union of a statement on the ministry and ordination based on the Free Church Federal Council's Declaration of Faith, and the tightening up of conditions for non-collegiate candidates entering the ministry.[49] In January 1922 it reconsidered the nature of the ceremony marking the inclusion of a minister in the Union's accredited list, and the wording of its recommendation was strengthened. It was agreed that 'all ministers passing from the Probationary List to the Ministerial List . . . should be set apart to the ministry of the Church within the Baptist Union in a service of consecration and prayer'.[50] Its recommendations were accepted by the Council on the following day.

In March 1922 the Council also agreed to changes in the ministerial recognition rules, chiefly aimed at making it more difficult for non-collegiate ministers to be accredited. They were required to be under 35 years old, to give evidence of three years satisfactory pastoral work, and to pass an examination set by the Union, before joining the list of probationers. After at least another three years ministry and a second examination, they could join the ministerial list.[51] The proposals were brought to the 1922 Assembly, where they faced substantial opposition, and were referred back to the committee for further consideration without a vote being taken. The imposition of an upper age limit was a particularly contentious suggestion.[52]

In September and November 1922 the Ministerial Recognition Committee attempted to find a compromise between the Union's need to tighten up entry requirements for admission to the accredited list and the Assembly's resistance to raising barriers for admission to the ministry. After three meetings it could only agree that 'an exhaustive enquiry into the question of the ministry, and especially as to the training of the ministry' should be undertaken.[53] The committee appointed by the Council to do this met over three days in January 1923. It drew up a compromise, and with one or two minor amendments, its recommended course of action was supported by both the Council and the 1923 Assembly.

On the question of relationships between the Union and the colleges, and the need to secure a higher standard of candidates, the special committee agreed on the formation of a standing joint committee, to be given the title of the United Collegiate Board. It also agreed that a ceremony at the annual Assembly should be held to mark the accreditation of new ministers, carefully avoiding controversial terminology, such as the use of the term ordination, simply suggesting it should be 'an appropriate service'. It recommended that the proposed upper-age limit for non-collegiate candidates should be abandoned. It also drew up a statement on ordination. One of the sentences is this statement, urging that no minister should 'take part in, or otherwise sanction, the ordination of a pastor to a Baptist Church who is not duly accredited', proved contentious and was later omitted.[54]

The opening section of the statement on the Ministry and Ordination, as agreed by the 1923 Assembly, was worded as follows:

Affirming the doctrine of the priesthood of all believers and the obligation resting upon them to fulfil their vocation according to the gift bestowed upon them:

By the *Ministry* we mean an office within the Church of Christ (not a sacerdotal order) conferred through the call of the Holy Spirit and attested by a particular or local Church.

By *Ordination* we mean the act of the Church by which it delegates to a person ministerial functions which no man can properly take upon himself.[55]

It went on to say that ordination should take place in the church to which the minister was called, preferably after the approval of the appropriate association. It also made provision for the ordination of ministers other than to the pastorate of a local church.

The 1923 attempt to define what Baptists meant by 'the ministry' and 'ordination', brief as it was, was important in their developing understanding of these key concepts. It became an important reference point for the denomination for many years afterwards, being printed annually in the *Baptist Handbook*.[56] It gave formal sanction to the use of terms about which there had been considerable ambivalence, especially since the middle of the nineteenth century. Baptists had always rejected a sacramental or priestly view of ministry, and in their eagerness to oppose Anglo-Catholicism had sometimes turned their backs on the high estimation of the pastor's place in local church life characteristic of their earlier history.[57] The 1923 statement is indicative more of a move towards a catholic view of ministry, however, than a return to the older Baptist concept of ministry, as the reference to 'an office within the Church of Christ' made clear.

The statement was also important within the particular context of Shakespeare's reforms, and especially for his commitment to church unity. In asserting that Baptists took the ministry and ordination seriously as important elements of their ecclesiology, it helped meet doubts expressed about this by members of the Church of England in the reunion discussions at this time.[58] On the other hand, the statement's clear emphasis on the role of the local church in ordination, and its lack of reference to the Union, or any form of wider recognition or accreditation, showed signs of a retreat from Shakespeare's moves towards the centralisation of the ministry. The omission of the special committee's original sentence urging ministers not to sanction the ordination of unaccredited candidates was very significant in this regard. The role of the wider church in ordination was limited simply to the 'desirability' of the local association's approval of any ordinations.

On balance, then, the acceptance by the 1923 Assembly of this statement on the ministry, and its support for the committee's recommendations on ministerial recognition, must be regarded as significant reversals for Shakespeare. Two of his main goals were to draw Baptists closer to the Anglicans in their practice of ministry, and to reduce substantially the opportunities available for non-college trained candidates to become accredited ministers. He achieved some progress over the former, but taken as a whole, no substantial advances were really made towards either goal.

A sense of uncertainty hung over the ministry. Shakespeare's attempts to overcome the difficulties of recognition and support by means of greater involvement by the Union had met with only limited success. At a meeting of the officers of the Union in April 1923 Shakespeare painted a gloomy picture of the state of the denomination. Among many problems he outlined, there was, he said, a 'restlessness' over ministerial pensions and 'a dearth of suitable candidates for the ministry'. Yet another special committee was set up.[59] At the Assembly a few days later the incoming President, W. E. Blomfield, gave his address on 'The Ministry and the Churches'. He bemoaned the poor quality of ministerial candidates and the still unacceptably high proportion of ministers without any specialist training, 800 out of a total of 2,000, according to his figures. 'We must enthrone in the minds of our churches a worthy conception of the ministerial office', he said, and take concerted action to secure a trained ministry.[60] It was almost as if there had been no progress since the same pleas had been made before the war.

The difficulties of the Union in trying to take over responsibility for all recognised ministers is further illustrated by a decision forced on it in July 1922. An important element of the 1916 Scheme was the Union's task of stationing ministers who were unable to secure an invitation from a church in pastorless churches for twelve months. The Superintendents concluded in 1922 that this was no longer feasible, and the policy was abandoned.[61] There were still calls for a greater degree of co-ordinated, centralised control over the ministry, for example by Blomfield at the 1923 Assembly, but this ideal seemed further than ever from fulfilment.

One aspect of the 1916 Scheme had, however, proved generally success-ful. This was the mechanism for ministerial settlement operated by the Superintendents. It made few financial demands on the Union, and as long as no element of compulsion was introduced, it did not fundamentally chal-lenge the right of the local church to call its own minister, nor the right of the ministers to accept or reject an invitation from a church. The Superintendents met on a monthly basis with Shakespeare at Baptist Church House, and by the end of the war were making recommendations about min-isterial movement on a significant scale.[62] The numbers increased as time went on.[63] A lot depended on how sensitively the Superintendents exercised their responsibilities in this regard. In spite of some initial suspicion, there is no evidence that the process invited any real controversy, and seems to have been well received. The Superintendents themselves were from the start intended to have a greater role than simply assisting ministerial settle-ment, and were frequently unofficially, and seemingly affectionately, described as Baptist bishops.[64] Shakespeare involved them in a wide range of matters apart from settlement issues, including the raising of the annual collection for the Sustentation Fund and the grouping of churches.

5.1.5 Evangelism

In 1922 and 1923 there was a renewed emphasis on the need for the denom-ination to take up the challenge of evangelism. Shakespeare himself, throughout the last year of his active time in office, made this a priority. One of the things that impressed itself each year upon Baptists, and all the other Free Church denominations, was that their slow but steady decline, that had begun in 1907, was showing no signs of being reversed. The end of the war brought no respite to this discouraging trend, confounding the hopes of many. Membership figures for English Baptists in 1920 were 10,000 down on those for 1914, and although there was some small advances in the early twenties, the pre-war levels were never regained. Currie gives the figure of Baptists in England as 264,923 in 1914 and 254,908 in 1920 (the peak was 267,737 in 1907). The number did not reach 260,000 again.[65]

It was hoped that the implementation of the 1916 Scheme would lead to a reversal of the pre-war decline by improving the effectiveness of the min-istry. The fact that this did not happen resulted in greater financial pressure on the Sustentation Fund, and this was another reason for attention to the need for greater efforts in outreach through evangelism. The large number of ministers in smaller churches supported by the Union gave rise to concern about their apparent lack of growth, and their apparently limited impact on their areas. There were accusations that the Sustentation Fund was keeping some 'duffers' in the ministry.[66] In March 1922 the Fund's Executive Committee decided to send a letter to all aided ministers in churches of under 60 members urging greater efforts in evangelism and among young people.

Concern was expressed that 'in some instances, even in the midst of considerable populations, the work of the Church seems to be absolutely stagnant'. The committee looked at a number of individual churches that were causing particular concern. It concluded that, in one case, 'a more aggressive minister should be appointed', and in another, suggested that 'a little more energy be put into the work'. It was decided by the committee to arrange a series of area conferences, to which all aided ministers would be invited.[67] In July Shakespeare conferred with the Superintendents during a five-day residential meeting in Brighton. He secured their support and co-operation in organising the proposed conferences. He also addressed them 'with regard to the condition of the Churches and the work of the Superintendents, after which details were given by each Superintendent as to what was being done in his Area to carry through the campaign of evangelism'.[68]

In November 1922 the *Baptist Times* printed a letter from Shakespeare to all ministers entitled 'Evangelization: Methods and Suggestions', in which he listed a number of suggested approaches to evangelism and gave information about suitable material available from Baptist Church House.[69] During November and December the newspaper included several special reports of evangelistic activity undertaken by the churches. During the same period Shakespeare and T. S. Penny, the chairman of the Superintendents' Board, attended the area conferences of aided ministers organised by the Superintendents to enquire about evangelistic activity and to urge the ministers to greater efforts.

These conferences gave rise to considerable controversy. In January the Council received a strongly worded letter from the Yorkshire Association protesting at 'the invidious distinctions being made between members of the ministry on matters of common interest', and expressing the hope that this was not the official policy of the Baptist Union. Similar complaints were received from other associations in the North of England. In response, the Council expressed its support for Shakespeare and Penny, and justified the decision to involve only grant-aided ministers on the grounds that the Union had a duty to ensure the effective use of denominational funds.[70] In February Shakespeare and Penny briefed the Superintendents on the conferences, and gave specific comments on a number of individual situations, including in at least one case the recommendation that the Union's grant be discontinued at the end of that year.[71]

The autumn evangelistic campaign, and Shakespeare's experiences during his attendance at the area conferences, did little to reassure him about the state of the denomination. There was an air of despondency emanating from Baptist Church House during the spring of 1923 over both the ministry and the churches' evangelistic efforts, intimately connected to each other in Shakespeare's mind. The *Baptist Times* wrote of the need for a 'healthy discontent', outlining some of the more critical inadequacies of the denomination.[72] The newspaper was keen not to implicate Shakespeare himself in the growing sense of despondency in the denomination. A fortnight later it published a eulogy that went even further than its previous tributes, saying,

> How greatly we rejoice that Dr. Shakespeare continues with us, and that his health has been so wonderfully maintained! . . . It is not an exaggeration to say that that our beloved leader is in the very fullness of his powers. His long experience and his devoted service have mellowed and deepened his life, so that his recent conferences with aided pastors were nothing short of a benediction.[73]

Arrangements for a major conference in January 1924 were put in place, at which the most critical issues could be addressed. In the event, this had to be postponed because of Shakespeare's breakdown in health in the autumn, and he was never able to participate in the thorough-going assessment of denominational problems that he had planned.

5.2 Resignation

In April 1921, following the death of his friend George Gould,[74] the publication of T. R. Glover's hostile *The Free Churches and Re-Union* and a long period of trying ill health, Shakespeare informed the Superintendents that he intended to retire at the 1922 spring Assembly. This was due to take place shortly after his 65th birthday.[75] The Superintendents greeted this news with 'consternation'. When he told the Council a week later, it immediately and unanimously passed a resolution 'deeply regretting' Shakespeare's decision, and expressed the hope that he would be able to continue in office 'for a considerable time to come'.[76] Shakespeare nevertheless announced at the Assembly that he would not be seeking re-election as Secretary in twelve month's time. He said he had achieved his two main objectives, the erection of a denominational headquarters in London and the establishment of the Sustentation Fund.[77]

In July, however, Shakespeare was able to tell the Council that the previous two weeks had seen a marked improvement in his health. 'He had regained the faculty of natural sleep, and with that the black cloud of depression which had rested upon his mind and heart had been lifted'. Many of the associations had written to urge him to withdraw his threatened resignation, and a resolution expressing the hope that he would continue was passed by the Council 'with great acclamation'.[78] Following an optimistic consultation with a medical specialist in September he told the November Council meeting that he would be fit enough to continue in office, and offered to withdraw his notice of resignation. This was accepted with enthusiasm. In spite of his promise to delegate as much work as possible, and to give up most of his outside engagements, his level of activity showed no signs of diminishing.[79] For the next two years Shakespeare's health remained reasonably good.

At about the same time as Shakespeare's continuance in office beyond 1922 was announced, an article appeared on the front page of an American Baptist journal, *The Western Recorder,* denouncing Shakespeare and other leading figures in the Union for their involvement in the reunion discussions with the Church of England. They were accused of endeavouring to establish by law a Free Church of England, in which episcopal ordination would be required of all Nonconformist ministers. Doubt was cast on their personal integrity in trying to push this through. Subsequent issues of the *Western Recorder* also questioned their doctrinal orthodoxy. In January 1922 a summary of the contents of these articles was given in the *Baptist Times*, and their author, A. C. Dixon, challenged to produce evidence to back up his 'unwarrantable statements'.[80] Later in the year, articles by Dixon and J. C. Carlile, President of the Union in 1921, and one of the targets of Dixon's attacks, appeared in the *Baptist Times*. Dixon refused to withdraw any of his accusations, and Carlile accused them of being 'insulting' and 'untrue'. 'In England, such things are not done', he said [81]

This bad-tempered clash highlighted a substantial gulf between Baptists in America and England, not only over reunion, but also over other doctrinal matters. Dixon was one of the leaders of a growing and militant conservative section within the Northern Baptist Convention. In 1923 he broke away from the Convention to form the fundamentalist Baptist Bible Union. He understood English Baptist church life, having served as pastor of the non-Union Metropolitan Tabernacle between 1911 and 1919.[82] His views may not have been representative of general Baptist opinion, either in America or England, but his opposition to Shakespeare did reflect the growing strength of theological conservatism among Baptists in the 1920's, particularly in America. Doctrinal controversy there, over such matters as the inspiration of Scripture and the atonement, was intense and bitter, especially within the Northern Convention.

In Britain, theologically conservative opinion among the Baptists centred round the figure of James Mountain, minister of the Tunbridge Wells Free Church, and the British Baptist Bible Union. The Fellowship of Independent Evangelical Churches, which was formed in 1922, was also attractive to those Baptists who were uneasy about what they considered to be modernist or liberal tendencies in the Baptist Union. Shakespeare's pursuit of reunion with the Church of England was a particular target for their criticism. They also attacked prominent liberal Baptist scholars, including T. R. Glover, who opposed Shakespeare, and Wheeler Robinson, who supported him. Bebbington suggests that the centralisation of the denomination under Shakespeare, and his editorial control of the *Baptist Times*, hindered the spread of fundamentalism among English Baptists at this time, and prevented the more conservative elements from becoming as prominent a part of denominational life as was the case across the Atlantic. There were few opportunities for groups like the Baptist Bible Union to disseminate their views.[83] They were, however, a new source of hostility to Shakespeare, a hostility that was grounded in theological conservatism.

The growing theological conservatism of some Baptists after the war was the result of several factors. One was a natural reaction against German higher criticism, which had in earlier years generally been held in high regard. R. J. Campbell's move from the Nonconformist ministry and his ordination as a priest in the Church of England in 1916 was another. Campbell was famous for his exposition of modernist, liberal views in *The New Theology*, published in 1907, while he was minister of the Congregational City Temple. During the war he not only joined the Church of England, but also repudiated the views he had expressed in *The New Theology*. His about turn did considerable harm to the cause of liberal evangelicalism with which he had been so closely associated. Fear of the growing strength of Anglo-Catholicism within the Church of England was an ever-present spur to some. Appeals for a return to the fundamentals of Scripture by organisations like the Protestant Truth Society became more insistent. The birth and early growth of Pentecostalism from about 1907 onwards brought 'vigorous reinforcement to the conservative wing of Evangelicalism',[84] and the proliferation of conservative University Christian Unions, in direct opposition to the Student Christian Movement, had a similar effect. Shakespeare was handicapped by this changing theological climate, especially as he was an advocate of greater unity, not polarisation, among the churches, and also of the value of modern scholarship for ministers.

Political events also played their part in the last months of Shakespeare's time in office. Lloyd George's resignation from the premiership occurred in October 1922, following the decision by Conservative Party back-benchers to dissolve the Government coalition. This was followed in November by a General Election in which both sections of the Liberal Party experienced a disastrous defeat, and after which the Labour Party became the official Opposition. Shakespeare and the *Baptist Times* persisted in their dogged support of Lloyd George and his National Liberals, but became increasingly isolated in doing so.[85] Shakespeare's personal loyalty to Lloyd George was reinforced when his son Geoffrey was elected as National Liberal Member of Parliament for Wellingborough in 1922, having served as Lloyd George's personal secretary for some time previously.

Liberal Prime Ministers had led the country continuously for almost seventeen years since Balfour's resignation in 1905, and for most of that time the Free Churches had enjoyed unprecedented access to political power. The events of the autumn of 1922 finally confirmed that the war had ushered in a new political era, extinguishing the remaining embers of Victorian and Edwardian Liberalism. For Shakespeare, who had been active once again in trying to secure Free Church support for Lloyd George earlier in 1922, this meant that the influence and status he had possessed as a result of his association with the Prime Minister had disappeared. Within a few months, there was a further indication of Shakespeare's waning influence, this time within his own denomination. His fiercest critic, T. R. Glover, was elected Vice-President of the Union at the 1923 Assembly.

At the 1923 Baptist World Alliance Congress in Stockholm Baptist opposition to many of the views associated with Shakespeare became clearer still. Plans for a third Congress in Berlin, in 1916, had been abandoned because of the war. In July 1920 a conference was held in London to draw up a strategy for the Alliance, in the light of the disruption caused by the war on the continent. Shakespeare was still the Eastern Secretary of the Alliance, but European leadership passed increasingly to J. H. Rushbrooke, who was made 'European Commissioner' at this conference. Some of the money raised for the 1920 Baptist United Fund was allocated to help rebuild Baptist work on the continent,[86] and Rushbrooke travelled widely during 1921 and 1922 in both Europe and America, rebuilding international Baptist contacts. It was decided to hold the third World Congress in Stockholm, in 1923. As the time for this drew nearer, tensions became apparent, largely due to doctrinal differences and controversy over Shakespeare's pursuit of reunion. W. Y. Fullerton, Home Secretary of the Baptist Missionary Society, referred to the need to silence 'divisive whisperings', in his preview of the event.[87] The Southern Baptists threatened not to support Shakespeare's reappointment as Eastern Secretary, and were only persuaded to do so at the Congress after the intervention of Rushbrooke.[88]

Two events in particular made the Stockholm Congress important for Shakespeare. One was the invitation to him from the Swedish Lutheran Archbishop, Nathan Soderblom, a prominent supporter of the reunion movement, to preach in Uppsala Cathedral at the start of the Congress. This was intended as an acknowledgement of Shakespeare's work for Christian unity, and constituted in itself a significant gesture in support of this cause.

J. C. Carlile, who accompanied Shakespeare to the Cathedral in Uppsala, and read from the Bible in the service, later described him as 'suffering torment as a result of the depletion of nervous energy'.[89] Shakespeare was deeply moved by the Archbishop's invitation, later calling it ' a remarkable expression of a new attitude and feeling for which I thank God'.[90] In his sermon he described Archbishop Soderblom as 'the central figure of Protestant Europe in Peace and Unity'. He took as his text a verse from Luke's Gospel: 'And Jesus said unto him, 'No man, having put his hand to the plough, and looking back, is fit for the Kingdom of God''. He began by stating what he believed were the main priorities for the Church of that time:

> The supreme work of the Church is to win the world for God . . . But there are two great tasks to which the Church has set its hand in these later days. The first is peace - international peace . . . The Church must press for reason, arbitration, and the reference of disputes to international tribunals . . .

The other problem of our time is Church Unity. Indeed the two are very closely related, for men will only deride Churches which desire peace everywhere except among themselves. Warring Churches cannot speak convincingly to a warring world.[91]

He expressed his own commitment to continue the struggle for unity in the church, and finished with an illustration of a Welsh preacher who, observing a farmer's cart going home after a day's work in the fields, said to his wife, 'when my work is done and the harvest reaped, may God give me a place in the harvest home'. 'We repeat that prayer', Shakespeare said.

The event might have been auspicious for the cause of church unity, but was not a happy one for Shakespeare personally. No doubt the lack of harmony at the Congress as well as recent discouragements in England had lowered his spirits. The account of his sermon given in the *Baptist Times* indicates that the circumstances were far from ideal.[92] The Cathedral's acoustics were poor, and the repetition of the sermon, which was first read in Swedish then preached in English, lessened its impact. On his way into the pulpit, Shakespeare was distressed when he accidentally knocked the pulpit Bible to the floor, and according to Carlile, was not able to regain his composure. He was afterwards reduced to tears, telling Carlile that 'the falling of that Bible is the sign that my work is done'.[93]

The other significant event for Shakespeare was the decision of the Congress to publish a message 'to the Baptist Brotherhood, to other Christian Brethren, and to the World'. It was mainly the work of the incoming President of the Alliance, E. Y. Mullins. Mullins had been President of the American Southern Baptist Convention since 1899, and the Convention had agreed a very similar statement three years earlier.[94] It was described as a 'declaration of Baptist principles and purposes', and was clearly, if not deliberately, antipathetic in spirit to Shakespeare's commitment to reunion. It contained nothing of a positive nature on the search for church unity, declaring,

We cannot unite with others in any centralised ecclesiastical organisation wielding power over the individual conscience . . . We cannot accept the conception of ordination made valid through a historic succession in the ministry . . . the ministry can possess no sacerdotal powers. They are called to the special tasks of preaching and teaching and administration.

Under the heading 'The Baptist Faith and Mission', the statement said that 'infant baptism is utterly irreconcilable with the ideal of a spiritual Christianity'. Under 'Religious Liberty and its applications' it went on:

No human authority of any kind . . . has any right to repress or hinder or thwart any man or group of men in the exercise of religious belief or worship . . . Religious liberty is inconsistent with any union of church and State. It is inconsistent with any special favour by the State towards one or more religious groups . . . It is inconsistent with priestly and episcopal authority and infant baptism.[95]

There is no record of any direct response from Shakespeare to this statement, which was a comprehensive demolition of his careful attempt to build closer relationships with the Church of England, especially as it was explicitly addressed to 'other Christian brethren', much as the Lambeth Appeal had been addressed to 'all Christian people'. Davidson regarded it as marking the end of any realistic hopes of success in the Lambeth talks.[96] Its publication came very shortly after the reception of the Church of England memorandum on the status of existing Free Church ministers at the Lambeth Palace talks, which was equally damaging in its own way to the cause of unity.[97] Shakespeare was caught in a pincer movement. On the one hand was his own increasingly conservative denomination, led by the Americans, and on the other was the intransigently episcopal Church of England. Either would have been sufficient to make the prospect of unity extremely difficult, but the existence of both made it an impossibility.

Although the Baptists' message was American in origin, it was carried by the whole Congress 'with acclamation',[98] and was greeted with enthusiasm by many, and probably most, English Baptists. Fullerton at the Baptist Missionary Society welcomed it, saying that it 'should go far to clear our position amongst other churches, and to establish it amongst ourselves'.[99] One correspondent in the *Baptist Times* described it as 'the most wonderful evangelical declaration that has ever been made by the Baptists since the days of the Reformation'.[100] Some voices were raised against it, however. Greenhough, the longstanding ally of Shakespeare, spoke of the 'illusory atmosphere and spiritual glamour of Stockholm'. He believed that the Baptist World Alliance had diverted the sympathies and prayers from 'the larger Christian union for which our Lord prayed and which is the great necessity of the hour'.[101]

A great deal of correspondence was received by the *Baptist Times* in the autumn of 1923, mostly raising grave doubts about the value of continuing in the reunion discussions.[102]. Shakespeare himself recommenced his work at Baptist Church House on his return from Sweden. In September he spoke at a service to mark the unveiling of a memorial for James Thew, the minister of the Leicester church he had attended as a teenager, and who had exercised such a strategic influence on him.[103] In October, he gave what was to prove his last public address at Carlile's church in Folkestone, on the occasion of his friend's 25th anniversary as pastor there.[104]

The first intimation that Shakespeare had suffered a serious break-down in his health came on 17 October, when a committee meeting at Baptist Church House was informed that because of 'eye trouble' he 'had been ordered complete rest for some weeks'.[105] In November the Council was informed that the problem with his sight was improving.[106] Carlile agreed to deputise for Shakespeare during his absence. In January 1924 Shakespeare was still not well enough to return to work, but the Council received a letter from him in which he expressed the hope that his health would soon be restored. His most serious problem, he said, was sleeplessness. In characteristically indomitable fashion, he also expressed the hope that the Council would 'be unanimous in its decisions regarding Christian unity'.[107] In February the Superintendents heard with 'great satisfaction' of Shakespeare's progress, and in March the Council responded in a similar way to the same news.[108] In April the *Baptist Times* reported that his health was 'increasingly healthy' and that he was 'stronger and better in every way'.[109]

In the meantime, quite a storm was brewing over the forthcoming annual Assembly in Cardiff and how the matter of reunion would be treated. Glover, as incoming President, knew that his election the previous year was, at least in part, a protest against Shakespeare's policy over reunion, and did not believe opposition to it could or should be silenced any longer. In the autumn of 1923 Glover was conducting a lecture tour in America, and in November wrote to Carlile making his views clear:

> And here I have to try to tell you how sick the whole thing makes me. I don't know if you realise what a shindig we are in for at Cardiff. The stoppers have been on for years, and now it will be off. I was elected as a protest against Shakespeare, and he can't keep the Federal Council's reply back. It will not be approved, and I will be no party to muzzling the Assembly . . .. I am sorry for any man threatened with any degree of loss of sight. But can't you get him to realise how to avoid this explosion? . . . Shakespeare doesn't realise how people feel his abandonment of our position. You know quite well that he has left his original Baptist ideas. . . . Now you can do us all a signal service. Get Shakespeare to accept a pension.

Glover also gave vent to his feelings about Shakespeare's style of leadership in general. 'How I hate that Church House', he wrote, 'top and bottom, and all the toadying sneaking cadging atmosphere!' He believed that Shakespeare used the *Baptist Times* unfairly to promote his unrepresentative views, and by so doing had 'brought the paper down from a paying concern to need a subsidy'.[110]

Glover was unable or unwilling to use the *Baptist Times* as a means of communicating his views, but articles for and against his well-known position did appear there. The principal protagonists in the reunion debate undertaken in its columns were Gilbert Laws of Norwich, the minister of Shakespeare's old St. Mary's Church in Norwich, and M. E. Aubrey of

Cambridge, both prominent younger ministers in the denomination. Laws took Shakespeare's side, accusing Glover of being 'confused and unfair in his criticisms'.[111] Aubrey defended Glover, and described the Anglican understanding of episcopacy as 'both spiritually and historically wrong and dangerous'. Laws responded by protesting at the manner in which Shakespeare and other respected denominational leaders of many years standing were being presented as 'masked conspirators'.

Carlile, deputising for Shakespeare at Baptist Church House, sought to quieten things down by reassuring the newspaper's readers that the denomination had not been in any way committed to episcopal ordination, or anything else, by the Lambeth conferences.[112] Glover himself found other ways of communicating his views, and occasionally used his regular religious column in the *Daily News* to do so. In two articles in February 1924 he presented as an awful nightmare the prospect of a standardised United Church, dominated by ecclesiastical officials. Two months later he asked, 'why should it be so constantly dinned into us that a divided Church militates against the world's acceptance of Christ?' Division may actually be a sign of health, he believed, and was certainly preferable to the 'ludicrous and pathetic' attempt to muffle differences.[113]

In February, the 1923 President, W. E. Blomfield, who was himself not sympathetic to 'the Lambeth ideal', wrote to Glover urging him not to insist on a debate on reunion at Cardiff, particularly in view of Shakespeare's poor health. He believed that the atmosphere such a debate would generate would be destructive to anything positive Glover might want to achieve.[114] It seems that Glover agreed to this, as no debate was held. A paragraph was added to the Council's report to the Assembly, however, suggested by Carlile, apparently in response to Glover's concerns, 'noting' progress towards unity, emphasising Baptist beliefs in believers baptism and the priesthood of all believers, and correcting any possible misunderstandings by insisting that the Union was not committed to any particular proposals for reunion.[115] Glover had personal sympathy for Shakespeare, but dreaded the prospect of his health recovering and his return to Baptist Church House. He told Carlile that he thought the Council's successful efforts in 1921 to 'fetch him back for a second disaster' after his notice of resignation the previous year were 'feckless' and feared the same thing might happen again.[116]

On the eve of the 1924 Assembly Shakespeare put an end to the uncertainty by writing a letter of resignation, following insistent medical advice. The letter was read to the Assembly by Herbert Marnham, the Union treasurer, together with other letters from Shakespeare's doctors referring to his medical condition. It was clear from his letter that Shakespeare had taken the decision to resign with the greatest reluctance. His physical strength was slowly returning, he said, and he was not conscious of any diminution of his mental powers, but his sight was only partial, and he did not possess the unimpaired energy required to continue his work as secretary of the Union.

'Even you who are my best friends cannot realise with what distress I have come to this decision', he went on. 'It was my dream to crown my life's work by securing adequate superannuation for our aged ministers, but God has willed it otherwise'. In retirement, he hoped to be able to continue helping with the work of the Union.[117] It was clearly understood that, this time, the resignation was not going to be rescinded. His 67th birthday had taken place about three weeks before.

It fell to Glover as President to propose and present a suitable resolution to the Assembly, by means of which the denomination could express its feelings about this momentous event. He did so in generous terms, referring to Shakespeare's achievement in teaching 'all Baptists to form larger ideals for their Church, and conceive of it as a great society'. He spoke of his leadership of the Free Churches, his promotion of the role of women, and his commitment to raising the standard of ministerial support and training.[118] The tributes to Shakespeare were warm and appreciative. Gilbert Laws informed the audience that the value of the Union's invested capital and property had risen to about £750,000, and its annual income had increased nearly four-fold since 1898.[119]

Glover also had the responsibility of ensuring that the Shakespeares were adequately provided for in retirement, and to this end organised a special fund for their benefit.[120] The task of supervising the Union's adjustment to life without Shakespeare was a considerable one, as the Union of 1924 was largely Shakespeare's own creation. Protracted and sometimes confidential conferences from July onwards discussed the organisation of the Union and the editorship of the *Baptist Times*. The position of Shakespeare's brother Alfred, who had worked with him in various capacities, particularly as subeditor of the newspaper, and his personal secretary W. H. Ball, were among those that had to be dealt with (they both continued to work at Baptist Church House).[121] In January 1925 the Secretariat Committee recommended M. E. Aubrey for the post of secretary of the Union, Carlile and Rushbrooke having indicated they did not want to be considered.[122] Aubrey was appointed at the Assembly that year.

Shakespeare retained an interest in the affairs of the Union, and on occasion visited Baptist Church House, but suffered a serious relapse in health in September 1924, and according to his obituary in the *Baptist Times*, 'sank into a profound melancholy from which it was impossible to rouse him'.[123] 'Poor Shakespeare!' wrote the Congregationalist J. D. Jones in his autobiography: 'Something like religious melancholy laid hold of him towards the end of his life. He doubted his own redemption and refused to be comforted'.[124] He steadfastly refused various honours that were pressed upon him. In 1925 Shakespeare had a cerebral haemorrhage, and for much of the last three years of his life he was 'helpless and speechless'.[125] He died following a stroke not long before his 71st birthday on 12th March 1928. Following his death, the Council recorded its feelings about the man who was described by J. H. Rushbrooke as 'the real founder of the Baptist Union'[126]:

> We have felt the thrill of his leadership in great enterprises, and we have watched with pride and thankfulness the growth of our Denomination in prestige and influence under his direction. Whatever some of us may have thought about some of Dr. Shakespeare's policies, we have all been united in a great sense of pride that he belonged to us.[127]

In retrospect, it is unfortunate that Shakespeare did not retire as he had intended in 1922, although whether he was the kind of man who could have survived retirement for long is debatable. His constant demands upon himself, both physically and mentally, were immense, and this pressure was eventually bound to take a heavy toll. An additional burden was that the last few months of his time at Baptist Church House were a period of considerable personal disappointment. Above all, it was becoming more and more evident that his ambitious vision of church unity, which he had embraced during the war, was unrealistic and would never be achieved. The theological undercurrents, both within his own denomination and within the Church of England, made unity of the kind he sought impossible. He was unable, having taken up this cause, to lay it down, even when it threatened his other aims, such as Free Church unity and the ordination of women.

There is an almost fatalistic atmosphere surrounding the post-war years. Shakespeare was able to make progress with hardly any of his cherished ambitions, with the possible exception of the work of the ten Superintendents, with whom he regularly met, and through whom he sought to continue shaping the denomination's life. On the other hand, he was equally unable to withdraw, or hand the leadership of the denomination over to others. His resignation was forced from him by poor health, although it is clear now that his important work had already really been completed several years before. Baptists continued to admire and respect him, even when they disagreed with him, but in the post-war years he seemed to have lost touch with their underlying desires and needs. Shakespeare could not get the institutions he had created adapt to circumstances that had changed enormously, nor could he set them free to discover a new role without him.

The war itself cast its shadow over the whole of Shakespeare's post-war work, and was the biggest single factor in shaping it. Some of the ideals that drove him forward had their roots in earlier years, but were branded into his consciousness during the war. This was so with respect to reunion with the Church of England, which had hardly featured at all in his writing or speaking before 1914. It was so also with respect to his ambition for the acceptance of the ministry of women. The war enabled him to achieve objectives that he had long cherished, such as an adequate and centralised scheme for the sustenance of the ministry, and the federation of the Free Churches. The difficulty he faced in the post-war period was to maintain and build on what had been created in the exceptional circumstances of the years between 1914 and 1918.

Shakespeare also found that some key aspects of his work before 1914 took on a very different character after 1918. His involvement with the Baptist World Alliance became a very different matter in the changed theological and international climate of the 1920's. The institutional development of the Baptist Union itself, and the denomination as a whole, which had so dominated his early years, seemed to feature little after 1918. This was partly because he had by then achieved most of what he had wanted to do, but also because his interests had moved on to a new and broader sphere.

Shakespeare's changing relationship with Lloyd George provides an illustration of his changing fortunes before, during and after the war. There was a sense of excitement and progress about association with a Baptist Chancellor before the war, bringing with it the apparent possibilities for almost limitless influence in the life of the nation. The war itself dramatically increased these, especially after 1916. By the beginning of 1919 it became suddenly obvious that there were disadvantages as well as advantages of such an association. Powerful social and political forces were at work, and what had seemed secure ground a few years before could be relied upon no longer. Less than four years later, the opportunities Lloyd George had presented to Shakespeare and his other Free Church supporters disappeared altogether. A new era had dawned, and old loyalties and ideals had become irrelevant. In a similar way, the excitement and potential for change and advance among Baptists generally in the pre-war years gave way to later disappointment. The opportunities presented by the war for increasing the pace of change proved, in the end, illusory, in the face of the realities of the post-war world.

1. *BT* 1 June 1900.
2. *BT* 24 May 1901.
3. *HB*, 1911 (p. 220).
4. BU Minute Book, 3 October 1910.
5. *BT* 29 November 1912.
6. BU Minute Book, 14 January 1914.
7. The modern deaconess movement started within German Protestantism in the early nineteenth century. Deaconesses were ordained in the Church of England from the 1860's, and the Methodists and the Church of Scotland followed this example in the 1880's. See Briggs, *English Baptists* pp. 278-89 for an account of the role of women in Baptist churches during the nineteenth century.
8. See Doris M. Rose, *Baptist Deaconesses* (Carey Kingsgate Press Ltd.: London, 1954) p. 14.
9. *BT* 12 January 1917.
10. BU Minute Book, 1918 (p. 180a).
11. BU Minute Book, 1 April 1919.

12. BU Minute Book, 12 June and 24 July 1919.
13. Shakespeare, *Churches* p. 143.
14. *BT* 19 September and 17 October 1919.
15. *BT* 24 October 1919.
16. Sparkes, *Ministry* p. 32.
17. BU Minute Book, 16 March 1920. More details about the Baptist United Fund are given on p. 145.
18. BU Minute Book, 28 April 1921. Dunn's letter was written on 27 April, and was received at an emergency meeting of the committee on the following day.
19. BU Minute Book, 21 April 1921.
20. BU Minute Book, 8 June 1923.
21. The actual title 'Baptist Zenana Mission' was not adopted until 1897.
22. BU Minute Book, 19 November 1918.
23. BU Minute Book, 16 December 1919. This Commission does not seem to have been very effective, as the Ministerial Recognition Committee asked for a fresh enquiry into the question of the ministry in 1922 (BU Minute Book, 21 November 1922). See references to the Commission on pp. 145-6 and p. 148.
24. *DT* 28 May 1920.
25. Sparkes, *Ministry* p. 32-5. For many years after this the Union produced a separate list of accredited women ministers.
26. The innovative title of Sisterhood was soon abandoned after Shakespeare's departure and the original term Deaconess re-introduced.
27. In 1979 the deaconess order was discontinued and the remaining deaconesses ordained to full ministerial status (McBeth, p. 516).
28. Sparkes *Home Mission* p. 80.
29. *Ibid.* pp. 75 and 78.
30. BU Minute Book, 14 July 1919.
31. The minimum level of stipend varied according to where the minister's church was situated and his family circumstances. The lowest minimum set for a married Baptist minister was set at £120 in 1916, rising to £130 in 1917, where it remained until at least 1920. The equivalent Primitive Methodist and Wesleyan figures (for 1919) were £140 and £175 respectively (Sparkes, *Home Mission* pp. 70-5). The Federal Council annual meeting in September 1920 heard that the Baptist minimum was £160 (although according to Sparkes this was not actually achieved until 1922), compared with £240 for the Congregationalists and £250 for the Primitive Methodists. (*Federal Council Minute Book*, 21 September 1920).
32. *BT* 5 September 1919.
33. Sparkes, *Home Mission* p. 71.
34. BU Minute Book, 16 December 1919.
35. *BT* 9 and 16 April 1920.
36. *BT* 14 May 1920.
37. *BT* 10 December 1920.
38. Sparkes, *Home Mission* pp. 79-80. It was agreed that 'an accredited minister ought to have a stipend of at least £250 per annum', but grants were available to support ministers receiving stipends between £160 and £250, and even less than £160 in some circumstances.
39. BU Minute Book, 15 October 1919.
40. *BT* 23 April 1920.

41. BU Minute Book, 13 December 1921.
42. Although the terms 'preacher' and 'pastor' indicate different kinds of ministry, they were often used interchangeably, and Union recognition involved little difference between the two. The usual preference for the former reflects the Baptist emphasis on preaching for the pastoral office.
43. The reorganisation of the Local Preachers' Federation and the Union's recognition of lay ministers were discussed several times in 1922. See BU Minute Book, 9 January 1922, 21 March 1922, 10 July 1922 and 20 November 1922.
44. BU Minute Book, 13 February 1923.
45. *HB* 1905 p. 186.
46. The Local Preachers' Federation of December 1921 became the Lay Preachers Federation of July 1922.
47. BU Minute Book, 30 November 1920.
48. *BT* 15 July 1921.
49. BU Minute Book, 16-17 November 1921.
50. BU Minute Book, 16 January 1922.
51. BU Minute Book, 21 March 1922.
52. *BT* 12 May 1922.
53. BU Minute Book, 25 September, 7 and 21 November 1922.
54. BU Minute Book 2-4 January and 20 March 1923.
55. The statement is reproduced in Roger Hayden (ed.) *Baptist Union Documents 1948-1977* (BHS: London, 1980) pp. 85-6.
56. See Hayden, *Documents* p. 72.
57. Michael Walker describes the impact of the Catholic Revival on Baptists, along with other Nonconformists, in his *Baptists at the Table: The Theology of the Lord's Supper amongst English Baptists in the Nineteenth Century* (BHS: Didcot, 1992) pp. 85-90. In some respects, especially as regards the priesthood and the eucharist, there was a strong reaction against it; in others, such as in architecture and music, its influence can be clearly seen, although it was rarely acknowledged.
58. See, for example, Arthur Headlam, writing of the need for the Church of England to recognise the orders and sacraments of non-episcopal churches in preparation for the Lambeth Conference. He insisted that carelessness and indifference as to form should not be tolerated (Arthur C. Headlam, *The Doctrine of the Church and Christian Reunion* (John Murray: London, 1920) p. 306.
59. BU Minute Book, 19 April 1923.
60. *BT* 27 April 1923.
61. BU Minute Book, 3-7 July 1922.
62. BU Minute Book, 14 January and 12 February 1919. At the Superintendents' meetings on those days 88 and 61 recommendations respectively were made.
63. BU Minute Book, 10 September 1919. 139 recommendations were made.
64. E.g. in an article from the *Daily News* reprinted in the *Baptist Times* on 28 May 1920, in which the new Baptist system of bishops and dioceses was described as necessary for the raising of the Baptist United Fund; in an article by F. C. Spurr in the *Baptist Times* on 1 July 1921; and in an article by Donald MacLean entitled 'The Newest Baptist Bishop' about the appointment of a new Superintendent in September 1921(*BT* 30 September 1921).
65. Currie, *Churches and Churchgoers* pp. 149-50.
66. *BT* 9 March 1923.

67. BU Minute Book, 20 March 1922.
68. BU Minute Book, 3-7 July 1922.
69. *BT* 3 November 1922.
70. BU Minute Book, 16 January 1923.
71. BU Minute Book, 9 February 1923.
72. *BT* 6 April 1923.
73. *BT* 20 April 1923.
74. See p. 121.
75. BU Minute Book, 22 April 1921.
76. BU Minute Book, 28 April 1921.
77. *BT* 29 April 1921. It was at this Assembly that Archbishop Lang gave his address on the Lambeth Appeal, which Shakespeare greeted with such enthusiasm (see pp. 120-1).
78. BU Minute Book, 12 July 1921; *BT* 15 July 1921.
79. BU Minute Book, 15 November 1921. In spite of his promise to avoid outside engagements, Shakespeare agreed to be appointed as one of the Federal Council's three secretaries in the autumn of 1921, following the end of his two-year term of office as Moderator. He continued to be heavily involved in the reunion discussions at Lambeth Palace.
80. *BT* 27 January 1922.
81. *BT* 9 June 1922.
82. D. W. Bebbington, 'Baptists and Fundamentalism in Inter-War Britain', in Keith Robbins (ed.), *Protestant Evangelicalism* (Oxford: 1990) p. 313 and McBeth, p. 756.
83. Bebbington, *Fundamentalism*, pp. 324-6.
84. D. W. Bebbington, *Evangelicalism in Modern Britain: a history from the 1730's to the 1980's* (Unwin and Hyman: London, 1989) p. 198.
85. In January 1922 Shakespeare described Lloyd George as 'one of the most indomitable, gallant, wonderful figures in the history of the world', mainly because of the Irish settlement. Lloyd George was still courting Free Church leaders, and in February he invited them to another breakfast in Downing Street (Koss, *Nonconformity* pp. 159-60).
86. See pp. 141: 145 for further details of the Baptist United Fund.
87. W. Y. Fullerton, 'The Stockholm Congress and Exhibition', *BQ* vol. 1 (July 1923) p. 291.
88. Green, pp. 103-4.
89. Carlile, *My Life* p. 167.
90. W. T. Whitley (ed.), *Third Baptist World Congress* (Kingsgate Press: London, 1923) p. (vii).
91. *Ibid.*, pp. 31-6.
92. *BT* 3 August 1923.
93. Carlile, *My Life* p. 167.
94. McBeth, p. 677.
95. *BT* 24 August 1923.
96. Davidson Papers, vol. 264 p. 60.
97. See p. 126.
98. *BT* 14 September 1923.
99. Fullerton, 'Stockholm' pp. 291-3.

100. *BT* 14 September 1923.
101. *BT* 12 October 1923.
102. See, for example, a resolution from the Northern Baptist Association (*BT* 19 October 1923). On 2 November 1923 the editor said 'a great many letters' had been received on the subject.
103. *BT* 21 September 1923. See p. 14.
104. *BT* 19 October 1923.
105. BU Minute Book, 17 October 1923.
106. BU Minute Book, 20 November 1923. At this meeting, while discussion was underway, John Clifford died. He had earlier expressed the hope that Shakespeare would recover and go on to lead the Union 'for years to come'.
107. BU Minute Book, 15 January 1924.
108. BU Minute Book, 13 February and 18 March 1924.
109. *BT* 18 April 1924.
110. T. R. Glover correspondence, box 16. The letter, written from San Francisco, was dated 30 November 1923. The Federal Council's reply to which Glover refers is its cautious support for continuing reunion negotiations, expressed at its annual meetings in the autumn of 1923.
111. *BT* 21 December 1923.
112. See *BT* 28 December 1923, 11, 18 and 25 January 1924. It is ironic that while the chief opposition to Shakespeare came from the conservative wing of the denomination, Glover was himself theologically liberal.
113. *DN* 9 and 16 February and 5 April 1924.
114. T. R. Glover correspondence, box 6. Blomfield's letters were dated 1 and 8 February 1924.
115. BU Minute Book, 18 March 1924.
116. T. R. Glover correspondence, box 16. Glover's letter to Carlile is dated 10 March 1924. It included the statement (referring to Shakespeare), 'I do not like his policies; but I do not want to see disaster for him'.
117. BU Minute Book, 7 May 1924; *BT* 9 May 1924.
118. *BT* 16 May 1924.
119. *BT* 9 May 1924.
120. BU Minute Book, 11 June 1924.
121. BU Minute Book, 21 July 1924.
122. BU Minute Book, 20 January 1925.
123. *BT* 15 March 1928.
124. J. D. Jones, p. 209.
125. *BT* 15 March 1928.
126. *Ibid.*.
127. *Ibid.*.

CHAPTER SIX

Shakespeare's Legacy

6.1 Shakespeare and the 'Dissolution of Dissent'[1]

Patterns of growth and decline among the main Nonconformist denominations became increasingly similar as the nineteenth century progressed. The
most obvious feature was a gradual but persistent numerical decline that
began in about mid-century. This was obscured to some extent by several
factors. One was the intermittent reversal of this downward trend during
periods of revival. Another was the fact that membership statistics themselves rose, virtually without exception, year by year until 1906. This was
misleading because it did not take into account two other trends working in
the opposite direction. The first of these was the diminishing number of
Nonconformist adherents. The proportion fell substantially, in relation to
members, as the century went on. The second was the steady increase in the
general population as a whole.[2]

The vitality and growth of Nonconformity, such a dramatic feature of
English society in the early 1800's, was in decline from mid-century
onwards. There were various reasons for this, many external to
Nonconformity itself. Changes within the Nonconformist denominations
probably also played a significant role. Attention has been drawn to a number of these, and their effect on growth rates, by Deryck Lovegrove, Derek
Tidball, Alan Gilbert and others. It has been suggested that the increasing
tendency for evangelism to be co-ordinated and controlled by central
denominational bodies from 1830 onwards, with a resulting diminution of
local initiatives, led to a reduction in evangelistic effectiveness.[3] As
Nonconformists became more conscious of their identity and place in society, both at the local and national level, more of their energy was directed
towards the improvement of their worship, buildings and organisation.
Increasing attention was given to the more easily managed recruitment of
new members from within the circle of adherents, rather than devoting
energy to the unpredictable task of evangelism among outsiders, so that
growth became 'endogenous' rather than 'exogenous'.[4] The development of
an elaborate 'penumbra' of organisations linked to individual churches was
often seen as the best way of enlarging this circle. This was, of course, only
possible for the larger churches. The role of the ministry became increasingly important as the denominations became more institutionally elaborate.
The responsibilities and involvement of the laity, a central factor in earlier
growth, tended to diminish. The ministerial office became more formalised,
and the distinction between lay and ordained ministry more clearly drawn.[5]

These processes were part of the institutionalisation of Nonconformity, and contributed to its declining vitality. Shakespeare believed, contrary to what appears to have been the case, that the strengthening of both national denominational machinery and the ordained ministry was central to the task of revitalising Baptist fortunes. He was particularly conscious of what he considered to be the failings of the Baptists compared to the other Nonconformist denominations, several of which were more prominent and prestigious. This was particularly apparent in the case of the Wesleyans, who were constitutionally organised as a national church, and whose organisation was historically highly centralised. It was also true of the Congregationalists, who shared an ecclesiology very similar to that of the Baptists. The Congregational Union was, at the time of Shakespeare's appointment, a much stronger body than the Baptist Union, largely as a result of the work of the gifted administrator Alexander Hannay, secretary of the Congregational Union in the 1870's and 80's. The principal cause of the relative lack of effective national co-ordination of effort among Baptists was their doctrinal and ecclesiastical disunity, especially before the amalgamation of the Union with the General Baptist Association in 1891.[6]

There is an irony about Shakespeare's determined pursuit of nationally co-ordinated effort in the interests of the denomination. It was precisely in Hannay's time that the Congregationalists began to show a relative decline compared to the still disunited Baptists. Charles Booth's commendation of Baptist success in London suggests that, in the metropolis at least, the lack of any co-ordinated direction of mission around the turn of the century did not result in any disadvantage compared to the other denominations.[7] Halévy considered the 'fissiparous tendencies' in congregational Nonconformity, for which the Baptists, among the main denominations, were probably the best known, to constitute its 'very essence', enabling it to develop and grow 'by division and schism rather than by organisation'.[8] It would be wrong to draw the conclusion from this that Baptists had no sense of common identity. Their unique baptismal practice was a strong uniting force, and even their diversity itself drew them together, expressing as it did their commitment to congregational independence.[9]

From mid-century, the Union and the Assemblies it organised were significant expressions of Baptist unity. Shakespeare built on this growing denominational consciousness, and it was he who was primarily responsible for drawing the disparate elements of the denomination together into a coherent whole. He could not have done this without the compliance of most Baptists, and the enthusiastic support of many, but his single-minded and determined commitment to what he considered to be the modernisation of the denomination, his organisational genius, and his capacity for hard work, were an important part of the process. The denomination thus embodied itself and became a meaningful ecclesiastical entity under the banner of the Union.

As a strategy for dealing with decline this did not succeed. The new denominational institutions created by Shakespeare, and the prestige they brought with them, along with his efforts to raise the standing of the ministry, may have captured the imagination and commitment of many Baptists at first, but the expectation of a return to growth attached to them failed to materialise. The transition from a relative to an absolute decline in membership statistics in 1907 was an unavoidable sign of this failure, and in spite of hopes for the contrary, it was not reversed. The increased and co-ordinated resources in the hands of the Union seemed less adequate than ever for meeting the challenges of mission, and the quality of ministerial candidates showed no signs of improving. Shakespeare's response was to call for even greater unity of effort, and to devote his energy to winning over the sceptics in the colleges and the churches. The organisational unity he had already won was remarkable, however, and even his considerable powers of persuasion could achieve no more. By the end of the war, his energies were primarily devoted elsewhere, to a wider unity.

What Baptists were experiencing was common to the other Nonconformist denominations, and parallels with the Congregationalists in particular were very marked.[10] By the 1920's, a sense of hopelessness about the task of evangelising the nation was pervasive. What was unusual about the Baptists was the enormous effort that had gone into the re-organisation of the denomination before the war, in an effort to prevent the realisation of their fears about the future. This made the sense of disappointment even greater.

The statistics of decline suggest that the war itself had little impact on the steady decline of Nonconformity. There was no sudden change during the war, or in the immediate post-war years. If anything, the indication is of a slight recovery in the early 1920's. The shadow of the war was cast over everything that took place after 1914, but it did not appear to change one way or another a trend that had longer term causes.

S. J. D. Green has argued that 'the burden of institutional proliferation' among the churches in industrial Yorkshire during the early twentieth century, intended as an answer to the erosive effects of secularisation, actually hastened it.[11] According to Green, the chief consequence of the attempt to extend the churches' influence in society by means of increasing the number of church-based organisations was the imposition of extra demands of time and money on existing church members. It did not lead to any significant increase in personal religious commitment on the part of those outside the church. Even among church people themselves, the policy of institutional proliferation had in the long run a negative effect. The ideal of the voluntary religious organisation extending its influence into surrounding society began to lose its hold on them in the face of increasing public or other secular provision of the social and educational services traditionally associated with the churches.

Green's analysis may also have relevance at the national level. The institutional elaboration of the Union led to extra financial demands, but otherwise it did little to encourage greater personal commitment or involvement on the part of the average church member. Responsibility for its administration remained in the hands of a relatively small number of denominational officials and leaders, and effective participation by the wider church community was very limited. The policy of expanding the organisational scope of the denomination may, perversely, have contributed to Baptist decline, rather than growth. Religious decline between 1870 and 1920 in industrial Yorkshire, Green believed, was not simply the consequence of a general loss of religious faith, leading to a decline in church attendance. It was also the direct result of changes in the churches themselves as they tried, through institutional expansion, to be more accessible to contemporary society. It led to a diminished level of personal commitment, less frequent attendance and, in time, a loss of faith. He wrote:

> Conventional wisdom and common sense suggest that the people stopped going to church because they no longer believed what the churches taught them. Perhaps the causal mechanism was really closer to the opposite; they stopped believing because they stopped going. If so, the decline of the churches in early twentieth-century Britain turns out to have been very significant, after all.[12]

It is unlikely that institutional change was the major factor in the long process of church decline. However, Green's argument has parallels with the findings of Gilbert and others about the impact of institutionalisation on Nonconformity in the first half of the nineteenth century, and it seems likely that it was a significant one.

Shakespeare's persistent belief that centralised co-ordination of effort and resources was required if evangelistic effectiveness was to be restored, and a return to growth achieved, seems to have been mistaken. Continuing decline was by 1898 probably inevitable. It seems unlikely, however, that a denomination that owed its past vigour and growth to the local and the spontaneous could ever recover that vitality by means of institutionalisation.

One of the features of English Nonconformity in the late nineteenth and early twentieth centuries was the emergence of new religious movements and organisations. There were several Protestant evangelical church bodies in England that, while small, and often sectarian in character, were growing quickly. They varied in character, from the rigidly hierarchical Salvation Army to the independently organised Open Brethren. Some, like the Salvation Army, the Churches of Christ and the Pentecostals, saw themselves as entirely independent of the existing churches, several originating in splits from the mainstream denominations, and developing in time into denominations in their own right. Others, like the Keswick movement, operated within the existing denominational framework. A large number of independent missionary agencies also emerged following the example of the pioneering China Inland Mission, founded in 1865. Some of these, like the London City Mission and a host of smaller missions, were concerned with domestic, rather than foreign, missionary work. There were also a large number of mainly small independent chapels and Gospel Halls. John Kent estimates that, in London, the combined attendance at the various 'fringe Protestant' places of worship in 1903 exceeded that of the largest of the major denominations.[13]

These churches, missions and other bodies usually emerged in reaction to the existing denominations, even when they were not the result of schismatic division. They frequently regarded the traditional churches as clerical and bureaucratic as well as doctrinally suspect. The anarchic spontaneity that had characterised much of Nonconformity itself a century before could now be found beyond its bounds, as a new form of dissent. There was a mutual desire to keep a substantial distance between the new groups and the existing denominations. Most denominational leaders carefully avoided association with what they considered to be poorly trained and uncultured preachers. They were themselves still struggling to overcome this same stigma.

If official Nonconformity turned its back on those new churches that were exhibiting the fastest growth, the same cannot be said about its attitude towards the Church of England. It seemed at times to be obsessed with the established church, in a mixture of hostility, rivalry, envy and admiration. This can, perhaps, be understood in view of the long history of antipathy between them, and the Nonconformists' long campaign for acceptance as equals. Robert Horton's *The Dissolution of Dissent* (1902) can be taken as expressing a fairly representative view.[14] Its main theme is the relationship between Nonconformity and the Church of England. Horton identified the three main complaints Nonconformists had about the Church. These were the religious establishment, liturgical worship and 'sacerdotalism'. He affirmed the importance of Nonconformity in the history of the religion of England, and the positive nature of its contribution. He went on to advocate its incorporation within the Church of England. Speaking of the Nonconformist churches, he wrote that the English Church 'should enlarge its borders to embrace them'.[15] He believed that a dissolution of dissent of this kind, whereby it could be welcomed within the Church of England without surrendering either its principles or its essential character, would be of mutual benefit. The emulation of the Church was a common feature of Nonconformity around the turn of the century, particularly in the buildings it erected and changes in its forms of worship. Hostility to the growing strength of Anglo-Catholicism within the Church was another, and the combination of the two, together with its long desire for acceptance on equal terms, led to the kind of ambivalent fascination which Horton describes.

Shakespeare, whose later vision of unity with the Church of England was like that of Horton, shared most Nonconformists' disdain for the new dissent, and their fascination with the Church of England. This is shown by his pursuit of a more cultured ministry and a respected place for the Union in national life, as well as his desire to nurture his relationship with Davidson and Lang. He was joined in this by many leading Baptists, and gave forceful expression to his feelings through his editorial control of the *Baptist Times*.

Many of the new groups, including the Brethren, the Churches of Christ and the Pentecostals, as well as many of the independent churches and missions, had a considerable affinity with the Baptists, mainly because of a common baptismal practice. According to earlier terminology, before the emergence of the Union as an effective national umbrella body, they might well have been accepted as Baptist. The denomination, even as late as the 1880's, was a loosely organised and disparate body of churches, containing a number of different groupings, of which the Union was but one. By the 1920's, however, the Union was so closely associated with the denomination that it had become virtually coterminous with it. Churches of a Baptist persuasion, along with their associations, were required either to accept the Union's authority or be excluded from the mainstream of denominational life.[16] Shakespeare's insistence on identifying the Union with the denomination, together with the institutional strengthening of the Union, meant that the division between official (i.e. Union) Baptist churches and organisations on the one hand, and unofficial Baptists on the other, became deep-seated and permanent. Without this insistence, it is possible that a broader understanding of what it mean to be 'Baptist' could have emerged, with a very different subsequent history for the denomination.

Baptists' search for the acceptance and respect of society, and particularly of the Church of England, culminated during and immediately after the war in the novel experience of having a Baptist Prime Minister, and in the recognition given to them by the Lambeth Appeal. These developments constituted, in effect, an invitation to take a place on the stage of national public life. Nonconformity did not disappear in the sense of becoming an integral part of the Church of England, as Horton and Shakespeare desired, but its essential character was diluted as a result of this social integration. As Horton realised in 1917, 'so soon as the English church sees the right of Free Churchmen to be, she will be in the way of making their existence unnecessary'.[17] Whatever the balance of advantage for the cause of religion in England as a whole might have been, there is little doubt that although the structures of Nonconformity continued in place, its ability to make a distinct contribution to English church life was markedly reduced.

As the notion of Nonconformity became less meaningful to Nonconformists, it was increasingly replaced by the concept of the Free Churches. This process had begun with the emergence of the National Free Church Council in the 1890's, which set the scene for many Nonconformists' self-understanding for much of the following century. Many regarded it as heralding a new Free Church of England. The National Council did not fulfil the hopes of its founders, and the founding of the Federal Council in 1919 constituted a renewed attempt to revive the Free Church ideal. This move represented the hopes of many for a deeper unity, this time through a federation of the denominations, rather than a popular movement at the local level. The Federal Council was no more successful in establishing Free Church identity than the National Council had been, however. The preoccupation of Shakespeare and others in the early years of the Federal Council with unity with the Church of England, confusion over the relationship with the older National Council and Shakespeare's poor health while he was Moderator all contributed to this failure.

Also important was the fact that Shakespeare's vision and desire for unity was not matched by any proper consideration of its ecclesiological implications for the participating denominations. With the Church of England, actions to demonstrate unity did not take place while contentious issues remained unidentified and unaddressed, much to Shakespeare's personal disappointment. Once they had been, organisational unity was seen to be a premature and unrealistic goal. The Free Churches, in contrast, established an institutional expression of unity in the Federal Council before the key differences between the denominations had been identified. In the years leading up to the formation of the Council Shakespeare constantly emphasised what they held in common, and the need for unity, but there was a marked reluctance to face up to their differences. He seemed to believe that a combination of exhortation and action would cause the underlying tensions over such things as church government, the ministry and baptism to disappear. This led to a form of unity that was little more than a hollow institutional shell masking important divisions.

The Federal Council proved valuable as a forum for enabling the Nonconformist denominations to co-operate. It also provided a means whereby they could be represented collectively where this was appropriate. These were substantial gains, and there have been benefits from them throughout the eighty years since. As a mechanism for achieving greater institutional unity, and promoting the Free Church ideal, however, the Council was not able to win any significant degree of confidence from the denominations, or support among the churches.

6.2 Changes in Baptist Church Polity

6.2.1 Denominational Leadership

Shakespeare's personal contribution was a major factor behind denominational change. It is true that the desire for greater denominational cohesion under the banner of the Union was widespread among Baptists at the time of his appointment. The erection of a London headquarters, the raising of a substantial capital fund to mark the new century and the Union's acquisition of an official denominational newspaper all met denominational aspirations that existed independently of Shakespeare. Concern about the quality and support of the ministry was also widespread. It was Shakespeare's ability and drive, however, that enabled these aspirations and concerns to be met. He did more than simply respond to an agenda set by others, bringing forward radical new ideas and direction. His commitment to a centrally co-ordinated approach to church extension, first expressed publicly in 1892 and put into effect through the Twentieth Century Fund was one example of this. The notion of the ministry as the responsibility of the whole denomination rather than the local church, and the acceptance of the ordained ministry of women also went beyond the thinking of most Baptists at the time.

Shakespeare's visionary leadership was manifested by his imaginative seizure of the opportunities that the mood for reform in the denomination presented to him. He was not satisfied with half measures. His ambitious designs for Baptist Church House are a good example of this, as was his systematic use of the *Baptist Times* to promote the Union's policy. His innovative approach to reforming the Union, his willingness to embrace the task of creating the Baptist World Alliance and his original approach to solving the problem of ministerial settlement, reflect a mind that was creative and bold. At least until 1916, a constant and sometimes bewildering stream of proposals about how denominational life could be improved flowed from his office. This was sometimes diverted, but never stemmed, by setbacks or opposition.

Shakespeare combined imagination and vision with a formidable organisational ability and capacity for work. His committee responsibilities at Baptist Church House were enormously demanding, and in most of the Union committees he was the main driving force behind their work. Apart from the periods when his health prevented it, he was almost always present, sometimes attending as many as five Union committee meetings in one afternoon.[18]

It is difficult to avoid the conclusion that Shakespeare was the most important single element in the changes in the denomination during his time in office. It is doubtful whether the Union structures were able to contain and channel his energies effectively, especially as they were to a large extent his creation in the first place. Of the official positions in the Union other than his own, the Presidency was the most influential, but was limited by being an annual appointment, and was intended to be inspirational rather than directing in Union affairs. As long as the Union's role was limited, its secretary's power was limited too. Once the Union took on the functions of a co-ordinating body for the whole denomination, and its powers grew, the secretary became, potentially at least, the most influential figure in the denomination. He was responsible for all paid Union staff and had considerable freedom to determine how and when matters were dealt with by the

Council and the Assembly. The longer he remained in office the greater his power became. For those who founded and reconstituted the Union in 1813 and 1832, the possibility that the secretary of the Union might enjoy a powerful position of church leadership among Baptists would have been unthinkable, but this was the situation a hundred years later.

The General Secretary of the Union has continued to be the central denominational figure among English Baptists, and looked to for leadership. The holders of the post since Shakespeare have, like him, served for long periods of time, with the exception of his immediate successor, J. C. Carlile, whose appointment was only intended to be a temporary measure. There were only three during the 57 years following M. E. Aubrey's appointment in 1925.[19] They all played a dominant role in denominational affairs. Shakespeare established this pattern of leadership by the General Secretary of the Union.

6.2.2 The Union

Of the changes that took place under Shakespeare, one of the most important and lasting, and one that he consistently promoted, was the shift in the focus of denominational life away from the local congregations and associations towards the Union. This centralisation was the inevitable consequence of several factors: the growing financial resources of the Union, the increased importance and rigour of ministerial accreditation by the Union, the virtual Union monopoly of denominational publications through its Publications Department and its ownership of the *Baptist Times*, the impressive new Baptist Church House, the transfer of responsibility for grant support for ministers from the associations to the Unions and the appointment of the Superintendents.

The fact of this change in the denomination's orientation and structure of authority could not be denied, but its real significance was a matter of some controversy. Those who advocated it usually denied that it amounted to an abandonment of traditional Baptist congregational church government, and claimed that it simply did away with the out-dated and harmful elements of independency. They maintained that it enabled local churches to co-operate more effectively in mission, and to have available to them a better qualified ministry, without taking away their essential autonomy. Sometimes the example of seventeenth-century Baptists was cited, with their sense of associational interdependence. Some advocated applying the term Church to the whole Baptist community as well as local congregations, speaking openly about the concept of a national Baptist Church. Others condemned what they saw as interference by the denominational hierarchy in affairs that were rightly the prerogative of the local church, guided by the Spirit of Christ as it met to seek His will. The impersonal and bureaucratic decision-making of Union committees, they said, was destructive of the whole concept of the

Church on which the denomination was founded.

This argument among Baptists about the rights and wrongs of a more centralised church polity has been a continuing feature of denominational life
ever since. In the 1940's there was a sharp disagreement between Ernest
Payne, tutor at Regent's Park College (by then in Oxford) and from 1951
General Secretary of the Union, and Arthur Dakin, Principal of Bristol
Baptist College, over the matter. Their contrasting concepts of the Baptist
ministry revealed the same underlying ecclesiological tension. In a booklet
entitled *The Baptist View of the Church and Ministry*, Dakin argued that
Baptist ecclesiology started with the local church, and that Baptists 'work
up to such central organisation as on that basis can be achieved'. This principle, he wrote, was 'fundamental' to their church polity.[20] According to
Dakin, a Baptist minister was consequently by definition a person called to,
and exercising, a ministry within a local church. Ministry, he wrote, must
be defined in terms of the local church, not a central authority. The status
of minister did not derive from a relationship with the Baptist Union, he
believed, but with a local church.[21]

Payne responded in the same year, 1944, with his *The Fellowship of
Believers: Baptist Thought and Practice Yesterday and Today*. In it, he
described Dakin's publication as a 'provocative but not very happily named
booklet'.[22] A foreword by Wheeler Robinson, the leading Baptist scholar
who had been one of Shakespeare's most enthusiastic supporters a quarter
of a century before, questioned the principle of congregationalism, and
Payne gave a forceful defence of the importance of the Union in Baptist
church polity. He criticised 'the exaggerated independence, self-sufficiency
and atomism which have sometimes been favoured of recent days',[23] and
commended the 'steady movement of events . . . towards the linking of each
individual minister with the Baptist Union as representing the whole Baptist
community'.[24] Payne was an admirer of Shakespeare and the part he played
in the development of the denomination, and in his own promotion of the
Union in Baptist life he built on the work done by his predecessor.[25]

A statement approved by the Council in 1948 called *The Baptist Doctrine
of the Church* supported the position taken by Payne (and by Shakespeare
before him),[26] as did the 1961 document *The Doctrine of the Ministry*, which
concluded that the Baptist Union was responsible for the maintenance of the
ministry.[27] *The Doctrine of the Ministry* acknowledged that differences of
opinion still remained among Baptists over the question of whether the minister was 'only a minister of the local church in which he served, or of a
wider fellowship'.[28] The nature of the relationships between the different
manifestations of the Church, at local and wider levels, and how these
should be reflected in church polity, have continued to pose difficult questions for Baptists.[29]

The pursuit of the right balance of authority between the Union, as the
institutional expression of the national community of Baptists, and the local

church, has become one of the central ecclesiastical issues confronted by Baptists since Shakespeare. It was only in the twentieth century that the Union became an important feature in the debate on church polity.[30] The emergence of the Union under Shakespeare cannot really be described, as Payne does, as 'a steady shift' of emphasis towards a more centralised ecclesiology. This may have been true of the development of the Union in the closing decades of the nineteenth century, but in the twenty or so years after 1898 it amounted to a sudden leap. The dramatic and permanent decline in the importance of the associations, and their subordination to the Union, has been one of the most important elements of this. These changes have determined the character of subsequent debates on church polity within the denomination. Their significance, and Shakespeare's role in bringing them about, has not always been acknowledged.

6.2.3 Baptist Ministry

Shakespeare's pre-occupation with the ministry was one of the most characteristic features of his life and work. The desire to see a more adequate provision for the support of ministers and greater ministerial 'efficiency' determined many of his ambitions for his denomination. Shakespeare was motivated, not only by a desire to see ministers properly supported and the conviction that the churches' prosperity depended above all on the ministry, but also by a high, indeed almost priestly, concept of the ministerial office. For him, the idea of the ministry as a separated body of men and women consecrated to God for spiritual leadership and service in the church made the responsibility for its selection, training, accreditation and provision, which he believed was held by the Union, a serious and sacred one. His efforts were aimed at restoring a status for ministers that he believed had been lost, but, in promoting a denominational and clerical concept of ministry, he was attempting to establish something completely new among Baptists.

English Baptists have continued since Shakespeare's time to practice ordination only once, at the beginning of a person's ministry, as a solemn setting apart for ministry, and to link this with denominational accreditation. To this extent the pattern set at the beginning of the twentieth century has been maintained. Ordination is for ministry among the churches of the Baptist Union, rather than for a particular local ministry. Baptists have historically seen the call to the ministry of a particular local church as a call to ministry within the whole Church of Christ,[31] but a denominational understanding of ordination is essentially a twentieth-century phenomenon. The post-war discussions within the Union about lay ministry[32] can only be understood in the light of a newly established distinction between the laity and the ordained ministry. It resulted in ambivalence about the status of non-ordained ministers. The official adoption of the term 'lay' as opposed to 'local' put them firmly in the camp of the laity. The elaboration of recognition procedures, on the other hand, gave them a quasi-clerical status. Baptists have tended to retreat from Shakespeare's high and clerical view of ministry since his departure, but most of the practices and institutions he created have remained. He put in place the ecclesiastical framework within which subsequent debates have occurred.

Non-English Baptists have often been the ones most eager to challenge a 'clerical' model of ministry. The Australian, Ruth Sampson, has been critical of 'the grossly disproportionate level of resources committed to the training of the few for ministry'. The limitation of ordination to so few 'ministers' leads, she believes, to an unbalanced view of ministry and a devaluing of the ministry of the 'laity'. She advocates the abandonment of the idea of ordination as 'admission to a special status group within the church at large', preferring a much more locally orientated view of ministry and ordination as 'commissioning for a particular ministry' within a local church.[33]

Baptist ordination practice has varied over time and from place to place. Variation is a natural consequence of the denomination's polity. It is nevertheless important to recognise that the clerical character of ministry in England during most of the twentieth century marks it out as significantly different from earlier practice. It may be possible to reconcile this with the two Baptist principles of the priesthood of all believers and the centrality of the local church as the primary context for ministry, but it nevertheless introduces an element of ambiguity. Shakespeare was responsible for institutionalising this uncertainty about ministry, and English Baptist thinking on the subject has been coloured by this ever since.

6.2.4 Superintendency

Confusion over the precise ecclesiological status and role of the Superintendents has gone hand in hand with a general appreciation of the ministry they have exercised. Personally, Shakespeare was ready to see them as Baptist bishops, and this terminology was not uncommon in Baptist circles in the early years of their existence. In part, this enthusiasm for episcopacy was due to Shakespeare's desire for union with the Church of England, but he was advocating its introduction, both within his own denomination and among the Free Churches generally, some time before any serious consideration had been given to any wider union. Unfortunately, neither he nor anyone else in the denomination gave a serious ecclesiological explanation of the step that was being taken. The Superintendents had no formal service of recognition or consecration to mark their appointment.

The origin of the Superintendency can only be understood in the light of Shakespeare's conviction that the ministry was above all the responsibility of the Union. His goal in establishing the 1916 Scheme was to forge a vital relationship between it and all accredited ministers. The Superintendents, as ministers appointed by, and in the service of, the Union, were part of this Scheme, having a specific role in ministerial deployment. Shakespeare's ambitions for the ministry proved beyond his ability to realise in full, but the Superintendents have remained as the chief monument to his original vision.

In the face of the lack of definition about their position, and the novelty of their appointment, how is it that the Superintendents have maintained their position within denominational life? One possible answer to this question can be found in seeing the Superintendents as fulfilling the role historically undertaken by the associations. When they were appointed it was made clear that they would combine their new duties with those of association secretary, several holding that position already. They took over all responsibilities previously held by the associations for ministerial settlement. At the same time, the associations' role as grant-making bodies for the support of churches and ministers was relinquished as the Sustentation Scheme came into effect. The associations did not disappear, but as their responsibilities for the ministry had been reduced, and with the appointment by the Union of the Superintendents to act as their leading officers, their importance as expressions of inter-church fellowship was greatly weakened. To a significant extent, their place in the denomination was taken over by the new Union appointments.

The prime responsibility of the Superintendents was for ministers, rather than the churches directly. Their appointment drew the ministry and the Union closer together. It also introduced a separation, as far as the churches were concerned, between matters that were directly related to the ministry and those that were not. The Superintendents naturally sometimes got involved in non-ministerial concerns, but their appointment had the effect of demonstrating that the Union's relationship with the churches was centred on the ministry. They can therefore be seen as a sign of Shakespeare's tendency to view the denomination predominantly in terms of its ministers rather than its churches.

Superintendency and associating had very different origins and character, and represent different approaches to denominational life. The associations were historically the product of local churches and ministers desiring fellowship with each other in order to fulfil their work more effectively. They consisted of individual churches relating to each other on a mutual basis. Superintendency was the product of Shakespeare's conviction that the work of the churches could only be done by means of a centralised administrative structure, dependent on the Union, for the direction of the ministry. The task of seriously evaluating the respective tasks of the Superintendents and the associations, and the relationship between them, has been taken up by the denomination, really for the first time, only at the close of the twentieth century.[34] It cannot be understood apart from the reforms put in place by Shakespeare.

6.2.5 Baptists and Ecumenism

Baptists reacted against Shakespeare's ecumenical adventures following his resignation in 1924 and the suspension of the Lambeth talks the following year. The prevailing mood in the denomination became unsympathetic to the stance he had taken. At the 1926 Assembly a reply to the Lambeth Appeal was unanimously agreed. This reply was largely the work of the incoming President, J. H. Rushbrooke. In his presidential address, entitled 'Protestant of the Protestants', Rushbrooke elaborated on its contents. He had fostered closer relationships with the American Baptists, and particularly with the new Southern Baptist President of the World Alliance, E. Y. Mullins, since the 1923 Stockholm Congress, and had been appointed Eastern Secretary in succession to Shakespeare early in 1925.

The 1926 reply amounted to a polite but uncompromising rejection of the Appeal. It expressed no desire for greater organisational unity between the churches, and asserted the right of every local church to self-government. It rejected any relation with the State that might impair this. It described infant baptism as 'subversive' of the Baptist conception of the church as a 'fellowship of believers'. It explicitly rejected the notion that the efficacy of the Lord's Supper depended on the episcopal ordination of the celebrant, and the concept of the ministry as a 'separated order of priests'. It concluded by stating that 'union of such a kind as the Bishops have contemplated is not possible for us'.[35]

The long awaited World Conference on Faith and Order was eventually held in Lausanne in 1927. Under Shakespeare, the Union had been actively involved in preparation for this, but within a few months of his resignation its Faith and Order Committee was dissolved.[36] It was decided not to send any official Union representatives to Lausanne. Instead, a copy of the 1926 reply to the Lambeth Appeal was regarded as a sufficient contribution from English Baptists. A few Baptists did nevertheless play an active role in the Faith and Order movement during the inter-war period, notably W. T. Whitley and Hugh Martin, and the Union Secretary Aubrey served on its Continuation Committee from 1929 onwards. In spite of Payne's remark that 'many British Baptists were deeply disappointed' at the decision not to send any delegates to Lausanne,[37] it seems clear that the general stance of the denomination, like that of the Southern Baptists, had become essentially anti-ecumenical.

Discussions within the Federal Council about achieving a greater degree of unity among the Free Churches took place in the 1930's, centring mainly on the possibility of the Congregationalists, Presbyterians and Baptists moving closer together. Anthony Cross considers these discussions to be 'the most vigorous debate on Christian unity' among Baptists since the turn of the century.[38] They came to an end with the Union Council's rejection of a plan for unity drawn up by the Free Church Unity Group in 1937. The prospects for any kind of organic unity were by then as remote as ever. The most significant development was the agreement to amalgamate the two Free Church Councils, an event that took place in 1941. This was more a case of organisational rationalisation than any significant step towards substantial unity.

Baptists as a whole never really shared Shakespeare's great vision of church unity. Even when he was most deeply involved in discussions, first with the other Free Churches, and then with the Church of England, between 1916 and 1923, the local churches did not participate significantly in the debate. Votes at Assemblies that did not commit the churches to do anything were never a reliable way of gauging real feeling. Events following Shakespeare's departure showed that most Baptists were unwilling to be flexible over the central issues involved in organic union, such as baptism, episcopal ordination and congregational church government.

One of the most striking things about Shakespeare's strategy was his readiness to belittle the importance of these issues. Baptism, for example, later recognised as a fundamental obstacle to unity as far as Baptists were concerned, was rarely addressed in the immediate post-war years. Shakespeare regarded differences over the nature of the ministry, episcopacy, congregational church government and the relations between Church and State as of secondary importance, compared with the over-riding imperative of unity. He believed that the gap between himself and the Church of England could be bridged, and committed himself to the task of persuading others to agree. Once the churches had come together in one great national organisation, he thought, different practices could be reconciled on the basis of good will and mutual respect. He appeared to overlook or ignore the fact that the Federal Council was a body that had no ecclesiastical authority. In its short history there had been no opportunity to address the differences between the Free Church denominations themselves, or to win the confidence of the denominational authorities. The truth was that the Council's deliberations and decisions committed nobody to anything, and were little more than empty gestures.

The belief that unity could be achieved organisationally, without addressing the primary doctrinal and ecclesiological causes of division, led to almost inevitable disappointment. As an ecumenical strategy, it was profoundly flawed. The *Churches at the Cross Roads* may well, as Hastings said, be 'one of the most important books of twentieth-century English Christianity', but surely not because it sets out 'the logic of the forthcoming ecumenical movement'.[39] Rather, it sets out Shakespeare's passion for unity, which had little to do with logic. That passion was Shakespeare's greatest contribution to the ecumenical debates of the twentieth century.

One of the consequences of the lengthy negotiations Shakespeare instigated with the Church of England was that the issues he himself regarded as secondary were eventually forced upon the attention of Baptists, in spite of his desire to avoid them. Central differences were thus gradually clarified. In the 1920's, one of the most important of these was the ministry. Before the Lambeth Palace conversations, there had been widespread but imprecise talk within the denomination about the Superintendents being really Bishops in all but name, about a ministry that belonged to the Union rather than to the local churches, and about the possibility of a central act of ordination. The word 'ordination' was avoided, but it is hard to avoid the implications of the phrase 'set apart to the ministry of the Church . . . in a service of consecration and prayer'.[40] Shakespeare was sympathetic to these ideas, although he was usually careful to avoid unnecessary controversy by making them explicit. They were, as people like T. R. Glover recognised, quite revolutionary in terms of traditional Baptist ecclesiology. The conversations at Lambeth Palace helped to expose the ambiguities they raised for the future direction of Baptist church polity, by addressing the issue of the ministry directly. The various reports and responses that were issued not only helped clarify differences between the churches, but also led to Baptists defining their own position more precisely The 1926 Baptist reply to the Lambeth Appeal would have been a disappointment to Shakespeare, but in the longer term it helped to put future discussions on unity onto a more realistic and honest basis by making it clearer where Baptists stood.

Shakespeare's passion for unity also meant that the disunity of the English churches was brought to the attention of Baptists in a way they could not ignore. Throughout the following 75 years, there have been several leading Baptists who have played prominent roles in the cause of reunion, Hugh Martin and Ernest Payne being among the most prominent. They did this in spite of opposition from many others in the denomination. Shakespeare's place as a pioneering Baptist ecumenist has been an important dimension of the denomination's twentieth-century history.

The search for organisational unity has been an important feature of the other Nonconformist denominations since the Great War, and Shakespeare's indirect contribution to that process should be acknowledged. The two most important concrete achievements have been the unification of Methodism in 1932 and the union of the majority of the member churches of the Congregational Church in England and Wales with the Presbyterian Church of England to form the United Reformed Church in 1972. Methodist unity reinforced the dominant position of Methodism in English Nonconformity, adding the Primitive and United Methodists to the Wesleyans, already the largest Nonconformist body. Formal discussions about union between the Presbyterians and Congregationalists were held intermittently from 1932 onwards. Shakespeare's pioneering work through the United Board and the Federal Council helped to set the scene for these important developments, which changed the face of twentieth-century English Nonconformity.

Shakespeare's primary motivation in pursuing reunion does not seem to have been ideological, in the sense that he saw a united English Church as a goal in itself. Rather his interest was in the Church's mission. He was passionate about the need to make the impact of the Church and its message more effective in national life. *The Churches at the Cross Roads* did not lay down a doctrinal or Biblical basis for unity. Its concern was how disunity hindered the common mission of the churches. A similar motivation had stimulated his concern for church extension in the 1890's and for the renewal of the Union and the ministry in the early years of the century. He did not believe that a fragmented, unorganised response to the challenges posed by contemporary society would ever achieve anything of any lasting value, and he constantly pleaded for greater co-ordination of effort and resources at both the denominational and the wider church level. He told the Assembly in 1908 that the first cause of Baptists' 'arrested progress' was 'our defective denominational system'.[41] He pleaded with the Free Churches from 1910 onwards for 'much fuller co-operation'.[42] During and after the war, he became even more convinced that a divided Church could never respond adequately to the needs and opportunities it faced.

Shakespeare was drawn onto an ever-broadening stage as his forty years in ministry progressed and his abilities recognised more widely. His ministry began at St. Mary's Baptist Church in Norwich, and ended with a prominent role in national Church life. At each point he sought to bring to bear his commitment to effective organisation and co-ordinated effort in mission. It is remarkable how the son of a Baptist manse in a small town in the North Riding of Yorkshire with an obscure early upbringing could become a prominent player on such a stage.

6.3 Conclusion

In an obituary, J. H. Rushbrooke described Shakespeare as 'the real founder of the Baptist Union'.[43] Charles Brown acknowledged at Shakespeare's memorial service in North Finchley that he 'created the modern Baptist Union'.[44] Arthur Porritt, editor of the *Christian World*, similarly described him as the 'Maker of the Baptist Denomination'.[45] These tributes reflect the undoubted fact that Shakespeare was a builder of institutions. He created, by means of his prodigious energy, powers of persuasion and organising skill, the modern Union and many other Baptist institutions, as well as the United Chaplaincy Board and the Federal Council. Subsequent years have seen these organisations modified, but they have, in general, survived in a similar state to when they were first put in place. Twentieth-century Baptists owe to him the institutional framework of their denomination, and especially the central authority of the Baptist Union, which has enabled them to make a corporate contribution to national life and to co-ordinate their work at a national level.

The construction of this institutional framework involved radical changes to Baptist church polity. The influence of the Union was broadened and deepened, the concept of the ministry underwent some quite profound transformations and the importance of the historic associations diminished substantially. Church life at the local level was inevitably affected by this. The principal change was in a significant modification of congregational church government. Officially, the principle of congregationalism was consistently upheld, but the reforms, accompanied as they were by frequent and vehement attacks on the churches' 'selfish independency' and isolationism changed the way it was understood. The typical local church found itself dependent to an unprecedented degree on the Union for information, finance and ministry.

Shakespeare saw no contradiction between this and the Baptist ecclesiology he inherited. He claimed to be upholding genuine Baptist values and priorities, adapting them to modern needs. Indeed, he would like to have seen his reforms taken much further. It is true that flexibility and pragmatism had been characteristic features of the denomination's church polity, and a measure of variety had enabled widely differing approaches to be called 'Baptist'. Those advocating change have always been encouraged by the fact that 'Baptists are not the heirs of any single, consistent ecclesiastical tradition'.[46] This has been especially true of relationships between local churches. Harrison observed this in his sociological study of American Baptists. 'Baptists,' he wrote, 'did not develop an explicit conception of the relation which must exist between the various parts of the church as a social institution'.[47]

In spite of the ecclesiological variety among Baptists, there were fundamental principles lying at the heart of their understanding of the church. These had their roots in the denomination's seventeenth century origins, and were centred on the notion of the church as a gathered congregation of believers. The members, having individually professed their faith through baptism, voluntarily came together in a solemn mutual commitment, sometimes expressed in terms of a church covenant. Such a congregation, it was believed, constituted a true and complete church, corporately receiving from Christ the authority it needed for the ordering of church life. Church bodies that lay beyond the local congregation, including associations, societies and the Union were historically based on this foundation. The autonomy of the local church was the spring from which Baptist ecclesiology flowed. It sometimes flowed in different directions, and took different forms, but its source was a common one.

Shakespeare effectively reversed this direction. His starting point was the Union and its need to become an effective national organisation, rather than the churches. As a consequence, he sought not so much to build the wider expressions of church life on the foundation provided by the local congregations, but to press the congregations to adapt to meet the needs of the wider church. Local churches' inherent insufficiency as an adequate basis for ministry and mission was a constant theme in his writing and speaking.

Congregational church government was not for him a positive and potentially fruitful basis on which Baptists could build, but a hindrance they had to overcome if they were to survive and prosper.

Shakespeare argued that none of his reforms contradicted the essential freedom of the churches, and in a strictly constitutional sense this was true. Ecclesiastical authority was still formally vested in the local church. Real power, however, was increasingly held by the Union. Harrison's description of the American Baptist Convention was apt, when he wrote; 'the encroachment upon the freedom of the churches has been consistently counteracted by an official reaffirmation of the belief in congregational independence'.[48] Harrison believed that this unacknowledged centralisation of power in the theoretically congregational Convention, the American equivalent of the Union, created serious internal contradictions and anomalies. It was exercised through such things as the appointment and direction of staff, the control of channels of communication and the procurement and allocation of denominational finances. Because the Convention's power was officially unrecognised and therefore inadequately regulated, it was possible for charismatic leaders to exert a disproportionate influence within the denomination, creating confusion about where true authority lay. It also led to an innate institutional conservatism greater than that of more 'highly rationalised ecclesiastical organisations', as there were no clear mechanisms for change.[49] Harrison argued that the authority of the various church bodies, from the local church to the central institutions, needed to be more openly recognised and defined. He also argued that the best way of achieving a healthy balance of power between churches and the Convention was by the restoration of effective local associations of churches, in order to create a 'balancing authority'.[50]

Harrison's analysis of the American Baptist Convention has obvious parallels to the development of the Union under Shakespeare, in spite of the cultural and historical differences between them.[51] It suggests that one of the most significant institutional changes under Shakespeare, and possibly one of the most damaging for the effective exercise of local church authority within the denomination, was the decline of the associations.

There was a strong desire among Baptists at the turn of the century for denominational reform. Shakespeare devoted his skill and energy to give that desire effective institutional expression. His achievements were substantial and lasting. By not basing them securely on the ecclesiology that lay at the heart of Baptist denominational identity he institutionalised a sense of ambiguity and confusion about the nature of the relationship between the Union and the churches. He left Baptists without a clear sense of where responsibility for mission and ministry really lay. The institutional framework the denomination inherited from him has survived substantially intact, as has the uncertainty to which it gave rise.

1. At least two books about Nonconformity have adopted this title - those by Robert Horton in 1902 and Mark D. Johnson in 1987.
2. See p. 13.
3. Deryck W. Lovegrove, *Established Church, Sectarian People: Itinerancy and the Transformation of English Dissent, 1780-1830* (Cambridge University Press: Cambridge, 1988) p. 104.   Derek J. Tidball, 'English Nonconformist Home Missions 1796-1901' (University of Keele *PhD* thesis, 1991) p. 326.
4. Gilbert, *Growth and Decline* p. (viii).
5. *Ibid.*, pp. 375-400.
6. See p. 9-10.
7. Booth, *Life and Labour* (series 3 vol. 7) pp. 124 and 128.
8. Elie Halévy, *The Rule of Democracy - 1905-1914* (Ernest Benn Ltd.: London, 1961) p. 74.
9. This unity in diversity is reflected in the Union's 'Declaration of Principle' of 1873. Abandoning earlier attempts to define a doctrinal basis, this simply states, 'in this Union it is fully recognised that every separate church has liberty to interpret and administer the laws of Christ, and that the immersion of believers is the only Christian baptism' (Sparkes, *Constitutions* p. 13). It was not until Shakespeare's revised constitution of 1904 that this declaration was expanded to include a fuller statement of Baptist principles.
10. An analysis of the remarkable similarities between the development of the Congregational and Baptist Unions during this period lies beyond the scope of this book. The two bodies seemed to stimulate each other to move in the same direction. Like the Baptists, the Congregationalists adopted a new constitution in 1904, by which denominational life was centralised. The Congregationalists seem to have been more successful than Shakespeare has in giving executive power to a central Council. A scheme for ministerial recognition was adopted, after several years of debate and revision, in 1912, and this was accompanied by the raising of a central fund for the augmenting of ministerial stipends between 1909 and 1913. A Scheme for Provinces and Moderators, which showed an almost exact parallel to the Baptist Areas and Superintendents, was put in place in 1919, about three years after the Baptist scheme. Most of these reforms took place under the Secretaryship of R. J. Wells, whose period of office (1905-1923) roughly corresponded to that of Shakespeare. Tudor Jones, having outlined these events in his history of Congregationalism, goes on to describe the growing sense of dismay and crisis within the denomination in the 1920's (see R. Tudor Jones, *Congregationalism in England 1662-1962* (Independent Press: London, 1962) pp. 376-388).
11. S. J. D. Green, *Religion in the age of decline: organisation and experience in industrial Yorkshire, 1870-1920* (Cambridge University Press: Cambridge, 1996).
12. *Ibid.*, pp. 389-390.
13. John Kent, *Holding the Fort: Studies in Victorian Revivalism* (Epworth Press: London, 1978) p. 300.
14. Horton was a prominent Congregationalist minister and President of the National Free Church Council in 1905.
15. Horton, *Dissent* p. 111.
16. They were mainly of a theologically conservative or reformed persuasion, including churches belonging to the Strict and Particular Baptist Associations and those that joined the Fellowship of Independent Evangelical Churches, founded in 1922.

17. Cited in Johnson, *Dissolution* p. 225.
18. On 15 March 1915, for example, Shakespeare attended the Scholarship Committee at 12 noon, the Annuity Fund Committee at 1.45 p.m., the Publicity Department Committee at 3 p.m., the Finance Committee at 4 p.m. and the Ministerial Recognition Committee at 5 p.m. (see BU Minute Book).
19 M. E. Aubrey (1925-1951), E. A. Payne (1951-1967) and D. S. Russell (1967-1982).
20. Dakin, p. 5.
21. *Ibid.*, pp. 41-8.
22. Payne, *Fellowship* p. 13.
23. *Ibid.*, p. 37.
24. *Ibid.*, p. 54.
25. Payne's favourable assessment of Shakespeare is demonstrated in many of his writings, especially in *Union* pp. 156-193. It seems, however, that his view of the benefit of a strong Union was somewhat modified in subsequent years. In a chapter added to a later edition of *The Fellowship of Believers*, published in 1952, he admitted that the growth in centralised denominational organisation had been accompanied by a disturbing decline in responsible churchmanship at the local level (see *Fellowship* pp. 114-127).
26. BUGBI, *The Baptist Doctrine of the Church* (Carey Kingsgate Press: London, 1948). See especially sections 3(e) and 4.
27. L. G. Champion *et al*, 'The Doctrine of the Ministry', in Hayden, *Documents*, pp. 13-54. See especially pp. 42-5.
28. *Ibid.*, p. 33.
29. See, for example, *The Nature of the Assembly and the Council of the Baptist Union of Great Britain* (BUGB: Didcot, 1994).
30. The Twentieth Century has also seen the emergence of Baptist institutions expressing denominational identity beyond national boundaries, notably the Baptist World Alliance (1905) and the European Baptist Federation (1948).
31. e.g. Champion, *Ministry* p. 20.
32. See pp. 145-7.
33. Ruth Sampson, 'United or Separated In the Ministry of the Church' in William H. Brackney (ed.), *Faith, Life and Witness (papers of the study and research division of the BWA: 1986-1990)* (Samford University Press: Birmingham, Alabama, 1990) pp. 325-34.
34. See the Union reports *Transforming Superintendency* (BUGB: Didcot, 1996) and *Relating and Resourcing* (BUGB: Didcot, 1998). The Union's *Report on the Commission on the Associations* (BUGB: Didcot, 1964) and *Working Together* (1973), both found in Hayden, *Documents*, do not deal with the Superintendents.
35. The full text of the reply is given in Payne, *Baptist Union* pp. 279-282. Cross draws attention to the importance of the baptism issue in the 1926 reply, one that had been regarded as secondary by Shakespeare (*Baptism and the Baptists*, pp. 62-3).
36. BU Minute Book, 7 July 1924.
37. Payne, *Baptist Union* p. 197.
38. Anthony R. Cross, 'Revd Dr Hugh Martin: Ecumenist' p. 76.
39. Hastings, p. 98.
40. BU Minute Book, 16 January 1922.
41. Shakespeare, *Arrested Progress* p. 9.

42. Shakespeare, 'Free Churches', p. 6.
43. *BT* 15 March 1928.
44. *BT* 22 March 1928.
45. *CW* 15 March 1928.
46. Hudson, *Baptist Concepts* p. 1.
47. Harrison, *Authority* p. 35.
48. *Ibid.*, p. 205.
49. *Ibid.*, pp. 74-7; 129; 206; 218-221.
50. *Ibid.*, pp. 218; 224.
51. It is worth bearing in mind that Harrison is not describing one particular Convention, but the general pattern of Baptist life in a number of American Conventions. This makes the applicability to the English scene more telling.

BIBLIOGRAPHY

(For published works, the place of publication is London unless otherwise specified).

1. Primary Sources

1.1 Archival Sources

(i) **Angus Library (Regent's Park College, Oxford):**
Ball, W. H., *Materials* (part of the E. A. Payne collection).
Baptist Union, *Minute Books* (1897-1925).
Inter-Collegiate Board, *Minutes* (1912-1916).
Payne, E. A., *Papers.*

(ii) **Devon and Cornwall Baptist Association:**
Minute Books and *Annual Reports* (1885-1921).

(iii) **Dr. Williams's Library, London:**
Free Church Council, *Reports* and *Minute Books* (1919-24).
Shakespeare, J. H., *Letter to R. F. Horton* (21 November 1923).

(iv) **House of Lords' Record Office:**
Lloyd-George, *Papers.*

(v) **Lambeth Palace Library:**
Davidson Papers (vols. 261-4).
Headlam Papers (vols. 2628-30).
Lambeth Conference Papers (vol. 113)
Tatlow Correspondence.

(vi) **Norfolk Record Office and Reference Library:**
Hewett, Maurice F., *Collection of Material in Preparation for an Historical Record of the Baptists in Norfolk and their Churches.*
St. Mary's Baptist Church, Norwich, *Deacons' Minute Book* (1882-1898); *Church Minute Book* (1882-1899); *1890/1 Year Book.*
Hipper, Kenneth, *Rev J. H. Shakespeare MA 1857-1928.*

(vii) **St. John's College, Cambridge:**
T. R. Glover Correspondence.

(viii) **Shakespeare family's private papers:**
Illuminated Address Presented to J. H. Shakespeare (October 1919).
Townsend, C. M., *The Life and Work of J. H. Shakespeare.*

1.2 Newspapers

Baptist
Baptist Times and Freeman
British Weekly
Christian World
Daily Chronicle
Daily News
Daily Sketch
Freeman
Manchester Guardian
Times

1.3 Books, Articles etc. published before 1930

Ainsworth, Henry, *The Communion of Saints: A Treatise of the fellowship, that the faithful have with God, and His Angels, and one with another; in this present life* (1641).

Arnold, Matthew, *Culture and Anarchy: an essay in political and social criticism* (John Murray: 1869).

Aubrey, M. E., 'The Future of Our Ministry' *BQ* vol. 1 (October 1922) pp.170-9.

Baptist Union, *Baptist Handbooks (1898-1921)* (BUGBI).
- *Reply to the Lambeth Appeal (1926)* (In J. H. Rushbrooke, *Faith of the Baptists* (see below).
- *The First Baptist World Congress: London, July 11-19, 1905. Authorised Record of proceedings* (BUGBI: 1905).

Baptist World Alliance, *The Baptist World Alliance: Second Congress. Philadelphia, June 19-25, 1911. Record of proceedings* (1911).

Bell, G. K. A. (ed.), *Documents on Christian Unity 1920-1924* (Oxford University Press: 1924).

Booth, Charles, *Life and Labour of the People in London* (3rd Series) (MacMillan and Co. Ltd.: 1902).

Booth, William, *In Darkest England and The Way Out* (Salvation Army: 1890).

Cairns, D. S. (*et al*), *The Army and Religion: An Enquiry and its bearing upon the Religious Life of the Nation* (MacMillan and Co. Ltd.: 1919).

Calvin, John, *Institutes of the Christian Religion* (translated by John Allen, 1831).

Campbell, R. J., *A Spiritual Pilgrimage* (Williams and Norgate: 1916).
- *The New Theology* (Chapman and Hall Ltd.: 1907).

Carlile, J. C. *The Story of the English Baptists* (James Clarke and Co.: 1905).
- 'Realities of Today' in James Marchant (ed.), *The Coming Renaissance* (Kegan Paul, Trench and Trubner: 1923).

Carlyle, A. J. (*et al*), *Towards Reunion: being contributions to mutual understanding by Church of England and Free Church writers* (MacMillan and Co. Ltd.: 1919).

Clark, Henry W., *History of English Nonconformity (vol. II)* (Chapman and Hall Ltd.: 1913).

Clarke, W. K. Lowther (*ed.*), *Facing the Facts: or An Englishman's Religion* (James Nisbet and Co. Ltd.: 1912).

Colman, Helen Caroline, *Jeremiah James Colman: A Memoir* (Chiswick Press: 1905).

Cuff, W., *Fifty Years Ministry 1865-1915: Memoirs and Musings* (BUGBI: 1915).

Dale, A. W. W., *Life of R. W. Dale of Birmingham* (Hodder and Stoughton: 1902).

Dale, R. W., *A Manual of Congregational Principles (11th Edition)* (Congregational Union of England and Wales: 1920).

- *History of English Congregationalism* (2nd Edition) (Hodder and Stoughton: 1907).

- *The Evangelical Revival and other sermons* (Hodder and Stoughton: 1880).

Darlow, T. H., *William Robertson Nicoll: Life and Letters* (Hodder and Stoughton: 1925).

Dicey, A. V., *Lectures on the Relation between Law and Public Opinion in England during the Nineteenth Century* (2nd Edition) (MacMillan and Co.: 1924).

Dunkley, C., *The Official Report of the Church Congress, held at Norwich, on October 8-11th, 1895* (Bemrose and Sons: 1895).

Figgis, John Neville, *Civilisation at the Cross Roads* (Longmans, Green, and Co.: 1912).

Forsyth, P. T., 'The United States of the Church' in J. H. Shakespeare and P. T. Forsyth (eds.), *A United Free Church of England* (NCEFC: 1911) pp. 15-47.

- *The Church and the Sacraments* (Longmans, Green and Co.: 1917).

Free Church Council, *Order of Service for Service of National Thanksgiving in Albert Hall, 16 November 1918*.

- *The Free Churches and the Lambeth Appeal (Report of a Committee Appointed by the Federal Council of Evangelical Free Churches and the National Free Church Council)* (The Religious Tract Society:1921).

- *Year Books (1903-10)* (NCEFC).

Fuller, A. G., 'Memoir of the Rev. Andrew Fuller' in Andrew Fuller, *Principal Works and Remains* (Henry G. Bohn: 1852) pp. 1-116.

Fullerton, W. Y., *At the Sixtieth Milestone: Incidents of the Journey* (Marshall Brothers: 1917).

- *F. B. Meyer: A Biography* (Marshall, Morgan and Scott: 1929).

- 'The Stockholm Congress and Exhibition' *BQ* vol. 1 (July 1923) pp. 291-4.

Fullerton, W. Y., John Clifford and J. H. Shakespeare, *A message from the Baptist Union of Great Britain and Ireland to the Baptists of the United States of America* (1917).

Gairdner, W. H. T., *Edinburgh 1910: An account and interpretation of the World Missionary Conference* (Oliphant, Anderson and Ferrier: Edinburgh, 1910).

Glover, Richard, 'The Desirability of a Closer Connexion between the Baptist Union and the leading Baptist Societies' in *Baptist Handbook 1875* (BUGBI).

Glover, T. R., *Jesus in the Experience of Men* (SCM: 1921).

-   *The Free Churches and Re-Union* (W. Heffer and Sons Ltd.: Cambridge, 1921).

-   *The Jesus of History* (SCM: 1917).

-   *The Nature and Purpose of a Christian Society* (3rd Edition) (Headley Brothers: 1912).

Gould, G. P., and J. H. Shakespeare (compilers), *An Order for the Solemnisation of Matrimony together with an Order for the Burial of the Dead* (Kingsgate Press: no date).

Gray, W. Forbes (ed.), *Non-Church Going: Its Reasons and Remedies* (Oliphant, Anderson and Ferrier: Edinburgh, 1911).

Hamilton, J. Miller, 'Rev. J. H. Shakespeare, M. A.,' in *Baptist Magazine* vol. 83 (September 1891) pp. 385-91.

Head, F. W., 'The Church and the People' in C. F. G. Masterman (*et al*), *The Heart of the Empire: Discussions of Problems of Modern City Life in England, with an essay on Imperialism* (T. Fisher Unwin: 1901).

Horne, Silvester, *A Popular History of the Free Churches* (James Clarke and Co.: 1903).

Horton, Robert F., 'The Church of England, Established and Free' *Contemporary Review* (1915) pp. 600-608.

-   *The Dissolution of Dissent* (Arthur H. Stockwell:1902).

-   *The Reunion of English Christendom* (NCEFC: 1905).

-   *An Autobiography* (George Allen and Unwin: 1917).

Hughes, Dorothea Price, *The Life of Hugh Price Hughes* (Hodder and Stoughton: 1907).

Kempthorne, J. A., 'The Present Outlook' in W. K. Lowther Clarke (ed.), *Facing the Facts: or An Englishman's Religion* (James Nisbet and Co. Ltd.: 1912).

Lunn, Henry S., *Chapters from My Life: With Special Reference to Reunion* (Cassell and Company: 1918).

Makepeace, J. F., *All I Could Never Be* (Basil Blackwell: Oxford, 1924).

Marchant, James (ed.), *Dr. John Clifford, CH: Life, Letters and Reminiscences* (Cassell and Co.: 1924).

-   *The Coming Renaissance* (Kegan Paul, Trench and Trubner: 1923).

Masterman, C. F. G. (*et al*), *The Heart of the Empire: Discussions of Problems of Modern City Life in England, with an essay on Imperialism* (T. Fisher Unwin: 1901).

- *The Condition of England* (6th Edition) (Methuen and Co. Ltd.: 1911).
Money, L. G. Chiozza, *Riches and Poverty* (3rd Edition) (Methuen and Co.: 1906).
Morgan, J. Brown, 'The present Baptist Churches of Yorkshire' in *Baptists in Yorkshire, Lancashire, Cheshire and Cumberland* (augmented edition) (BHS: 1913), pp. 115-137.
Mudie-Smith, Richard, *The Religious Life of London* (Hodder and Stoughton: 1904).

Orchard, W. E., *The Outlook for Religion* (Cassell and Company: 1917).

Porritt, Arthur, *The Best I Remember* (Cassell and Company: 1922).

Robinson, H. Wheeler, *The Life and Faith of the Baptists* (Methuen and Co. Ltd.: 1927).
Rushbrooke, J. H. (*et al*), *The Faith of the Baptists: papers on belief and polity, being the substance of addresses delivered at the Assembly of the Baptist Union of Great Britain and Ireland held in Leeds, May 1926* (Kingsgate Press: 1926).

St. Mary's Baptist Church, *Re-Opening Services: Renovated St. Mary's* (St. Mary's Baptist Church: Norwich, 1886).
Selbie, W. B. (ed.), *The Life of Charles Silvester Horne* (Hodder and Stoughton: 1920).
- *Nonconformity: Its Origins and Progress* (Thornton Butterworth: 1912).
Shakespeare, J. H., *The Arrested Progress of the Church: An Address to the Spring Assembly of the Baptist Union of Great Britain and Ireland, 28 April 1908* (BUGBI: 1908).
- 'Address' *St. Mary's Magazine* vol. 3 (November 1898).
- *Baptist and Congregational Pioneers* (NCEFC: 1906).
- *Baptist Church Extension in Large Towns: A Paper read at the Assembly of the Baptist Union, 28 April 1892* (BUGBI: 1892).
- *The Churches at the Cross Roads: A Study in Church Unity* (Williams and Norgate: 1918).
- 'The Colleges and the Ministry' *Baptist Magazine* vol. 83 (February and June 1891) pp. 70-4 and 261-9.
- *The Duty of Christian Men in the Present Political Crisis: An Election Sermon* (Norfolk News Co. Ltd.: Norwich, 1885).
- *The Free Churches at the Cross Roads* (NCEFC: 1916).
- 'The Great Need' in J. Marchant (ed.), *The Coming Renaissance* (Kegan Paul, Trench and Trubner: 1923) pp. 79ff.
- *The Issues of Agnosticism and Faith: A Sermon* (Norfolk News Co. Ltd.: Norwich, 1889).
- *Sermon* (delivered at St. Mary's Baptist Chapel on 28 December 1884) (in Angus Library, Regent's Park College, Oxford)

- *The Story of the Twentieth Century Fund* (BUGBI: 1904).
- 'Studies in Theology: Sin; Grace; The Incarnation; The Meaning of the Cross' *Baptist Magazine* vol. 91 (July, August, October and December 1899) pp. 308-13; 372-7; 462-9; 557-62.
- *The Two Republics* (Evangelical Information Committee:1918).

Shakespeare, J. H., and G. P. Gould, *A Manual for Free Church Ministers* (no date).

Shakespeare, J. H., and P. T. Forsyth, *A United Free Church of England* (NCEFC: 1911).

Shillito, E., *The Hope and Mission of the Free Churches* (T. C. and E. C. Jack: no date: ?1912).

Skeats, Herbert S., and Charles Miall, *History of the Free Churches of England 1688-1891* (Alexander and Shepheard: 1891).

Slosser, Gaius Jackson, *Christian Unity: Its History and Challenge in all Communions, in all Lands* (Kegan Paul, Trench, Trubner and Co.: 1929).

Society for Promoting Christian Knowledge, *Documents Bearing on the Problem of Christian Unity and Fellowship 1916-1920* (The MacMillan Company: 1920)

Spurr, Frederic C., *Some Chaplains in Khaki: An Account of the Work of Chaplains of the United Navy and Army Board* (H. R. Allensen Ltd. and The Kingsgate Press: 1916).

Stead, W. T., *The Revival of 1905* (The 'Review of Reviews' Publishing Office: 1905).

Stoughton, John, *Religion in England from 1800-1850. A history, with a postscript on subsequent events* (vol. II) (Hodder and Stoughton: 1884).

Tipple, S. A., *Spoken Words of Prayer and Praise* (James Clarke and Co.: 1912).

Tyrrell, George, *Christianity at the Cross-Roads* (Longmans, Green and Co.: 1913).

Whitley, W. T. (ed.), *Third Baptist World Congress, Stockholm, July 21-7, 1923. Record of Proceedings* (Kingsgate Press: 1923).
- *The Baptists of London 1612-1928: Their fellowship, their expansion, with notes on their 850 churches* (Kingsgate Press: 1928).

Williams, Charles, *The Principles and Practices of the Baptists* (James Clarke and Co.: no date: ?1903).

Williams, T. Rhondda (ed.), *The True Revival Versus Torreyism* (Percy Lund, Humphries and Co. Ltd.: 1904).

Williamson, David, *Life of Alexander MacLaren: Preacher and Expositor* (James Clarke and Co.: no date: ?1910).

Willis, Irene Cooper, *How We went into the War: A Study of Liberal Idealism* (The National Labour Press, Ltd.: 1918).

2. Secondary Sources

A Jones, Peter d', *The Christian Socialist Revival 1877-1914: Religion, Class and Social Conscience in late Victorian England* (Princeton University Press: Princeton, New Jersey, 1968).

Adams, William Scovell, *Edwardian Heritage: A Study in British History 1901-1906* (Frederick Muller Ltd.: 1949).

Aubrey, M. E., 'John Howard Shakespeare, 1857-1928' *BQ* vol. 17 (July 1957) pp. 99-108.

Baker, Derek (ed.), *Renaissance and Renewal in Christian History: Papers read at the 15th Summer Meeting and the 16th Winter Meeting of the Ecclesiastical History Society (Church History* vol. 13*)* (Basil Blackwell: 1977).

Baptist History Society, *English Baptist Records 2: Church Book, St. Andrews Street Baptist Church, Cambridge, 1720-1832* (BHS: Didcot, 1991).

Baptist Union, *The Baptist Doctrine of the Church* (The Carey Kingsgate Press: 1948).

- *The Meaning and Practice of Ordination among Baptists* (BUGBI: 1957).

- *The Nature of the Assembly and the Council of the Baptist Union of Great Britain* (BUGB: Didcot, 1994).

- *Relating and Resourcing: The Report of the Task Group on Associating* (BUGB: Didcot, 1998).

- *Transforming Superintendency: The Report of the General Superintendency Review Group* (BUGB: Didcot, 1996).

Bartlett, Alan Bennett, 'The Churches in Bermondsey 1880-1939' (University of Birmingham *PhD* 1987).

Baxter, Colin Benjamin, 'A Study of Organisational Growth and Development of the Congregational, Presbyterian and United Reformed Churches' (Brunel University *DPhil* 1981).

Beasley-Murray, Paul, *Radical Believers* (BUGB: Didcot, 1992).

Bebbington, D. W., 'Baptist Members of Parliament, 1847-1914' *BQ* vol. 29 (April 1981) pp. 51-64.

Bebbington, D. W., 'Baptists and Fundamentalism in Inter-War Britain' in Keith Robbins (ed.), *Protestant Evangelicalism* (Oxford University Press: 1990) pp. 297-326.

- 'Baptists and Politics since 1914' in K. W. Clements (ed.), *Baptists in the Twentieth Century* (BHS: 1983) pp. 76-90.

- *Evangelicalism in Modern Britain: A history from the 1730's to the 1980's* (Unwin Hyman: 1989).

- 'Gladstone and the Baptists' *BQ* vol. 26 (1976) pp. 224-239.

- *The Nonconformist Conscience: Chapel and Politics: 1870-1914* (George Allen and Unwin: 1982).

- *Victorian Nonconformity* (Headstart History: 1992).

- *William Ewart Gladstone: Faith and Politics in Victorian Britain* (Eerdmans: Grand Rapids, 1993).

Bedarida, Francois, *A Social History of England 1851-1990 (2nd Edition)* (Routledge: 1991).

Bell, G. K. A., *Randall Davidson: Archbishop of Canterbury (3rd Edition)* (Oxford University Press: 1952).

Bennett, G. V. and J. D. Walsh (eds.), *Essays in Modern English Church History: in Memory of Norman Sykes* (Oxford University Press: New York, 1966).

Binfield, Clyde, 'Asquith: The Formation of a Prime Minister' *The Journal of the United Reformed Church History Society* vol. 2 (April 1981) pp. 204-242.

- 'English free churchmen and a national style' in Stuart Mews (ed.), *Religion and National Identity (Church History* vol. 18*)* (Basil Blackwell: Oxford, 1982) pp. 519-532.

- 'Hebrews Hellenized? English Evangelical Nonconformity and Culture, 1840-1940' in S. Gilley and W. J. Sheils (eds.) *A History of Religion in Britain* (Blackwell: Oxford 1994) pp. 322-345.

- *Pastors and People: The Biography of a Baptist Church: Queen's Road, Coventry* (Queen's Road Baptist Church: Coventry, 1984).

- *So Down to Prayers: Studies in English Nonconformity 1780-1920* (M. Dent and Sons Ltd.: 1977).

- 'Towards an Appreciation of Baptist Architecture' in K. W. Clements (ed.), *Baptists in the Twentieth Century* (BHS: 1983).

Bonsall, H. Edgar, and Edwin H. Robertson, *The Dream of An Ideal City: Westbourne Park 1877-1977* (Westbourne Park Baptist Church: 1978).

Bowers, Faith, 'Bloomsbury Chapel 1848-1905' (London University (King's College, London *MPhil* 1984).

Brachlow, Stephen, *The Communion of Saints: Radical Puritan and Separatist Ecclesiology 1570-1625* (Oxford University Press: New York, 1988).

Brackney, William H. (ed.), *Faith Life and Witness* (Samford University Press: Birmingham, Alabama, 1990).

- (ed.), *Baptist Life and Thought: 1600-1980: A Source Book* (Judson Press: Valley Forge, 1983).

- *The Baptists* (Greenwood Press: New York, 1988).

Bradley, Ian, *The Call to Seriousness: The Evangelical Impact on the Victorians* (Jonathan Cape: 1976).

Briggs, J. H. Y., 'Baptists and Higher Education in England' in William H. Brackney (ed.), *Faith, Life and Witness* (Samford University Press: Birmingham, Alabama, 1990).

- 'Charles Haddon Spurgeon and the Baptist Denomination in Nineteenth Century Britain' *BQ* vol. 31 (January 1986) pp. 218-40.

- *The English Baptists of the Nineteenth Century* (BHS: Didcot, 1994).

- 'Evangelical Ecumenism: The Amalgamation of General and Particular Baptists in 1891' *BQ* vol. 34 (July and October 1991) pp. 99-110 and pp. 160-7.

Briggs, John, and Ian Sellers (eds.), *Victorian Nonconformity* (Edward Arnold: 1973).

Broomfield, Gerald, *Anglican and Free Church Ministries: Unification through Reciprocal Supplementary Ordination* (SPCK: 1944).

Brown, Kenneth D., 'College Principals - a Cause of Nonconformist Decay?' *Journal of Ecclesiastical History* vol. 38 (1987) pp. 236-253.

- 'Patterns of Baptist Ministry in the Twentieth Century' *BQ* vol. 33 (April 1989) pp. 81ff.

- *A Social History of the Nonconformist Ministry in England and Wales, 1800-1930* (Clarendon Press: Oxford, 1988).

- 'An Unsettled Ministry? Some Aspects of Nineteenth Century British Nonconformity' *Church History* vol. 56 (June 1987) pp. 204-23.

Brown, Raymond, *The English Baptists of the Eighteenth Century* (BHS: 1986).

Carey, Pearce, 'Regent's as I knew it' *BQ* vol. 8 (July 1936) pp. 136-9.

Carlile, J. C., *My Life's Little Day* (Blackie and Son Ltd.: 1935).

Cecil, Robert, *Life in Edwardian England* (B. T. Batsford: 1969).

Chadwick, Owen, *The Victorian Church, Part II* (2nd Edition) (Adam and Charles Black: 1972).

Chadwick, Rosemary, 'Independence or Co-operation? The Yorkshire Baptist Association, 1880-1914' *BQ* vol. 31 (October 1986) pp. 355-69.

Champion, J. A. I., *The Pillars of Priestcraft Shaken - the Church of England and its enemies: 1660-1730* (Cambridge University Press: Cambridge, 1992).

Champion, L. G., 'Baptist Church Life in the Twentieth Century' in K. W. Clements (ed.), *Baptists in the Twentieth Century* (BHS: 1983).

- 'Baptists and the Ministry: The Nature of Christian Ministry' *BQ* vol. 17 (October 1958) pp. 341-350.

- 'Evangelical Calvinism and the Structures of Baptist Church Life' *BQ* vol. 28 (July 1980) pp. 196-208.

Champion, L. G., Barrett J. O., and West, W. M. S., 'The Doctrine of the Ministry' in R. Hayden (ed.), *Baptist Union Documents, 1948-1977* (BHS: 1980).

Child, R. L., 'Baptists and the Reunion Movement' *BQ* vol. 10 (July 1941) pp. 392-7.

- *The General Superintendency (1915-1965)* (BUGBI: 1965).

Clark, N., 'The Meaning and Practice of Ordination' *BQ* vol. 17 (January 1958) pp. 197-205.

Clement, A. S. (ed.), *Baptists who made History: A Book about Great Baptists written by Baptists* (Carey Kingsgate Press: 1955).

Clements, Keith (ed.), *Baptists in the Twentieth Century* (BHS: 1983).

- *Lovers of Discord: Twentieth century theological controversies in England* (SPCK: 1988).

Clifford, Paul Rowntree, *Venture in Faith: The Story of the West Ham Central Mission* (The Carey Kingsgate Press: 1950).

Coggins, James Robert, *John Smyth's Congregation: English Separatism,*

Mennonite Influence, and the Elect Nation (Herald Press: Waterloo, Ontario, 1991).

Cole, C. Robert, and Michael E. Moody (eds.), *The Dissenting Tradition* (Ohio University Press: Athens, Ohio, 1975).

Collinson, Patrick, 'The English Conventicle' in W. J. Shiels and Diana Wood (eds.), *Voluntary Religion* (Basil Blackwell: Oxford, 1986) pp. 223-59.

- *Godly People: Essays on English Protestantism and Puritanism* (The Hambledon Press: 1983).

- 'Towards a Broader Understanding of the Early Dissenting Tradition' in C. Robert Cole and Michael E. Moody (eds.), *The Dissenting Tradition* (Ohio University Press: Athens, Ohio, 1975) pp. 3-38.

Cooper, R. E., *From Stepney to St. Giles: The Story of Regent's Park College 1810-1960* (The Carey Kingsgate Press: 1960).

Cox, Jeffrey, *The English Churches in a Secular Society. Lambeth 1870-1930* (Oxford University Press: 1982).

Cross, Anthony R., *Baptism and the Baptists: Theology and Practice in Twentieth -Century Britain* (Paternoster Press: Carlisle, 2000).
'Revd Dr Hugh Martin: Ecumenist', *BQ* vol. 37 (April 1997) pp. 71-86.

Cross, Claire, *Church and People 1450-1660: The Triumph of the Laity in the English Church* (Fontana Press: 1976).

Crossick, Geoffrey (ed.), *The Lower Middle Class in Britain 1870-1914* (Croom Helm: 1977).

Cuming, G. J., and Derek Baker (eds.), *Popular Belief and Practice (Studies in Church History* vol. 8) (Cambridge University Press: Cambridge, 1972).

Cunningham, Valentine, *Everywhere Spoken Against - Dissent in the Victorian Novel* (Clarendon Press: Oxford, 1975).

Currie, Robert, Alan Gilbert and Lee Horsley, *Churches and Churchgoers: Patterns of Church Growth in the British Isles since 1700* (Clarendon Press: Oxford, 1977).

Dakin, A., *The Baptist View of the Church and Ministry* (BUGBI: 1944).

Dangerfield, George, *The Strange Death of Liberal England* (1966 Edition) (MacGibbon and Kee: 1966).

David, Jacqueline, 'A Spiritual Pilgrimage: A Biographical Study of R. J. Campbell' (University of Birmingham *PhD* 1991).

Davie, Donald, *A Gathered Church: The Literature of the English Dissenting Interest, 1700-1930* (Routledge and Kegan Paul: 1978).

Davies, Horton, *The English Free Churches* (Oxford University Press: 1952).

- *A Mirror of the Ministry in Modern Novels* (Oxford University Press: New York, 1959).

- *Worship and Theology in England: From Newman to Martineau, 1850-1900* (Oxford University Press: 1962).

- *Worship and Theology in England: The Ecumenical Century, 1900-1965* (Princeton University Press: New Jersey, 1965).

Devlin, Carol A., 'The Eucharistic Procession of 1908: The Dilemma of the Liberal Government' *Church History* vol. 63 (September 1994) pp. 407-25.

Doyle, Barry M., 'Through the Windows of a Baptist Meeting House: Religion, Politics and the Nonconformist Conscience in the life of Sir George White MP' *BQ* vol. 36 (April 1996) pp. 294-307.

Drummond, Andrew L., *The Churches in English Fiction: A literary and historical study from the Regency to the present time, of British and American fiction* (Edgar Backus: Leicester, 1950).

Dyos, H. J., and Michael Wolff (eds.), *The Victorian City: Images and Realities* (vol. II) (Routledge and Kegan Paul: 1973).

Everitt, Alan, *The Pattern of Rural Dissent: the Nineteenth Century* (Leicester University Press: Leicester, 1972).

Feuchtwanger, E. J., *Democracy and Empire: Britain 1865-1914* (Edward Arnold: 1985).

Field, Clive, 'Adam and Eve: Gender in the English Free Church Constituency' *Journal of Ecclesiastical History* vol. 44 (January 1993) pp. 63-79.

Fraser, Derek (ed.), *Cities, Class and Communication: Essays in Honour of Asa Briggs* (Harvester Wheatsheaf: Hemel Hempstead, 1990).

Fraser, W. Hamish, 'From Civic Gospel to Municipal Socialism' in Derek Fraser (ed.), *Cities, Class and Communication: Essays in Honour of Asa Briggs* (Harvester Wheatsheaf: Hemel Hempstead, 1990) pp. 58-80.

Gilbert, Alan D., 'The Growth and Decline of Nonconformity in England and Wales, with Special Reference to the Period before 1850: An Historical Interpretation of Statistics of Religious Practice' (University of Oxford *DPhil* 1973).

-   *The Making of Post-Christian Britain: A history of the secularisation of modern society* (Longman Group: 1980).

-   *Religion and Society in Industrial England: Church, Chapel and Social Change 1740-1914* (Longman: 1976).

Gilbert, Bentley Brinkerhoff, *David Lloyd George: a political life: Organiser of Victory, 1912-1916* (Ohio State University Press: Columbus, 1992).

Gilley, S., and W. J. Sheils (eds.), *A History of Religion in Britain: practice and belief from Pre-Roman Times to the Present* (Blackwell: Oxford, 1994).

Glaser, John F., 'English Nonconformity and the Decline of Liberalism' *American Historical Review* vol. 63 (January 1958) pp. 352-363.

Glasse, James D., *Profession: Minister* (Abingdon: New York, 1968).

Glover, T. R., 'Nonconformity Old and New' in *Fifty Years: Memories and Contrasts: A Composite Picture of the Period 1882-1932* (Thornton Butterworth: 1932).

Glover, Willis B., *Evangelical Nonconformists and Higher Criticism in the Nineteenth Century* (Independent Press: 1954).

Gosse, Edmond, *Father and Son: A Study of Two Temperaments* (edited by James

Hepburn) (Oxford University Press: 1974) (first published in 1907).

Grant, John W., *Free Churchmanship in England: 1870-1940 (with special reference to Congregationalism)* (Independent Press: no date).

Green, Bernard, *Tomorrow's Man: A Biography of James Henry Rushbrooke* (Baptist Historical Society: Didcot, 1997).

Green, S. J. D., 'Religion and the Industrial Town, with Special Reference to the West Riding of Yorkshire, c1870-1920' (University of Oxford *DPhil* 1989).

- 'Religion and the Rise of Common Man: Mutual Improvement Societies, Religious Associations and Popular Education in Three Industrial Towns in the West Riding of Yorkshire c1850-1900' in Derek Fraser (ed.), *Cities, Class and Communication: Essays in Honour of Asa Briggs* (Harvester Wheatsheaf: Hemel Hempstead, 1990) pp. 25-43.

- *Religion in the age of decline: Organisation and Experience in Industrial Yorkshire, 1870-1920* (Cambridge University Press: Cambridge, 1996).

Grigg, John, *Lloyd George: From Peace to War. 1912-1916* (Methuen: 1985).

Halévy, Elie, *Imperialism and the Rise of Labour* (Ernest Benn: 1961).

- *The Rule of Democracy, 1905-1914* (Ernest Benn: 1961).

Hall, Basil, 'The Welsh Revival of 1904-5: A Critique' in G. J. Cuming and Derek Baker (eds.), *Studies in Church History* vol. 8 (1972) pp. 291ff.

Hall, Sidney, and Harry Mowvley, *Tradition and Challenge: The Story of Broadmead Baptist Church, Bristol, from 1685-1991* (Broadmead Baptist Church: Bristol, 1991).

Halsey, A. H., *Trends in British Society since 1900: A guide to the changing social structure of Britain* (The MacMillan Press: 1972).

Hancock, W. C. R., 'No Compromise: Nonconformity and Politics, 1893-1914' *BQ* vol. 34 (April 1995) pp. 56-69.

Harris, Jose, *Private Lives, Public Spirit - A Social History of Britain 1870-1914* (Oxford University Press: 1993).

Harrison, Archibald W., *The Evangelical Revival and Christian Reunion* (The Epworth Press: 1942).

Harrison, F. M. W., 'The Nottinghamshire Baptists: Mission, Worship and Training' *BQ* vol. 25 (July 1974) pp. 309-28.

- 'The Nottinghamshire Baptists: Polity' *BQ* vol. 25 (January 1974) pp. 212-231.

Harrison, Paul M., *Authority and Power in the Free Church Tradition: A Social Case Study of the American Baptist Convention* (Princeton University Press: Princeton, New Jersey, 1959).

Harrison, Rachel M., 'The Significance of the Ordained Ministry For the Members of the Baptist Union of Great Britain' (Heythrop College, London *MTh* 1988).

Hastings, Adrian, *A History of English Christianity. 1920-1985* (Collins: 1986).

Hayden, Roger (ed.), *Baptist Union Documents, 1948-1977* (BHS: 1980).

- *English Baptist History and Heritage* (BUGB: Didcot, 1990).

- 'Still at the Crossroads? - Revd. J. H. Shakespeare and Ecumenism' in K.

W.Clements (ed.), *Baptists in the Twentieth Century* (BHS: 1983) pp. 31.

Healey, F. G., *Rooted in Faith: Three Centuries of Nonconformity 1662-1962* (Independent Press: 1961).

Helmstadter, Richard J., and Bernard Lightmen (eds.), *Victorian Faith in Crisis: Essays on Continuity and Change in Nineteenth Century Religious Belief* (MacMillan Academic and Professional: 1990).

Hempton, David, 'Religious Life in Industrial Britain: 1830-1914' in S. Gilley and W. J. Sheils (eds.), *A History of Religion in Britain: practice and belief from Pre-Roman Times to the Present* (Blackwell: Oxford, 1994) pp. 306ff.

Hinchliff, Peter, 'Frederick Temple, Randall Davidson and the Coronation of Edward VII' *The Journal of Ecclesiastical History* vol. 48 (January 1997) pp. 71-99.

Hoover, A. J., *God, Germany and Britain in the Great War: A Study in Clerical Nationalism* (Praeger Publishers: New York, 1989).

Hopkins, Mark Thomas Eugene, 'Baptists, Congregationalists and Theological Change: Some Late Nineteenth Century Leaders and Controversies' (University of Oxford *DPhil* 1988).

Horst, Irvin Buckwalter, *The Radical Brethren: Anabaptism and the English Reformation to 1558* (B. de Graaf: Nieuwkoop,1972).

Hudson, W. S., 'Shifting Patterns of Church Order in the Twentieth Century' in Winthrop Still Hudson (ed.), *Baptist Concepts of the Church* (Judson Press: Pennsylvania, 1959) pp. 196ff.

Jackson, Eleanor M., 'Significant Developments in the History of 'Organised Ecumenism': 1910-1968' (University of Birmingham *MA* 1972).

Jewson, C. B., *The Baptists in Norfolk* (Carey Kingsgate Press: 1957).

- *St. Mary's in Four Centuries: 1669-1969* (St. Mary's Baptist Church: Norwich, 1969).

Johnson, Mark D., *The Dissolution of Dissent 1850-1918* (Garland Publishing: New York, 1987).

Johnson, W. Charles, *Encounter in London: The Story of the London Baptist Association 1865-1965* (Carey Kingsgate Press Ltd.: 1965).

Jones, J. D., *Three Score Years and Ten* (Hodder and Stoughton: 1940).

Jones, R. Tudur, *Congregationalism in England 1662-1962* (Independent Press Ltd.: 1962).

Jordan, E. K. H., *Free Church Unity: History of the Free Church Council Movement 1896-1941* (Lutterworth Press: 1956).

Keating, Peter (ed.), *Into Unknown England 1866-1913: Selections from the Social Explorers* (Manchester University Press/Fontana: Manchester, 1976).

Kent, John, *Holding the Fort: Studies in Victorian Revivalism* (Epworth Press: 1978).

- 'Hugh Price Hughes and the Nonconformist Conscience' in G. V. Bennett and J. D. Walsh (eds.), *Essays in Modern English Church History* (Oxford

University Press: New York, 1966) pp. 181-205.

- 'A late Nineteenth Century Nonconformist Renaissance' in Derek Baker (ed.) *Renaissance and Renewal in Christian History (Church History* vol. 13*)* (Basil Blackwell: Oxford, 1977) pp. 351-360.
- 'Models of the British Nonconformist Ministry' in N. Lash and J. Rhymer (eds.) *The Christian Priesthood* (Darton, Longman and Todd: 1970) pp. 83ff.

Kirkby, Arthur H., *Andrew Fuller (1754-1815)* (Independent Press Ltd.: 1961).

Klaassen, Walter (ed.), *Anabaptism in Outline: Selected Primary Sources* (Herald Press: Kitchener, Ontario, 1981).

Klaiber, A. J., *The Baptist Union General Superintendents: What they are and what they do?* (BUGBI: 1948).

Koss, Stephen, *Nonconformity in Modern British Politics* (B. T. Batsford: 1975).

Koss, Stephen, 'Lloyd George and Nonconformity: The Last Rally' *The English Historical Review* vol. 39 (January 1974) pp. 77-108.

Laquer, Thomas Walter, *Religion and Respectability: Sunday Schools and working class culture 1780-1850* (Yale University Press: 1976).

Lawrence, George W. Jnr., 'William Robertson Nicoll (1851-1923) and Religious Journalism in the Nineteenth Century' (University of Cambridge *PhD* 1954).

Lazell, David, *From the Forest I Came: The Story of Gipsy Rodney Smith MBE* (Concordia Press: 1970).

Lidgett, J. Scott, *My Guided Life* (Methuen and Co.: 1936).

Lloyd, Roger, *The Church of England 1900-1965* (SCM Press: 1966).

Lockhart, J. G., *Cosmo Gordon Lang* (Hodder and Stoughton: 1949).

Lockwood, David, *The Blackcoated Worker: A Study in Class Consciousness* (Unwin University Books: 1958).

Lord, F. Townley, *Baptist World Fellowship: A Short History of the Baptist World Alliance* (Carey Kingsgate Press: 1955).

Lovegrove, Deryck W., *Established Church, Sectarian People: Itinerancy and the Transformation of English Dissent, 1780-1830* (Cambridge University Press: Cambridge, 1988).

- 'Idealism and Association in Early Nineteenth Century Dissent' *Studies in Church History* vol. 23 (1986) pp. 303-17.

Lumpkin, William L., *Baptist Confessions of Faith* (The Judson Press: Philadelphia, 1959).

Luther, Martin, *Works (vols. 39, 40 and 41) (edited by Conrad Bergendoff)* (Fortress Press: Pennsylvania, 1958).

Macarthur, Arthur, 'The Background to the Formation of the United Reformed Church (Presbyterian and Congregational) in England and Wales in 1972' *Journal of the United Reformed Church History Society* vol. 4 (October 1987) pp. 3-22.

McBeth, H. Leon, *The Baptist Heritage - four centuries of Baptist Witness* (Broadman: Nashville, 1987).

Machin, G. I. T., *Politics and the Churches in Great Britain, 1869-1921* (Clarendon Press: Oxford, 1987).

McLeod, Hugh, *Class and Religion in the late Victorian City* (Croom Helm: 1974).

- *Religion and Society in England, 1850-1914* (MacMillan Press: 1996).

- 'White Collar Values and the Role of Religion' in Geoffrey Crossick (ed.), *The Lower Middle Class in Britain 1870-1914* (Croom Helm: 1977) pp. 61-88.

Manley, K. R., 'The Making of an Evangelical Baptist Leader' *BQ* vol. 26 (1976) pp. 254-74.

Maring, Norman H., 'Andrew Fuller's Doctrine of the Church' in Winthrop Still Hudson (ed.), *Baptist Concepts of the Church* (Judson Press: Pennsylvania, 1959) pp. 71-105.

Marwick, Arthur, *The Deluge: British Society and the First World War* (2nd edition) (MacMillan Education: 1991).

- 'The Impact of the First World War on British Society' *Journal of Contemporary History* vol. 3 (January 1968) pp. 51-63.

Matthew, H. C. G., *Gladstone: 1875-1898* (Clarendon Press: Oxford, 1995).

Mayor, S., 'English Nonconformity and the American Experience' *Journal of the United Reformed Church History Society* vol. 3 (1983-7) pp. 104-15.

- 'The Free Church Understanding of the Ministry in the Twentieth Century' *BQ* vol. 23 (July 1970) pp. 289-300.

Meller, H. E., *Leisure and the Changing City, 1870-1914* (Routledge and Kegan Paul: 1976).

Mews, Stuart Paul, 'Neo-orthodoxy, liberalism and War: Karl Barth, P. T. Forsyth and John Oman, 1914-1918' in Derek Baker (ed.), *Renaissance and Renewal in Christian History* (Basil Blackwell: Oxford, 1977) pp. 361-75.

- 'Religion and English Society in the First World War' (University of Cambridge *PhD* 1973).

Mitchell, Sheila, *'Not Disobedient . . .': A history of United Baptist Church, Leicester, including Harvey Lane 1760-1845, Belvoir Street 1845-1940 and Charles Street 1831-1940* (United Baptist Church: Leicester, 1984).

Moon, Norman S., *Education for Ministry* (Bristol Baptist College: Bristol, 1979).

Moore, James R., *Religion in Victorian Britain* (vol. III) (Manchester University Press: Manchester, 1988).

Moore, Robert, *Pitmen, Preachers and Politics: the effects of Methodism in a Durham mining community* (Cambridge University Press: Cambridge, 1974).

Morgan, Kenneth O., *The Age of Lloyd George* (George Allen and Unwin Ltd.: 1971).

Morgan, P. B., 'A Study of the Work of Revivalist Movements in Great Britain' (University of Oxford *BLitt* 1961).

Morris, J. N., *Religion and Urban Change: Croydon 1840-1914* (The Boydell Press: Woodbridge, 1992).

Munson, J. E. B., 'A Study of Nonconformity in Edwardian England as Revealed by the Passive Resistance Movement against the 1902 Education Act'

(University of Oxford *DPhil* 1973).
- *The Nonconformists: In search of a lost culture* (SPCK: 1991).

Neill, Stephen, *Men of Unity* (SCM Press: 1960).
Nicholls, Mike, *Lights to the World: A history of Spurgeon's College, 1856-1992* (Nuprint: Harpenden, 1994).
Nicholson, J. F. V., *The Ministry - a Baptist View* (BUGBI: 1976).
- 'The Office of 'Messenger' amongst British Baptists in the Seventeenth and Eighteenth Centuries' *BQ* vol. 17 (January 1958) pp. 206-25.
- 'Towards a Theology of Episcope Amongst Baptists' *BQ* vol. 30 (April 1984) pp. 265-81.
Niebuhr, H. Richard, *The Social Sources of Denominationalism* (The World Publishing Company: Cleveland, 1957).
Nowell-Smith, Simon (ed.), *Edwardian England 1901-1914* (Oxford University Press: 1964).
Nuttall, Geoffrey F., *Visible Saints: The Congregational Way, 1640-1660* (Basil Blackwell: Oxford, 1957).

O'Day, Alan, *The Edwardian Age: Conflict and Stability* (MacMillan Press: 1979).
O'Day, Rosemary, 'The Clerical Renaissance in Victorian England and Wales' in Gerald Parsons (ed.), *Religion in Victorian Britain 1: Traditions* (Open University: Manchester University Press, 1988) pp. 184ff.
Orr, J. Edwin, *The Second Evangelical Awakening in Britain* (Marshall, Morgan and Scott Ltd.: 1949).

Parsons, Gerald (ed.), *Religion in Victorian Britain I: Traditions* (Open University, Manchester University Press: Manchester, 1988).
Parsons, Gerald, 'Emotion and Piety: Revivalism and Ritualism in Victorian Christianity' in Gerald Parsons (ed.), *Religion in Victorian Britain 1: Traditions* (Open University: Manchester University Press, 1988) pp. 213ff.
- 'From Dissenters to Free Churchmen: the transitions of Victorian Nonconformity' in Gerald Parsons (ed.), *Religion in Victorian Britain 1: Traditions* (Open University: Manchester University Press, 1988) pp. 67ff.
Payne, E. A., 'Baptist-Congregationalist Relationships' *Congregational Quarterly* vol. 33 (July 1955) pp. 216-226.
- *The Baptist Union: a short history* (Carey Kingsgate Press Ltd.: 1959).
- *The Baptist Union and its Headquarters: a descriptive record prepared for the Jubilee of the opening of the Baptist Church House* (Carey Kingsgate Press: 1953).
- 'The Baptist Union - Looking Back' *BQ* vol. 12 (1948) pp. 267-74.
- 'Baptists and the Ministry' *BQ* vol. 25 (April 1973) pp. 51-8.
- *The Fellowship of Believers: Baptist Thought and Practice Yesterday and Today* (Carey Kingsgate Press: 1944).

- *The Free Church Tradition in the Life of England* (SCM Press: 1944).
- *The Free Churches and Episcopacy* (Carey Kingsgate Press: 1952).
- *Free Churchmen, Unrepentant and Repentant, and other papers* (Carey Kingsgate Press: 1965).
- *James Henry Rushbrooke: A Baptist Greatheart* (Carey Kingsgate Press: 1954)
- 'John Howard Shakespeare (1857-1928)' in A. S. Clement (ed.), *Baptists who made history: A Book about Great Baptists written by Baptists* (Carey Kingsgate Press: 1955).
- (ed.), *Studies in History and Religion* (Lutterworth Press: 1942).
Peaston, A. Elliott, *The Prayer Book Tradition in the Free Churches* (James Clarke and Co.: 1964).
Peel, Albert, *These Hundred Years: A History of the Congregational Union of England and Wales, 1831-1931* (Congregational Union of England and Wales: 1931).
Peel, Albert, and Leland H. Carlson (eds.), *The Writings of Robert Harrison and Robert Browne* (George Allen and Unwin: 1953).
Pelling, Henry, *Popular Politics and Society in Late Victorian Britain* (MacMillan and Co.: 1968).
Perkin, Harold, *The Rise of Professional Society: England since 1880* (Routledge: 1989).
Pike, E. Royston, *Human Documents of the Age of the Forsytes* (George Allen and Unwin Ltd.: 1969).
Price, Seymour J., 'William Thomas Whitley' *BQ* vol. 12 (1948) pp. 357-63.
Pugh, Martin, *State and Society: British Political and Social History 1870-1992* (Edward Arnold: 1994).

Randall, Ian, 'Mere Denominationalism - F. B. Meyer and Baptist Life' *BQ* vol. 35 (January 1993) pp. 19ff.
Read, Donald (ed.), *Edwardian England* (Croom Helm: 1982).
Reardon, Bernard M. G., *Religious Thought in the Victorian Age: A survey from Coleridge to Gore* (2nd edition) (Longman Group Ltd.: 1995).
Reynolds, G. G., '75 years of the General Superintendency - what next?' *BQ* vol. 34 (January 1992) pp. 229ff.
- *First Among Equals: A study of the basis of association and oversight among Baptist churches* (Berkshire, Southern and Oxfordshire and East Gloucester Baptist Associations: 1993).
Richard, Noel J., 'The Education Bill of 1906 and the Decline of Political Nonconformity' *The Journal of Ecclesiastical History* vol. 23 (January 1972) pp. 49-63.
Richards, Edgar, 'The Nature of the Free Church Ministry, with special reference to (a) The Writings of A. M. Fairbairn, J. Oman, P. T. Forsyth and J. Scott Lidgett, and (b) Recent Reunion Proposals' (University of London *PhD* 1967).
Rinaldi, Frank W., 'The Tribe of Dan: The New Connexion of General Baptists 1770-1891. A study in the transition from revival movement to established

denomination' (Glasgow University *PhD* 1996).

Robbins, Keith, 'The Churches in Edwardian Society' in Donald Read (ed.), *Edwardian England* (Croom Helm: 1982) pp. 112ff.

- *The Eclipse of a Great Power: Modern Britain: 1870-1975* (Longman: 1983).
- *History, Religion and identity in Modern Britain* (The Hambledon Press: 1993).
- (ed.)*Protestant Evangelicalism* (Oxford, 1990).
- 'The Spiritual Pilgrimage of the Rev. R. J. Campbell' *The Journal of Ecclesiastical History* vol. 30 (April 1979) pp. 261-76.

Rose, Doris M., *Baptist Deaconesses* (Carey Kingsgate Press: 1954).

Rouse, Ruth, and Stephen Neill (eds.), *A History of the Ecumenical Movement 1517-1948* (3rd edition) (World Council of Churches: Geneva, 1986).

Routley, Erik, *English Religious Dissent* (Cambridge University Press: Cambridge, 1960).

Russell, Anthony, *The Clerical Profession* (SPCK: 1980).

Russell, D. S., 'The Ministry and Sacraments' *BQ* vol. 17 (April 1957) pp. 67-73.

Sangster, Paul, *A History of the Free Churches* (Heinemann: 1983).

Searle, G. R., *The Liberal Party: Triumph and Disintegration, 1886-1929* (The MacMillan Press: 1992).

Sell, Alan P. F, *Dissenting Thought and the Life of the Churches - Studies in an English Tradition* (Mellen Research University Press: San Francisco, 1990).

- (ed.)*Protestant Nonconformists and the West Midlands of England* (Keele University Press: Keele, 1996).

Sellers, Ian (ed.), 'Edwardians, Anabaptists and the Problem of Baptist Origins' *BQ* vol. 29 (July 1981) pp. 97-112.

- 'Liverpool Nonconformity (1786-1914)' (Keele University *PhD* 1969).
- *Nineteenth Century Nonconformity* (Edward Arnold: 1977).
- *Our Heritage: The Baptists of Yorkshire, Lancashire and Cheshire 1647-1987* (Yorkshire Baptist Association: Leeds, 1987).
- 'W. T. Whitley: A Commemorative Essay' *BQ* vol. 37 (October 1997) pp. 159-73.

Sennett, Richard, *The Fall of Public Man* (Cambridge University Press: Cambridge, 1977).

Shakespeare, Geoffrey, 'John Howard Shakespeare' *BQ* vol. 17 (April 1957) pp. 51-2.

- *Let Candles Be Brought In* (MacDonald: 1949).
- 'The persecution of Baptists in Russia' *BQ* vol. 5 (April 1930) pp. 49-54.

Shakespeare, William, *Walking through Leaves* (privately published: 1996).

Sparkes, Douglas C., *An Accredited Ministry* (BHS: Didcot, 1996).

- 'Baptists and the Outbreak of the First World War' *BQ* vol. 26 (1975) pp. 74-93.
- *The Constitutions of the Baptist Union of Great Britain* (BHS: Didcot, 1996).
- *The Home Mission Story* (BHS: Didcot, 1995).

- *The Offices of the Baptist Union of Great Britain* (BHS: Didcot, 1996).
- *Pensions - Provision for Retired and Disabled Ministers* (BHS: Didcot, 1996).
Stanley, Brian, *The History of the Baptist Missionary Society* (T. and T. Clark: Edinburgh, 1992).

Tatlow, Tissington, *The Story of the Student Christian Movement of Great Britain and Ireland* (SCM Press: 1933).
Taylor, A. J. P., *Essays in English History* (Penguin Books: 1991).
- 'Prologue: the Year 1906' in Donald Read (ed.), *Edwardian England* (Croom Helm: 1982).
Thompson, David M. (ed.), *Denominationalism and Dissent, 1795-1835: a question of identity* (Dr. Williams's Trust: 1985).
- *Nonconformity in the Nineteenth Century* (Routledge and Kegan Paul: 1972).
- 'War, the Nation and the Kingdom of God: The Origins of the National Mission of Repentance and Hope, 1915-6' in W. J. Shiels (ed.), *The Church and War* (Basil Blackwell: 1983) pp. 337-50.
Thompson, John Handby, 'The Free Church Army Chaplain 1830-1930' (University of Sheffield *PhD* 1990).
Thompson, Paul, *The Edwardians: The Remaking of British Society* (Weidenfeld and Nicolson: 1975).
Tidball, Derek J., 'English Nonconformist Home Missions 1796-1901' (Keele University *PhD* 1991).
Tolmie, Murray, *The Triumph of the Saints: The Separate Churches of London 1616-1649* (Cambridge University Press: Cambridge, 1977).
Torbet, Robert G., *A History of the Baptists (Revised)* (Carey Kingsgate Press: 1966).
Townsend, Henry, *The Claims of the Free Churches* (Hodder and Stoughton: 1949).
Townsend, Michael, 'John Howard Shakespeare: Prophet of Ecumenism' *BQ* vol. 37 (April 1998) pp. 298-312.
Trevelyan, George Macaulay (*et al*), *Fifty Years: Memories and Contrasts: A Composite Picture of the Period 1882-1932* (Thornton Butterworth: 1932).
Tyson, John R., 'Lady Huntingdon's Reformation' *Church History* vol. 64 (1995) pp. 580-93.

Underwood, A. C., *A History of the English Baptists* (Carey Kingsgate Press: 1947).
Underwood, T. L., *Primitivism, Radicalism and the Lamb's War: The Baptist-Quaker Conflict in Seventeenth Century England* (Oxford University Press: New York, 1997).

Walker, Michael J., *Baptists at the Table: The Theology of the Lord's Supper among English Baptists in the Nineteenth Century* (BHS: Didcot, 1992).
Waller, P. J., *Democracy and Sectarianism: A political and social history of*

Liverpool 1868-1939 (Liverpool University Press: Liverpool, 1981).

Walsh, John, 'Origins of the Evangelical Revival' in G. V. Bennett and J. D. Walsh (eds.), *Essays in Modern English Church History* (Oxford University Press: New York, 1966) pp. 132-62.

- 'Religious Societies: Methodist and Evangelical 1738-1800' in W. J. Shiels and Diana Wood (eds.), *Voluntary Religion* (Basil Blackwell: Oxford, 1986) pp. 223-59.

Ward, W. R., 'The Baptists and the Transformation of the Church, 1780-1830' *BQ* vol. 25 (1974) pp. 167-84.

Watson, H. L., 'The General Superintendents' *BQ* vol. 25 (October 1973) pp. 146-50.

Watts, Michael R., *The Dissenters: From the Reformation to the French Revolution* (Clarendon Press: Oxford, 1978).

- *The Dissenters vol. II: The Expansion of Evangelical Nonconformity* (Clarendon Press: Oxford, 1995).

- 'John Clifford and Radical Nonconformity, 1836-1923' University of Oxford *DPhil* 1966).

Weaver, J. Denny, *Becoming Anabaptist: The Origin and Significance of Sixteenth Century Anabaptism* (Herald Press: Scottdale, Pennsylvania, 1987).

West, W. M. S., *Baptist Principles* (BUGB: 1960).

- *Baptists Together* (BHS: Didcot, 2000)

- 'The Revd. Secretary Aubrey' (Parts 1, 2 and 3) *BQ* vol. 34 (January, April and July 1992) pp. 199-213; 263-281; 320-336.

- 'The Young Mr. Aubrey' *BQ* vol. 33 (October 1990) pp. 351-363.

White, B. R. (ed.), *Association Records of the Particular Baptists of England, Wales and Ireland to 1660* (BHS: 1971).

- *Authority: a Baptist View* (BUGB: 1976).

- 'The Doctrine of the Church in the Particular Baptist Confession of 1644' *The Journal of Theological Studies (New Series)* vol. 19 (1968) pp. 570-90.

- *The English Baptists of the Seventeenth Century* (BHS: 1983).

- *The English Separatist Tradition: From the Marian Martyrs to the Pilgrim Fathers* (Oxford University Press: 1971).

White, John Wesley, 'The Influence of North American Evangelism in Great Britain Between 1830 and 1914 on the Origin and Development of the Ecumenical Movement' (University of Oxford *DPhil* 1963).

Whitley, W. T., *A History of British Baptists* (Revised Edition) (Kingsgate Press: 1932).

Wickham, E. R., *Church and People in an Industrial City* (Lutterworth Press: 1957).

Wilkes, John W., 'The Transformation of Dissent: a Review of the change from the Seventeenth to the Eighteenth Centuries' in C. Robert Cole and Michael E. Moody (eds.), *The Dissenting Tradition* (Ohio University Press: Athens, Ohio, 1975) pp. 108-22.

Wilkinson, Alan, *Dissent or Conform? War, Peace and the English Churches 1900-1945* (SCM Press Ltd.: 1986).

Wilkinson, Alan, *The Church of England and the First World War* (SPCK: 1978).

Willey, Basil, *Spots of Time: A Retrospect of the Years 1897-1920* (Chatto and Windus: 1965).

Williams, C. R., 'The Welsh Religious Revival, 1904-5' *British Journal of Sociology* vol. 3 (1952) pp. 242-59.

Williams, George Huntson, *The Radical Reformation* (Weidenfeld and Nicolson: 1962).

Wilson, Bryan, *Religion in Secular Society: A Sociological Comment* (C. A. Watts and Co.: 1966).

- *Religion in Sociological Perspective* (Oxford University Press: 1982).

Wilson, Trevor, *The Downfall of the Liberal Party 1914-1935* (Collins: 1966).

Wollaston, E. P. M., 'The First Moderators: 1919' *The Journal of the United Reformed Church History Society* vol. 5 (November 1994) pp. 298-301.

Wood, H. G., *Terrot Reaveley Glover: A Biography* (Cambridge University Press: Cambridge, 1953).

Yeo, Stephen, *Religion and Voluntary Organisations in Crisis* (Croom Helm: 1976).

Young, G. M., *Portrait of An Age: Victorian England* (annotated edition) (Oxford University Press: 1977).

Young, Kenneth, *Chapel: The joyous days and prayerful nights of the Nonconformists in their heyday, circa 1850-1950* (Eyre Methuen: 1972).

APPENDICES

1. John Howard Shakespeare: some key dates

16 April 1857: born in Malton in the North Riding of Yorkshire, to Benjamin and Mary Anne Shakespeare. Benjamin was the minister of Malton Baptist Church.

1863: moved to Derby, and afterwards to Leicester.

1875: started work as a clerk in London.

1878: entered Regent's Park College, London, to train for the Baptist ministry, having failed the entrance examination for the Civil Service.

1883: called to the pastorate of St. Mary's Baptist Church, Norwich. Married Amy Gertrude Goodman, the daughter of a Baptist minister.

1885: elected to the Council of the Baptist Union.

1892: made his mark in the denomination with an address at the national Assembly entitled 'Church Extension in Large Towns'.

1898: appointed Secretary of the Baptist Union. Moved back to London.

1899: the *Freeman* newspaper acquired by the Baptist Union, and subsequently published as the *Baptist Times and Freeman*.

1899-1902: raised the Twentieth Century Fund.

1903: the opening of Baptist Church House on Southampton Row.

1905: the formation of the Baptist World Alliance. Shakespeare appointed European Secretary.

1906: *Baptist and Congregational Pioneers* published.

1912-1914: the raising of the Sustentation Fund.

1914: the formation of the United Army Board, with Shakespeare as chairman.

1916: the implementation of the Ministerial Settlement and Sustentation Scheme, including the appointment of ten Area Superintendents. Shakespeare President of the National Free Church Council.

1918: *The Churches at the Cross Roads* published.

1919: the creation of the Free Church Federal Council, with Shakespeare as first Moderator.

1920-1923: led the Free Church response to the Lambeth Appeal in talks at Lambeth Palace.

1920: the raising of the Baptist United Fund (in conjunction with the Baptist Missionary Society).

1924: resignation from office on the grounds of poor health.

1925: cerebral haemorrhage results in a complete health breakdown.

12 March 1928: died following a stroke.

2. Baptist Union Presidents during Shakespeare's period in office[1]

1898-1899: Rev. Samuel Vincent.
1899-1900: Rev. John Clifford[2].
1900-1901: Rev. William Cuff.
1901-1902: Rev. Alexander MacLaren.
1902-1903: Rev. John R. Wood.
1903-1904: Alderman George White.
1904-1905: Rev. John Wilson.
1905-1906: His Honour Judge William Willis.
1906-1907: Rev. Frederick B. Meyer.
1907-1908: Rev. Principal William J. Henderson.
1908-1909: Rev. Charles Brown.
1909-1910: Rev. Principal John T. Marshall.
1910-1911: Sir George W. McAlpine.
1911-1912: Rev. Principal William Edwards.
1912-1913: Rev. John W. Ewing.
1913-1914: Rev. Principal George P. Gould.
1914-1915: Rev. Charles Joseph.
1915-1916: Rev. John T. Forbes.
1916-1917: Rev. Thomas Phillips.
1917-1918: Rev. William Y. Fullerton.
1918-1919: Rev. John E. Roberts.
1919-1920: Mr. Herbert Marnham.
1920-1921: Rev. David J. Hiley.
1921-1922: Rev. John C. Carlile.
1922-1923: Mr. John Chown[3].
1923-1924: Rev. Principal William E. Blomfield.
1924-1925: Mr. Terrot R. Glover.

1. From Payne, *Baptist Union* pp. 259-260.
2. Rev James Spurgeon was elected Vice-President, but died shortly before he was due to assume office as President. Clifford took his place at short notice, after being nominated by the Council.
3. Chown died after a few months in office and J. C. Carlile was appointed by the Council to complete his Presidential year.

ABBREVIATIONS

B: Baptist.
BHS: Baptist Historical Society.
BQ: *Baptist Quarterly.*
BT: *Baptist Times and Freeman* (prior to 1898 *Freeman*).
BU: Baptist Union.
BUGB: Baptist Union of Great Britain.
BUGBI: Baptist Union of Great Britain and Ireland.
BW: *British Weekly.*
BWA: Baptist World Alliance.
BWL: Baptist Women's League.
CW: *Christian World*
FCEFC: Federal Council of the Evangelical Free Churches.
HB: *Baptist Handbook.*
LPL: Lambeth Palace Library.
NCEFC: National Council of the Evangelical Free Churches.
SPCK: Society for Promoting Christian Knowledge.

INDEX

Accreditation 84f, 147ff

Addison, Christopher 100

Advisory Committee for Ministerial Removals 31

Ainsworth, Henry 4

American Baptists 41, 154, 182, 187

Anabaptists 1, 45f,

Anglo-Catholicism 54, 93, 110, 149, 155, 173

Angus, Joseph 9, 14

Annuity Fund 8, 26, 54, 144

"Arrested Progress" 63f, 185

Arthur, J. J. 142

Asquith, Herbert xiii, 99

Assemblies 36f, 43, 85, 146, 183, (seventeenth century) 4, (nineteenth century) 8, 170, (1889) 17, (1892) 17, (1898) 19, 25, (1900) 27, (1901) 27, 29, 38, (1902) 27f, (1903) 37, 55, (1904) 37, 56, (1905) 48, 57, (1906) 49, 57, 62, (1907) 58f, (1908) 63, 185, (1909) 65ff, (1910) 67ff, 71, (1911) 72, (1912) 72ff, (1914) 74f, 81 (1915) 78ff, (1916) 83, (1918) 105f, (1919) 114ff, 140, (1920) 141, (1921) 120, (1922) 124, 148, 153, (1923) 148ff, 156, (1924) 160f, (1925) 161, (1926) 182

Associations 35, 61, 66, 74, 76ff, 82, 85f, 124, 144, 177, 181, 186f, (Abingdon) 3f, (Devon and Cornwall) 54, (Lincolnshire) 5, (London) 140, (Midland) 2ff, (New Connexion) 5, 8ff, (Norfolk) 16, (Northamptonshire) 6, (seventeenth century) 2ff, (Southern) 84, (Strict and Particular) 86, (Yorkshire) 84, 152

Aubrey, M. E. 44, 159ff, 182

Augmentation Fund 31, 34

Balfour, A. J. 100

Ball, W. H. 41f, 118, 161

Baptism xvin, 1, 104, 115, 118, 124, 134n, 157f, 174, 182f, 186, 189n

Baptist 25f, 28, 32ff, 37, 48, 56ff, 62, 64ff, 69

Baptist and Congregational Pioneers xiii, 43ff

Baptist Annual Register 6

Baptist Assemblies (see Assemblies)

Baptist Argus 38

Baptist Bible Union 154

Baptist Church House xiii, 29ff, 43, 176f

Baptist Church Hymnal 33

Baptist Confessions of Faith 1ff

Baptist Handbook 13, 34, 56ff, 63, 146, 149

Baptist Historical Society 31, 63,

Baptist Insurance Company 31

Baptist Magazine 15, 17, 32f, 44

Baptist Manual 12

Baptist Missionary Society 6f, 8, 29, 36, 39, 74, 84, 114, 123, 141f, 145, 148, 156, 158

Baptist Navy and Army Church 102

Baptist Sisterhood 140ff

Baptist Times xiii, 25, 27, 29f, 31ff, 43f, 48, 56, 61f, 66f, 69, 71, 83, 94, 100f, 109, 139, 141, 144, 152f, 154, 158f, 161, 174, 176f

Baptist Tract and Book Society 33

Baptist Union xii, 7-9, 17, 19f, 25-60, 63, 66f, 72, 83, 84-91, 105f, 140ff,

145-151, 161, 170f, 174, 175-181, 185-7

Baptist Union Constitution 7f, 35-8, 79, 140,

Baptist Union Corporation 9

Baptist Union Council 17, 19, 29f, 35-8, 55, 58, 62, 65, 72f, 76, 78, 82f, 84f, 96, 114, 120, 124f, 140ff, 148, 152f, 159, 177f

Baptist Union Declaration of Principle 38, 188n

Baptist Union Statement on the Ministry (1923) 149

Baptist Union Ministerial Recognition Scheme (see Ministerial Recognition)

Baptist Union Ministerial Settlement and Sustentation Scheme (see Ministerial Settlement and Sustentation)

Baptist United Fund 141, 145, 156

Baptist Women's Century Fund League 27, 139

Baptist Women's League 74, 139f, 143

Baptist World Alliance xvi, 30, 38-41, 156ff, 176, 182, 189n

Baptist World Congress (1905) 38-41, 48, (1911) 68, 89n, (1923) 156ff, 182

Bateson, J. H. 98

Belvoir Street Baptist Church, Leicester 14

Benskin, F. G. 72

Blomfield, W. E. 51n, 61, 126, 160

Board of Introduction and Consultation 31, 61

Booth, Charles 11f, 170

Booth, Samuel Harris 8, 19, 41

Booth, General 11

Brethren 172, 174

Bristol Baptist College 6

British Weekly xiv, 38, 76, 99, 109, 121, 124

Brown, Charles 106, 135n, 185

Brown, Hugh 71

Browne, Robert 1, 46

Campbell, R. J. 155

Caravan Mission 140

Carey, William 6

Carlile, J. C. xiii, 45, 145, 154, 156f, 159ff, 177

Carson, Edward 100

China Inland Mission 173

Chivers, William 28, 55, 61

Christian World 43, 68, 83, 185

Church Congress in Norwich 18f

Church Extension 17f, 26, 31, 68, 127

Church of England i, 10, 18, 41, 45, 54, 93, 95, 96-9, 109-131, 143, 154f, 158, 173ff, 180, 183f

Church of England Memorandum on the Free Church Ministry (1923) 126

Church of Scotland 141

Churches at the Cross Roads xiiif, 14, 107-110, 141, 143, 183, 185

Churches of Christ 172, 174

Clark, Henry 46

Clifford, John xiv, 9, 11, 27f, 33, 39ff, 43, 73, 102, 110, 114, 116, 167n

Colleges 5, 8, 17, 35, 54f, 56, 58, 61, 63ff, 69f, 87n, 141, 149, 171

Collier, John 80, 117f

Commission of Enquiry on the Ministry 142, 145f, 148

Compton-Rickett, Joseph 99, 117

Congregationalists 10, 25f, 29, 38, 81, 88n, 94, 96f, 123, 131n, 170f, 182, 184

Cromwell, Oliver 10

Dafis, D. Ff. 34

Daily News 125, 160

Dakin, Arthur 178

Davidson, Randall 111, 119, 123, 130, 158, 174

Deaconesses 140f, 143
Derby, Lord 98
Disestablishment 99f, 110
Dixon, A. C. 154
Doddridge, Philip 4
Downgrade Controversy 9, 17, 55
Dunn, Kathleen, 140, 142f

Edinburgh World Missionary
    Conference (1910) xiii, 94, 111
Education Act (1870) 14, (1902) 39,
    45, 47, 93, 110
Edwards, Jonathan 6
Episcopal Church of America 94
Eucharistic Congress (1908) 110
European Baptist Congress (1908)
    40, 64
European Baptist Federation 189n
European (Eastern) Secretary of the
    Baptist World Alliance 40, 156,
    182
Ewing, John 83

Faith and Order Movement xiii, 80,
    94f, 110f, 113, 121, 127, 182
Federal Council of the Evangelical
    Free Churches xiif, xvi, 30, 103-
    110, 113, 115ff, 119f, 123-131,
    175, 182ff, 185
Fellowship of Independent
    Evangelical Churches 154, 188n
Forsyth, P. T. 105
Free Church Council (see Federal
    Council and National Council)
Freeman 10, 20, 26, 31, 43
French, Roland 72
Fuller, Andrew 6f
Fullerton, W. Y. 156, 158

Gates, Edith 142
General Baptists 1-5, 7-10, 12, 38,
    54, 79f, 170
General Elections (1906) 93, (1918)
    100f, (1922) 155

George V 101
Gladstone, W. E. 10
Glover, Richard 37, 39, 65ff, 69f, 74,
    114
Glover, T. R. 65, 74, 98, 114ff, 121-6,
    153f, 156, 159ff, 184
Golf 44
Gore, Charles 116
Gould, G. P. 79, 121, 153
Grantham, Thomas 38
Greenhough, J. G. 55ff, 59f, 62, 64f,
    71ff, 86n, 158
Gwynne, Bishop 97

Halevy, E 170
Hannay, Alexander 170
Hardy, Margaret 142
Havelock Hall 142, 145
Helwys, Thomas 1f, 46
Henderson, William 49, 58f
Home Missionary Society 7f
Home Work Fund 31, 34, 53, 82, 140
Horne, Silvester 11, 68, 88n
Horton, Robert 173
Hughes, Hugh Price 11, 15f, 31, 42,
    47, 109
Hungary 40

Illingworth, Percy 75, 96
Illuminated Address 117f
Inter-Collegiate Board 70 (see also
    United Collegiate Board)
Interdenominational Chaplaincy
    Advisory Committee 97f, 103

James, Mrs. Russell 139f
Johnson, Francis 46
Jones, J. D. 123, 128f, 161
Joseph, Charles 74

Keswick Movement 172
Kikuyu Conference 110
Kitchener, H. H. 96, 101

Labour Party 99, 155
Lambeth Appeal xiii, xvi, 114-128, 143, 158, 174, 182, 184
Lambeth Conference (1920) 116, 119f
Lambeth Quadrilateral 118
Lang, Cosmo Gordon 111, 120f, 123, 126, 174
Law, Bonar 100
Law, Thomas 68, 131n
Laws, Gilbert 159ff
Lay ministers 145ff
Liberal Party xiv, 75, 100, 155
Lidgett, J. Scott 112f, 120, 128
Lloyd George, David xiv, 39, 74, 96f, 99ff, 115, 155f, 163
Local Preachers' Federation 145f
Logan, J. Moffat 44, 66, 69
London Baptist Confessions (seventeenth century) 1ff
London City Mission 173
Lunn, Henry 16, 110
Lutheran Church 80

MacLaren, Alexander 29, 39, 41, 43
Makepeace, J. F. 14
Malines 126
Malton 13
Mansfield Conferences 112f, 116, 127, 135n
Marnham, Herbert 43, 106, 117, 144f, 160
Marshall, Newton H. 40
Martin, Hugh 182, 184
Mercier, Cardinal 126
Messengers 3ff, 79f
Methodists 4f, 10f, 15, 25f, 31, 42, 47, 62, 65, 70, 96ff, 103, 112f, 117, 119, 123, 126, 129, 141, 170, 184
Metropolitan Tabernacle 86
Meyer, F. B. 11, 41, 73, 99, 111, 140
Military Service Act (1916) 99
Ministerial Recognition 53-60, 71f,

79, 84f, 142f, 145-151
Ministerial Settlement and Sustentation xvi, 10, 44f, 55f, 61-85, 108, 121, 139f, 144ff, 148, 151, 153
Ministers' Home of Rest 31
Moody, D. L. 15
Mountain, James 105, 154
Mullins, E. Y. 39, 157, 182
Mursell, James P. 14

National Council of the Evangelical Free Churches 10f, 16, 67f, 80, 93-5, 99f, 103, 117, 127f, 131, 174f
New Connexion 5, 7-10, 12, 14, 80
Nexus Committee 117, 119, 127
Nicoll, Robertson xiv, 76, 99, 109f, 114
Nonconformity xiiff, 4, 10-13, 15f, 25, 31, 45ff, 93ff, 96-101, 104, 107, 110, 116f, 120, 130, 155, 169-175, 184
Northern Baptist Convention 154

Ordination 3, 53f, 109, 114f, 119f, 124, 126, 143, 146f, 149f, 154, 179f, 182, 184, (of women) 134n, 143

Parker, Joseph 47, 109
Particular Baptist Fund 83
Particular Baptists 1-5, 7f, 12, 80
Passive Resistance 39, 110
Payne, E. A. 9, 79, 178f, 182, 184
Penny, T. S. 152
Pentecostalism 155, 172, 174
Phillips, Thomas 67, 115
Porritt, Arthur 43, 100, 185
Presbyterians 10, 66, 96, 112, 120, 123, 126, 182, 184
Prestridge, J. N. 38f
Primitive Methodists 10, 97, 184
Probationer ministers 58f, 70, 72, 142, 148

Protestant Truth Society 155
Psalms and Hymns Trust 32f

Quakers 137n

Regent's Park Baptist Church 14, 142
Regent's Park College 9, 14f, 79, 121, 141, 148, 178
Rippon, John 6, 38
Roberts, J. E. 106, 112
Robertson, A. T. 38
Robinson, Henry Wheeler 49, 58, 148, 154, 178
Roman Catholics 97f, 126, 128
Rushbrooke, J. H. 40, 63, 67, 71, 74f, 80, 156, 161f, 182, 185
Ruth, T. E. 64, 87n

St. Mary's Baptist Church (Norwich) 9, 15-20, 35, 45, 109, 116, 185
Salvation Army 10, 137n, 140, 172
Separatism 1f, 46
Shakespeare, Alfred 32, 161
Shakespeare, Amy 15, 43
Shakespeare, Benjamin 13
Shakespeare, Geoffrey xiv, 14, 155
Shakespeare's ill health 19f, 27, 74, 114, 116-120, 128, 153, 158-162
Smyth, John 1, 46
Society for the Encouragement and Support of Itinerant Preaching 7
Soderblom, Nathan 156
Southern Baptist Convention 39, 156f, 182
Spurgeon, C. H. 9, 12, 17, 30, 33, 41, 54, 123
Spurgeon, James 27, 31
Spurgeon's College 65f, 70, 82, 84
Spurr, F. C. 96, 98
Stead, W. T. 10

Steadman, William 6
Stockwell, A. H. 31f
Strict Baptists 86, 188n
Student Christian Movement 111, 155
Superintendents xii, 30, 77-85, 108, 111, 121, 147, 150-3, 159, 162, 177, 180f

Tatlow, Tissington 111f
Taylor, Dan 5
Thew, James 9, 14, 55
Torrey-Alexander Mission 39
Twentieth Century Fund 25-31, 34f, 42ff, 55, 69, 73f, 139, 176

Unitarianism 5, 12
United Chaplaincy Board xvi, 30, 95-104, 113, 129, 184f
United Collegiate Board 149
United Free Church of England xiii, 68, 94, 98, 103f, 108, 111, 117, 128
United Methodists 10, 97, 184
United Reformed Church 184

Vincent, Samuel 25, 28

War Office 76, 96ff, 102
Wells, R. J. 96
Wesleyans (see Methodists)
Western Recorder 154
Weston, Frank 110
Whitley, W. T. 63, 112, 182
Willis, William 48f, 57
Women 107f, 139-143
Wynn, Walter 48, 56

Young People 31, 34, 107, 151

Studies in Baptist History and Thought

(All titles uniform with this volume)
Dates in bold are of projected publication
Volumes in this series are not always published in sequence

David Bebbington and Anthony R. Cross (eds)
Global Baptist History
(SBHT vol. 14)
This book brings together studies from the Second International Conference on
Baptist Studies which explore different facets of Baptist life and work especially
during the twentieth century.
2006 / 1-84227-214-4 / approx. 350pp

David Bebbington (ed.)
The Gospel in the World
International Baptist Studies
(SBHT vol. 1)
This volume of essays from the First International Conference on Baptist
Studies deals with a range of subjects spanning Britain, North America, Europe,
Asia and the Antipodes. Topics include studies on religious tolerance, the
communion controversy and the development of the international Baptist
community, and concludes with two important essays on the future of Baptist
life that pay special attention to the United States.
2002 / 1-84227-118-0 / xiv + 362pp

John H.Y. Briggs (ed.)
Pulpit and People
Studies in Eighteenth-Century English Baptist Life and Thought
(SBHT vol. 28)
The eighteenth century was a crucial time in Baptist history. The denomination
had its roots in seventeenth-century English Puritanism and Separatism and the
persecution of the Stuart kings with only a limited measure of freedom after
1689. Worse, however, was to follow for with toleration came doctrinal conflict,
a move away from central Christian understandings and a loss of evangelistic
urgency. Both spiritual and numerical decline ensued, to the extent that the
denomination was virtually reborn as rather belatedly it came to benefit from the
Evangelical Revival which brought new life to both Arminian and Calvinistic
Baptists. The papers in this volume study a denomination in transition, and
relate to theology, their views of the church and its mission, Baptist spirituality,
and engagements with radical politics.
2007 / 1-84227-403-1 / approx. 350pp

Damian Brot
Church of the Baptized or Church of Believers?
A Contribution to the Dialogue between the Catholic Church and the Free
Churches with Special Reference to Baptists
(SBHT vol. 26)
The dialogue between the Catholic Church and the Free Churches in Europe
has hardly taken place. This book pleads for a commencement of such a
conversation. It offers, among other things, an introduction to the American
and the international dialogues between Baptists and the Catholic Church and
strives to allow these conversations to become fruitful in the European context
as well.
2006 / 1-84227-334-5 / approx. 364pp

Dennis Bustin
Paradox and Perseverence
Hanserd Knollys, Particular Baptist Pioneer in Seventeenth-Century England
(SBHT vol. 23)
The seventeenth century was a significant period in English history during
which the people of England experienced unprecedented change and tumult in
all spheres of life. At the same time, the importance of order and the traditional
institutions of society were being reinforced. Hanserd Knollys, born during this
pivotal period, personified in his life the ambiguity, tension and paradox of it,
openly seeking change while at the same time cautiously embracing order. As a
founder and leader of the Particular Baptists in London and despite persecution
and personal hardship, he played a pivotal role in helping shape their identity
externally in society and, internally, as they moved toward becoming more
formalised by the end of the century.
2006 / 1-84227-259-4 / approx. 324pp

Anthony R. Cross
Baptism and the Baptists
Theology and Practice in Twentieth-Century Britain
(SBHT vol. 3)
At a time of renewed interest in baptism, *Baptism and the Baptists* is a detailed
study of twentieth-century baptismal theology and practice and the factors which
have influenced its development.
2000 / 0-85364-959-6 / xx + 530pp

Anthony R. Cross and Philip E. Thompson (eds)
Baptist Sacramentalism
(SBHT vol. 5)
This collection of essays includes biblical, historical and theological studies in the theology of the sacraments from a Baptist perspective. Subjects explored include the physical side of being spiritual, baptism, the Lord's supper, the church, ordination, preaching, worship, religious liberty and the issue of disestablishment.
2003 / 1-84227-119-9 / xvi + 278pp

Anthony R. Cross and Philip E. Thompson (eds)
Baptist Sacramentalism 2
(SBHT vol. 25)
This second collection of essays exploring various dimensions of sacramental theology from a Baptist perspective includes biblical, historical and theological studies from scholars from around the world.
2006 / 1-84227-325-6 / approx. 350pp

Paul S. Fiddes
Tracks and Traces
Baptist Identity in Church and Theology
(SBHT vol. 13)
This is a comprehensive, yet unusual, book on the faith and life of Baptist Christians. It explores the understanding of the church, ministry, sacraments and mission from a thoroughly theological perspective. In a series of interlinked essays, the author relates Baptist identity consistently to a theology of covenant and to participation in the triune communion of God.
2003 / 1-84227-120-2 / xvi + 304pp

Stanley K. Fowler
More Than a Symbol
The British Baptist Recovery of Baptismal Sacramentalism
(SBHT vol. 2)
Fowler surveys the entire scope of British Baptist literature from the seventeenth-century pioneers onwards. He shows that in the twentieth century leading British Baptist pastors and theologians recovered an understanding of baptism that connected experience with soteriology and that in doing so they were recovering what many of their forebears had taught.
2002 / 1-84227-052-4 / xvi + 276pp

Steven R. Harmon
Towards Baptist Catholicity
Essays on Tradition and the Baptist Vision
(SBHT vol. 27)
This series of essays contends that the reconstruction of the Baptist vision in the
wake of modernity's dissolution requires a retrieval of the ancient ecumenical
tradition that forms Christian identity through rehearsal and practice. Themes
explored include catholic identity as an emerging trend in Baptist theology,
tradition as a theological category in Baptist perspective, Baptist confessions
and the patristic tradition, worship as a principal bearer of tradition, and the role
of Baptist higher education in shaping the Christian vision.
2006 / 1-84227-362-0 / approx. 210pp

Michael A.G. Haykin (ed.)
'At the Pure Fountain of Thy Word'
Andrew Fuller as an Apologist
(SBHT vol. 6)
One of the greatest Baptist theologians of the eighteenth and early nineteenth
centuries, Andrew Fuller has not had justice done to him. There is little doubt
that Fuller's theology lay behind the revitalization of the Baptists in the late
eighteenth century and the first few decades of the nineteenth. This collection of
essays fills a much needed gap by examining a major area of Fuller's thought,
his work as an apologist.
2004 / 1-84227-171-7 / xxii + 276pp

Michael A.G. Haykin
Studies in Calvinistic Baptist Spirituality
(SBHT vol. 15)
In a day when spirituality is in vogue and Christian communities are looking for
guidance in this whole area, there is wisdom in looking to the past to find
untapped wells. The Calvinistic Baptists, heirs of the rich ecclesial experience in
the Puritan era of the seventeenth century, but, by the end of the eighteenth
century, also passionately engaged in the catholicity of the Evangelical Revivals,
are such a well. This collection of essays, covering such things as the Lord's
Supper, friendship and hymnody, seeks to draw out the spiritual riches of this
community for reflection and imitation in the present day.
2006 / 1-84227-149-0 / approx. 350pp

Brian Haymes, Anthony R. Cross and Ruth Gouldbourne
On Being the Church
Revisioning Baptist Identity
(SBHT vol. 21)

The aim of the book is to re-examine Baptist theology and practice in the light of the contemporary biblical, theological, ecumenical and missiological context drawing on historical and contemporary writings and issues. It is not a study in denominationalism but rather seeks to revision historical insights from the believers' church tradition for the sake of Baptists and other Christians in the context of the modern–postmodern context.

2006 / 1-84227-121-0 / approx. 350pp

Ken R. Manley
From Woolloomooloo to 'Eternity': A History of Australian Baptists
Volume 1: Growing an Australian Church (1831–1914)
Volume 2: A National Church in a Global Community (1914–2005)
(SBHT vols 16.1 and 16.2)

From their beginnings in Australia in 1831 with the first baptisms in Woolloomoolloo Bay in 1832, this pioneering study describes the quest of Baptists in the different colonies (states) to discover their identity as Australians and Baptists. Although institutional developments are analyzed and the roles of significant individuals traced, the major focus is on the social and theological dimensions of the Baptist movement.

2 vol. set 2006 / 1-84227-405-8 / approx. 900pp

Ken R. Manley
'Redeeming Love Proclaim'
John Rippon and the Baptists
(SBHT vol. 12)

A leading exponent of the new moderate Calvinism which brought new life to many Baptists, John Rippon (1751–1836) helped unite the Baptists at this significant time. His many writings expressed the denomination's growing maturity and mutual awareness of Baptists in Britain and America, and exerted a long-lasting influence on Baptist worship and devotion. In his various activities, Rippon helped conserve the heritage of Old Dissent and promoted the evangelicalism of the New Dissent

2004 / 1-84227-193-8 / xviii + 340pp

Peter J. Morden
Offering Christ to the World
Andrew Fuller and the Revival of English Particular Baptist Life
(SBHT vol. 8)
Andrew Fuller (1754–1815) was one of the foremost English Baptist ministers
of his day. His career as an Evangelical Baptist pastor, theologian, apologist and
missionary statesman coincided with the profound revitalization of the Particular
Baptist denomination to which he belonged. This study examines the key
aspects of the life and thought of this hugely significant figure, and gives
insights into the revival in which he played such a central part.
2003 / 1-84227-141-5 / xx + 202pp

Peter Naylor
Calvinism, Communion and the Baptists
A Study of English Calvinistic Baptists from the Late 1600s to the Early 1800s
(SBHT vol. 7)
Dr Naylor argues that the traditional link between 'high-Calvinism' and
'restricted communion' is in need of revision. He examines Baptist communion
controversies from the late 1600s to the early 1800s and also the theologies of
John Gill and Andrew Fuller.
2003 / 1-84227-142-3 / xx + 266pp

Ian M. Randall, Toivo Pilli and Anthony R. Cross (eds)
Baptist Identities
International Studies from the Seventeenth to the Twentieth Centuries
(SBHT vol. 19)
These papers represent the contributions of scholars from various parts of the
world as they consider the factors that have contributed to Baptist
distinctiveness in different countries and at different times. The volume includes
specific case studies as well as broader examinations of Baptist life in a
particular country or region. Together they represent an outstanding resource for
understanding Baptist identities.
2005 / 1-84227-215-2 / approx. 350pp

James M. Renihan
Edification and Beauty
The Practical Ecclesiology of the English Particular Baptists, 1675–1705
(SBHT vol. 17)
Edification and Beauty describes the practices of the Particular Baptist churches at the end of the seventeenth century in terms of three concentric circles: at the centre is the ecclesiological material in the Second London Confession, which is then fleshed out in the various published writings of the men associated with these churches, and, finally, expressed in the church books of the era.
2005 / 1-84227-251-9 / approx. 230pp

Frank Rinaldi
'The Tribe of Dan'
A Study of the New Connexion of General Baptists 1770–1891
(SBHT vol. 10)
'The Tribe of Dan' is a thematic study which explores the theology, organizational structure, evangelistic strategy, ministry and leadership of the New Connexion of General Baptists as it experienced the process of institutionalization in the transition from a revival movement to an established denomination.
2006 / 1-84227-143-1 / approx. 350pp

Peter Shepherd
The Making of a Modern Denomination
John Howard Shakespeare and the English Baptists 1898–1924
(SBHT vol. 4)
John Howard Shakespeare introduced revolutionary change to the Baptist denomination. The Baptist Union was transformed into a strong central institution and Baptist ministers were brought under its control. Further, Shakespeare's pursuit of church unity reveals him as one of the pioneering ecumenists of the twentieth century.
2001 / 1-84227-046-X / xviii + 220pp

Karen Smith
The Community and the Believers
A Study of Calvinistic Baptist Spirituality in Some Towns and Villages of Hampshire and the Borders of Wiltshire, c.1730–1830
(SBHT vol. 22)

The period from 1730 to 1830 was one of transition for Calvinistic Baptists. Confronted by the enthusiasm of the Evangelical Revival, congregations within the denomination as a whole were challenged to find a way to take account of the revival experience. This study examines the life and devotion of Calvinistic Baptists in Hampshire and Wiltshire during this period. Among this group of Baptists was the hymn writer, Anne Steele.

2005 / 1-84227-326-4 / approx. 280pp

Martin Sutherland
Dissenters in a 'Free Land'
Baptist Thought in New Zealand 1850–2000
(SBHT vol. 24)

Baptists in New Zealand were forced to recast their identity. Conventions of communication and association, state and ecumenical relations, even historical divisions and controversies had to be revised in the face of new topographies and constraints. As Baptists formed themselves in a fluid society they drew heavily on both international movements and local dynamics. This book traces the development of ideas which shaped institutions and styles in sometimes surprising ways.

2006 / 1-84227-327-2 / approx. 230pp

Brian Talbot
The Search for a Common Identity
The Origins of the Baptist Union of Scotland 1800–1870
(SBHT vol. 9)

In the period 1800 to 1827 there were three streams of Baptists in Scotland: Scotch, Haldaneite and 'English' Baptist. A strong commitment to home evangelization brought these three bodies closer together, leading to a merger of their home missionary societies in 1827. However, the first three attempts to form a union of churches failed, but by the 1860s a common understanding of their corporate identity was attained leading to the establishment of the Baptist Union of Scotland.

2003 / 1-84227-123-7 / xviii + 402pp

Philip E. Thompson
The Freedom of God
Towards Baptist Theology in Pneumatological Perspective
(SBHT vol. 20)
This study contends that the range of theological commitments of the early
Baptists are best understood in relation to their distinctive emphasis on the
freedom of God. Thompson traces how this was recast anthropocentrically,
leading to an emphasis upon human freedom from the nineteenth century
onwards. He seeks to recover the dynamism of the early vision via a
pneumatologically-oriented ecclesiology defining the church in terms of the
memory of God.
2006 / 1-84227-125-3 / approx. 350pp

Philip E. Thompson and Anthony R. Cross (eds)
Recycling the Past or Researching History?
Studies in Baptist Historiography and Myths
(SBHT vol. 11)
In this volume an international group of Baptist scholars examine and re-
examine areas of Baptist life and thought about which little is known or the
received wisdom is in need of revision. Historiographical studies include the
date Oxford Baptists joined the Abingdon Association, the death of the Fifth
Monarchist John Pendarves, eighteenth-century Calvinistic Baptists and the
political realm, confessional identity and denominational institutions, Baptist
community, ecclesiology, the priesthood of all believers, soteriology, Baptist
spirituality, Strict and Reformed Baptists, the role of women among British
Baptists, while various 'myths' challenged include the nature of high-Calvinism
in eighteenth-century England, baptismal anti-sacramentalism, episcopacy, and
Baptists and change.
2005 / 1-84227-122-9 / approx. 330pp

Linda Wilson
Marianne Farningham
A Plain Working Woman
(SBHT vol. 18)
Marianne Farningham, of College Street Baptist Chapel, Northampton, was a
household name in evangelical circles in the later nineteenth century. For over
fifty years she produced comment, poetry, biography and fiction for the popular
Christian press. This investigation uses her writings to explore the beliefs and
behaviour of evangelical Nonconformists, including Baptists, during these years.
2006 / 1-84227-124-5 / approx. 250pp

Other Paternoster titles
relating to Baptist history and thought

George R. Beasley-Murray
Baptism in the New Testament
(Paternoster Digital Library)
This is a welcome reprint of a classic text on baptism originally published in 1962 by one of the leading Baptist New Testament scholars of the twentieth century. Dr Beasley-Murray's comprehensive study begins by investigating the antecedents of Christian baptism. It then surveys the foundation of Christian baptism in the Gospels, its emergence in the Acts of the Apostles and development in the apostolic writings. Following a section relating baptism to New Testament doctrine, a substantial discussion of the origin and significance of infant baptism leads to a briefer consideration of baptismal reform and ecumenism.

2005 / 1-84227-300-0 / x + 422pp

Paul Beasley-Murray
Fearless for Truth
A Personal Portrait of the Life of George Beasley-Murray
Without a doubt George Beasley-Murray was one of the greatest Baptists of the twentieth century. A long-standing Principal of Spurgeon's College, he wrote more than twenty books and made significant contributions in the study of areas as diverse as baptism and eschatology, as well as writing highly respected commentaries on the Book of Revelation and John's Gospel.

2002 / 1-84227-134-2 / xii + 244pp

David Bebbington
Holiness in Nineteenth-Century England
(Studies in Christian History and Thought)
David Bebbington stresses the relationship of movements of spirituality to changes in their cultural setting, especially the legacies of the Enlightenment and Romanticism. He shows that these broad shifts in ideological mood had a profound effect on the ways in which piety was conceptualized and practised. Holiness was intimately bound up with the spirit of the age.

2000 / 0-85364-981-2 / viii + 98pp

Clyde Binfield
Victorian Nonconformity in Eastern England 1840–1885
(Studies in Evangelical History and Thought)
Studies of Victorian religion and society often concentrate on cities, suburbs, and industrialisation. This study provides a contrast. Victorian Eastern England—Essex, Suffolk, Norfolk, Cambridgeshire, and Huntingdonshire—was rural, traditional, relatively unchanging. That is nonetheless a caricature which discounts the industry in Norwich and Ipswich (as well as in Haverhill, Stowmarket and Leiston) and ignores the impact of London on Essex, of railways throughout the region, and of an ancient but changing university (Cambridge) on the county town which housed it. It also entirely ignores the political implications of such changes in a region noted for the variety of its religious Dissent since the seventeenth century. This book explores Victorian Eastern England and its Nonconformity. It brings to a wider readership a pioneering thesis which has made a major contribution to a fresh evolution of English religion and society.
2006 / 1-84227-216-0 / approx. 274pp

Edward W. Burrows
'To Me To Live Is Christ'
A Biography of Peter H. Barber
This book is about a remarkably gifted and energetic man of God. Peter H. Barber was born into a Brethren family in Edinburgh in 1930. In his youth he joined Charlotte Baptist Chapel and followed the call into Baptist ministry. For eighteen years he was the pioneer minister of the new congregation in the New Town of East Kilbride, which planted two further congregations. At the age of thirty-nine he served as Centenary President of the Baptist Union of Scotland and then exercised an influential ministry for over seven years in the well-known Upton Vale Baptist Church, Torquay. From 1980 until his death in 1994 he was General Secretary of the Baptist Union of Scotland. Through his work for the European Baptist Federation and the Baptist World Alliance he became a world Baptist statesman. He was President of the EBF during the upheaval that followed the collapse of Communism.
2005 / 1-84227-324-8 / xxii + 236pp

Christopher J. Clement
Religious Radicalism in England 1535–1565
(Rutherford Studies in Historical Theology)
In this valuable study Christopher Clement draws our attention to a varied assemblage of people who sought Christian faithfulness in the underworld of mid-Tudor England. Sympathetically and yet critically he assess their place in the history of English Protestantism, and by attentive listening he gives them a voice.
1997 / 0-946068-44-5 / xxii + 426pp

Anthony R. Cross (ed.)
Ecumenism and History
Studies in Honour of John H.Y. Briggs
(Studies in Christian History and Thought)
This collection of essays examines the inter-relationships between the two fields in which Professor Briggs has contributed so much: history—particularly Baptist and Nonconformist—and the ecumenical movement. With contributions from colleagues and former research students from Britain, Europe and North America, *Ecumenism and History* provides wide-ranging studies in important aspects of Christian history, theology and ecumenical studies.
2002 / 1-84227-135-0 / xx + 362pp

Keith E. Eitel
Paradigm Wars
The Southern Baptist International Mission Board
Faces the Third Millennium
(Regnum Studies in Mission)
The International Mission Board of the Southern Baptist Convention is the largest denominational mission agency in North America. This volume chronicles the historic and contemporary forces that led to the IMB's recent extensive reorganization, providing the most comprehensive case study to date of a historic mission agency restructuring to continue its mission purpose into the twenty-first century more effectively.
2000 / 1-870345-12-6 / x + 140pp

Ruth Gouldbourne
The Flesh and the Feminine
Gender and Theology in the Writings of Caspar Schwenckfeld
(Studies in Christian History and Thought)
Caspar Schwenckfeld and his movement exemplify one of the radical communities of the sixteenth century. Challenging theological and liturgical norms, they also found themselves challenging social and particularly gender assumptions. In this book, the issues of the relationship between radical theology and the understanding of gender are considered.
2005 / 1-84227-048-6 / approx. 304pp

David Hilborn
The Words of our Lips
Language-Use in Free Church Worship
(Paternoster Theological Monographs)
Studies of liturgical language have tended to focus on the written canons of
Roman Catholic and Anglican communities. By contrast, David Hilborn
analyses the more extemporary approach of English Nonconformity. Drawing
on recent developments in linguistic pragmatics, he explores similarities and
differences between 'fixed' and 'free' worship, and argues for the
interdependence of each.
2006 / 0-85364-977-4

Stephen R. Holmes
Listening to the Past
The Place of Tradition in Theology
Beginning with the question 'Why can't we just read the Bible?' Stephen
Holmes considers the place of tradition in theology, showing how the doctrine
of creation leads to an account of historical location and creaturely limitations as
essential aspects of our existence. For we cannot claim unmediated access to the
Scriptures without acknowledging the place of tradition: theology is an
irreducibly communal task. *Listening to the Past* is a sustained attempt to show
what listening to tradition involves, and how it can be used to aid theological
work today.
2002 / 1-84227-155-5 / xiv + 168pp

Mark Hopkins
Nonconformity's Romantic Generation
Evangelical and Liberal Theologies in Victorian England
(Studies in Evangelical History and Thought)
A study of the theological development of key leaders of the Baptist and
Congregational denominations at their period of greatest influence, including
C.H. Spurgeon and R.W. Dale, and of the controversies in which those among
them who embraced and rejected the liberal transformation of their evangelical
heritage opposed each other.
2004 / 1-84227-150-4 / xvi + 284pp

Galen K. Johnson
Prisoner of Conscience
John Bunyan on Self, Community and Christian Faith
(Studies in Christian History and Thought)
This is an interdisciplinary study of John Bunyan's understanding of conscience across his autobiographical, theological and fictional writings, investigating whether conscience always deserves fidelity, and how Bunyan's view of conscience affects his relationship both to modern Western individualism and historic Christianity.
2003 / 1-84227- 151-2 / xvi + 236pp

R.T. Kendall
Calvin and English Calvinism to 1649
(Studies in Christian History and Thought)
The author's thesis is that those who formed the Westminster Confession of Faith, which is regarded as Calvinism, in fact departed from John Calvin on two points: (1) the extent of the atonement and (2) the ground of assurance of salvation.
1997 / 0 85364-827-1 / xii + 264pp

Timothy Larsen
Friends of Religious Equality
Nonconformist Politics in Mid-Victorian England
During the middle decades of the nineteenth century the English Nonconformist community developed a coherent political philosophy of its own, of which a central tenet was the principle of religious equality (in contrast to the stereotype of Evangelical Dissenters). The Dissenting community fought for the civil rights of Roman Catholics, non-Christians and even atheists, on an issue of principle which had its flowering in the enthusiastic and undivided support which Nonconformity gave to the campaign for Jewish emancipation. This reissued study examines the political efforts and ideas of English Nonconformists during the period, covering the whole range of national issues raised, from state education to the Crimean War. It offers a case study of a theologically conservative group defending religious pluralism in the civic sphere, showing that the concept of religious equality was a grand vision at the centre of the political philosophy of the Dissenters.
2007 / 1-84227-402-3 / x + 300pp

Donald M. Lewis
Lighten Their Darkness
The Evangelical Mission to Working-Class London, 1828–1860
(Studies in Evangelical History and Thought)
This is a comprehensive and compelling study of the Church and the complexities of nineteenth-century London. Challenging our understanding of the culture in working London at this time, Lewis presents a well-structured and illustrated work that contributes substantially to the study of evangelicalism and mission in nineteenth-century Britain.
2001 / 1-84227-074-5 / xviii + 372pp

Stanley E. Porter and Anthony R. Cross (eds)
Semper Reformandum
Studies in Honour of Clark H. Pinnock
Clark Pinnock has clearly been one of the most important evangelical theologians of the last forty years in North America. Always provocative, especially in the wide range of opinions he has held and considered, Pinnock, himself a Baptist, has recently retired after twenty-five years of teaching at McMaster Divinity College. His colleagues and associates honour him in this volume by responding to his important theological work which has dealt with the essential topics of evangelical theology. These include Christian apologetics, biblical inspiration, the Holy Spirit and, perhaps most importantly in recent years, openness theology.
2003 / 1-84227-206-3 / xiv + 414pp

Meic Pearse
The Great Restoration
The Religious Radicals of the 16th and 17th Centuries
Pearse charts the rise and progress of continental Anabaptism – both evangelical and heretical – through the sixteenth century. He then follows the story of those English people who became impatient with Puritanism and separated – first from the Church of England and then from one another – to form the antecedents of later Congregationalists, Baptists and Quakers.
1998 / 0-85364-800-X / xii + 320pp

Charles Price and Ian M. Randall
Transforming Keswick
Transforming Keswick is a thorough, readable and detailed history of the convention. It will be of interest to those who know and love Keswick, those who are only just discovering it, and serious scholars eager to learn more about the history of God's dealings with his people.
2000 / 1-85078-350-0 / 288pp

Jim Purves
The Triune God and the Charismatic Movement
A Critical Appraisal from a Scottish Perspective
(Paternoster Theological Monographs)
All emotion and no theology? Or a fundamental challenge to reappraise and realign our trinitarian theology in the light of Christian experience? This study of charismatic renewal as it found expression within Scotland at the end of the twentieth century evaluates the use of Patristic, Reformed and contemporary models (including those of the Baptist Union of Scotland) of the Trinity in explaining the workings of the Holy Spirit.
2004 / 1-84227-321-3 / xxiv + 246pp

Ian M. Randall
Evangelical Experiences
A Study in the Spirituality of English Evangelicalism 1918–1939
(Studies in Evangelical History and Thought)
This book makes a detailed historical examination of evangelical spirituality between the First and Second World Wars. It shows how patterns of devotion led to tensions and divisions. In a wide-ranging study, Anglican, Wesleyan, Reformed and Pentecostal-charismatic spiritualities are analysed.
1999 / 0-85364-919-7 / xii + 310pp

Ian M. Randall
One Body in Christ
The History and Significance of the Evangelical Alliance
In 1846 the Evangelical Alliance was founded with the aim of bringing together evangelicals for common action. This book uses material not previously utilized to examine the history and significance of the Evangelical Alliance, a movement which has remained a powerful force for unity. At a time when evangelicals are growing world-wide, this book offers insights into the past which are relevant to contemporary issues.
2001 / 1-84227-089-3 / xii + 394pp

Ian M. Randall
Spirituality and Social Change
The Contribution of F.B. Meyer (1847–1929)
(Studies in Evangelical History and Thought)
This is a fresh appraisal of F.B. Meyer (1847–1929), a leading Free Church minister. Having been deeply affected by holiness spirituality, Meyer became the Keswick Convention's foremost international speaker. He combined spirituality with effective evangelism and socio-political activity. This study shows Meyer's significant contribution to spiritual renewal and social change.
2003 / 1-84227-195-4 / xx + 184pp

Geoffrey Robson
Dark Satanic Mills?
Religion and Irreligion in Birmingham and the Black Country
(Studies in Evangelical History and Thought)
This book analyses and interprets the nature and extent of popular Christian belief and practice in Birmingham and the Black Country during the first half of the nineteenth century, with particular reference to the impact of cholera epidemics and evangelism on church extension programmes.
2002 / 1-84227-102-4 / xiv + 294pp

Alan P.F. Sell
Enlightenment, Ecumenism, Evangel
Theological Themes and Thinkers 1550–2000
(Studies in Christian History and Thought)
This book consists of papers in which such interlocking topics as the Enlightenment, the problem of authority, the development of doctrine, spirituality, ecumenism, theological method and the heart of the gospel are discussed. Issues of significance to the church at large are explored with special reference to writers from the Reformed and Dissenting traditions.
2005 / 1-84227330-2 / xviii + 422pp

Alan P.F. Sell
Hinterland Theology
Some Reformed and Dissenting Adjustments
(Studies in Christian History and Thought)
Many books have been written on theology's 'giants' and significant trends, but what of those lesser-known writers who adjusted to them? In this book some hinterland theologians of the British Reformed and Dissenting traditions, who followed in the wake of toleration, the Evangelical Revival, the rise of modern biblical criticism and Karl Barth, are allowed to have their say. They include Thomas Ridgley, Ralph Wardlaw, T.V. Tymms and N.H.G. Robinson.
2006 / 1-84227-331-0

July 2005

Alan P.F. Sell and Anthony R. Cross (eds)
Protestant Nonconformity in the Twentieth Century
(Studies in Christian History and Thought)
In this collection of essays scholars representative of a number of Nonconformist traditions reflect thematically on Nonconformists' life and witness during the twentieth century. Among the subjects reviewed are biblical studies, theology, worship, evangelism and spirituality, and ecumenism. Over and above its immediate interest, this collection provides a marker to future scholars and others wishing to know how some of their forebears assessed Nonconformity's contribution to a variety of fields during the century leading up to Christianity's third millennium.

2003 / 1-84227-221-7 / x + 398pp

Mark Smith
Religion in Industrial Society
Oldham and Saddleworth 1740–1865
(Studies in Christian History and Thought)
This book analyses the way British churches sought to meet the challenge of industrialization and urbanization during the period 1740–1865. Working from a case-study of Oldham and Saddleworth, Mark Smith challenges the received view that the Anglican Church in the eighteenth century was characterized by complacency and inertia, and reveals Anglicanism's vigorous and creative response to the new conditions. He reassesses the significance of the centrally directed church reforms of the mid-nineteenth century, and emphasizes the importance of local energy and enthusiasm. Charting the growth of denominational pluralism in Oldham and Saddleworth, Dr Smith compares the strengths and weaknesses of the various Anglican and Nonconformist approaches to promoting church growth. He also demonstrates the extent to which all the churches participated in a common culture shaped by the influence of evangelicalism, and shows that active co-operation between the churches rather than denominational conflict dominated. This revised and updated edition of Dr Smith's challenging and original study makes an important contribution both to the social history of religion and to urban studies.

2006 / 1-84227-335-3 / approx. 300pp

July 2005

David M. Thompson
Baptism, Church and Society in Britain from the Evangelical Revival to *Baptism, Eucharist and Ministry*
The theology and practice of baptism have not received the attention they deserve. How important is faith? What does baptismal regeneration mean? Is baptism a bond of unity between Christians? This book discusses the theology of baptism and popular belief and practice in England and Wales from the Evangelical Revival to the publication of the World Council of Churches' consensus statement on *Baptism, Eucharist and Ministry* (1982).
2005 / 1-84227-393-0 / approx. 224pp

Martin Sutherland
Peace, Toleration and Decay
The Ecclesiology of Later Stuart Dissent
(Studies in Christian History and Thought)
This fresh analysis brings to light the complexity and fragility of the later Stuart Nonconformist consensus. Recent findings on wider seventeenth-century thought are incorporated into a new picture of the dynamics of Dissent and the roots of evangelicalism.
2003 / 1-84227-152-0 / xxii + 216pp

Haddon Willmer
Evangelicalism 1785–1835: An Essay (1962) and Reflections (2004)
(Studies in Evangelical History and Thought)
Awarded the Hulsean Prize in the University of Cambridge in 1962, this interpretation of a classic period of English Evangelicalism, by a young church historian, is now supplemented by reflections on Evangelicalism from the vantage point of a retired Professor of Theology.
2006 / 1-84227-219-5

Linda Wilson
Constrained by Zeal
Female Spirituality amongst Nonconformists 1825–1875
(Studies in Evangelical History and Thought)
Constrained by Zeal investigates the neglected area of Nonconformist female spirituality. Against the background of separate spheres, it analyses the experience of women from four denominations, and argues that the churches provided a 'third sphere' in which they could find opportunities for participation.
2000 / 0-85364-972-3 / xvi + 294pp

Nigel G. Wright
Disavowing Constantine
Mission, Church and the Social Order in the Theologies of
John Howard Yoder and Jürgen Moltmann
(Paternoster Theological Monographs)
This book is a timely restatement of a radical theology of church and state in the
Anabaptist and Baptist tradition. Dr Wright constructs his argument in dialogue
and debate with Yoder and Moltmann, major contributors to a free church
perspective.
2000 / 0-85364-978-2 / xvi + 252pp

Nigel G. Wright
Free Church, Free State
The Positive Baptist Vision
Free Church, Free State is a textbook on baptist ways of being church and a
proposal for the future of baptist churches in an ecumenical context. Nigel
Wright argues that both baptist (small 'b') and catholic (small 'c') church
traditions should seek to enrich and support each other as valid expressions of
the body of Christ without sacrificing what they hold dear. Written for pastors,
church planters, evangelists and preachers, Nigel Wright offers frameworks of
thought for baptists and non-baptists in their journey together following Christ.
2005 / 1-84227-353-1 / xxviii + 292

Nigel G. Wright
New Baptists, New Agenda
New Baptists, New Agenda is a timely contribution to the growing debate about
the health, shape and future of the Baptists. It considers the steady changes that
have taken place among Baptists in the last decade – changes of mood, style,
practice and structure – and encourages us to align these current movements and
questions with God's upward and future call. He contends that the true church
has yet to come: the church that currently exists is an anticipation of the joyful
gathering of all who have been called by the Spirit through Christ to the Father.
2002 / 1-84227-157-1 / x + 162pp

Paternoster
9 Holdom Avenue,
Bletchley,
Milton Keynes MK1 1QR,
United Kingdom
Web: www.authenticmedia.co.uk/paternoster

July 2005